PRETRIAL LITIGATION

IN A NUTSHELL

Third Edition

By

R. LAWRENCE DESSEM

Dean and Professor of Law
Mercer University

**WEST
GROUP**

A THOMSON COMPANY

ST. PAUL, MINN.
2001

West Group has created this publication to provide you with accurate and authoritative information concerning the subject matter covered. However, this publication was not necessarily prepared by persons licensed to practice law in a particular jurisdiction. West Group is not engaged in rendering legal or other professional advice, and this publication is not a substitute for the advice of an attorney. If you require legal or other expert advice, you should seek the services of a competent attorney or other professional.

Nutshell Series, In a Nutshell, the Nutshell Logo and the West Group symbol are registered trademarks used herein under license.

 TEXT IS PRINTED ON 10% POST CONSUMER RECYCLED PAPER

To My Family

*

PREFACE AND ACKNOWLEDGEMENTS

The West Nutshell Series is to serve as "a succinct exposition of the law to which a student or lawyer can turn for reliable guidance," and this third edition of *Pretrial Litigation in a Nutshell* is written with this purpose in mind.

As with the first and second editions of this book, the text discusses both the law governing the civil pretrial process and the skills that counsel must employ during pretrial proceedings. The law discussed is that applicable to federal civil proceedings, primarily the Federal Rules of Civil Procedure. As the result of major amendments to the Federal Rules that became effective on December 1, 2000, pretrial practice (particularly pretrial discovery and disclosure) has once again changed, and these changes are reflected and discussed in this third edition. State counterparts to the Federal Rules of Civil Procedure have been adopted in a majority of jurisdictions, and the pretrial skills considered in the text are essential to lawyers in both state and federal practice.

This text can be used as an assigned text in a law school or continuing legal education course in pretrial litigation. The text also should prove a useful supplement in civil procedure courses or clinical courses involving civil pretrial practice. In addition, attorneys embarking on a litigation practice or who do not regularly handle civil lawsuits may find the text useful with respect to pretrial practice.

I thank those who have supported me in writing this text and in all my other undertakings: my wife Beth Taylor Dessem and children Matthew, Lindsay, and Emily. My administrative assistant Debbie Manly and the staff of the Walter F. George School of Law of Mercer University also have provided significant help along the way. Those from whom I learned about pretrial litigation, and about being a lawyer, include Judge William K. Thomas and my friends and former colleagues in both the General Counsel's Office of the National Education Office and the Federal Programs Branch of the Civil Division of the United States Department of Justice. Finally, I appreciate the ability to use material from D. Binder & S. Price, *Legal Interviewing and Counseling: A Client-Centered Approach* (1977), which is reprinted with the permission of the West Group.

R. LAWRENCE DESSEM

Macon, Georgia
July 4, 2001

OUTLINE

OUTLINE

*

RESEARCH REFERENCES

Key Number System: Attorney And Client ⊂⇒63, 64, 101, 112, 112.50 (45k63, 45k64, 45k101, 45k112, 45k112.50); Compromise And Settlement ⊂⇒2-72 (89k2-89k72); Federal Civil Procedure ⊂⇒281-297, 671-786, 821-853, 921-940, 1261-1686, 1691-1850, 1921-1943, 2461-2570 (170ak281-170ak297, 170ak671-170ak786, 170ak821-170ak853, 170ak921-170ak940, 170ak1261-170ak1686, 170ak1691-170ak1850, 170ak1921-170ak1943, 170ak2461-170ak2570); Federal Courts ⊂⇒101-160 (170bk101-170bk160); Judgment ⊂⇒178-190 (228k178-228k190); Motions ⊂⇒1-66 (267k1-267k66); Parties ⊂⇒50-65 (287k50-287k65); Pleading ⊂⇒38.5-100, 138-150, 229-286 (302k38.5-302k100, 302k138-302k150, 302k229-302k286); Venue ⊂⇒33-84 (401k33-401k84).

Am Jur 2d, Counterclaim, Recoupment, and Setoff §§ 1 et seq.; Declaratory Judgments §§ 214-227; Depositions and Discovery §§ 1 et seq.; Federal Tax Enforcement §§ 994-996; Pleading §§ 1 et seq.; Pretrial Conference and Procedure §§ 1 et seq.; Trial §§ 6-17, 91-114

Corpus Juris Secundum, Depositions §§ 1 et seq.; Federal Civil Procedure §§ 818-839; Judgments §§ 930-941; Pleading §§ 1 et seq.; Set-off and Counterclaim §§ 1 et seq.

ALR Index: Consolidation and Merger of Offenses and Charges; Counterclaim and Setoff; Depositions; Preliminary or Pretrial Matters; Pretrial Conferences; Supplemental Pleading

ALR Digest: Action or Suit § 74; Depositions §§ 1 et seq.; Discovery and Inspection §§ 1 et seq.; Pleading §§ 168 et seq.; Trial § 1.7

Am Jur Legal Forms 2d, Counterclaim and Setoff §§ 76:1 et seq.

Am Jur Pleading and Practice (Rev), Counterclaim, Recoupment, and Setoff §§ 1 et seq.; Criminal Procedure §§ 131-179; Depositions and Discovery §§ 1 et seq.; Expert and Opinion Evidence §§ 31-42; Federal Criminal Procedure §§ 15-29, 98-108, 135-138; Federal Practice and Procedure §§ 745-832, 988-1004; Pleading §§ 1 et seq.; Pretrial Conference and Procedure §§ 1 et seq.

76 Am Jur Trials 127, Jury Selection and Voir Dire in Criminal Cases; 71 Am Jur Trials 1, How to Conduct International Discovery; 57 Am Jur Trials 155, Handling Fire Claims Out of Court; 51 Am Jur Trials 1, Managing Litigation; 47 Am Jur Trials 1, Environmental Law Litigation under CERCLA; 42 Am Jur Trials 313, Uses, Techniques, and Reliability of Polygraph Testing; 41 Am Jur Trials 349, Habeas Corpus: Pretrial Rulings; 27 Am Jur Trials 1, Representing the Mentally Disabled Criminal Defendant; 23 Am Jur Trials 95, The Use of Videotape In Civil Trial Preparation and Discov-

ery; 18 Am Jur Trials 1, Coram Nobis Practice In Criminal Cases; 5 Am Jur Trials 27, Pretrial Procedures and Motions In Criminal Cases; 5 Am Jur Trials 331, Excluding Illegally Obtained Evidence; 4 Am Jur Trials 659, Pretrial Conference; 4 Am Jur Trials 1, Discovery-Written Interrogatories; 4 Am Jur Trials 119, Discovery-Oral Depositions; 3 Am Jur Trials 681, Tactics and Strategy of Pleading; 2 Am Jur Trials 229, Locating and Interviewing Witnesses; 1 Am Jur Trials 1, Interviewing the Client

60 POF3d 175, Proof of Matters By Judicial Notice; 27 POF3d 489, Forensic Identification of Handwriting

45 POF2d 595, Protected Communication Between Physician and Patient; 33 POF2d 549, Criminal Law: Need for Disclosure of Identity of Informant; 19 POF2d 435, Lineups and Showups: Admissibility and Effect of Pretrial Identification; 18 POF2d 149, Excessive Bail; 14 POF2d 1, Reliability of Polygraph Examination

Use Westlaw® to Research the Law Governing Pretrial Litigation

Access Westlaw, the computer-assisted legal research service of West Group, to search a broad array of legal resources, including case law, statutes, practice guides, current developments, and various other types of information. Consult the online Westlaw Directory to determine databases specific to your needs.

Searching on Westlaw

With Westlaw, you can use the Natural Language search method, which allows you to simply describe your pretrial litigation issue in plain English. For example, to retrieve cases discussing objections to discovery on the basis that it is oppressive or an undue burden, access the U.S. District Courts Cases database (DCT) and type the following Natural Language description: **object to discovery that is oppressive (undue burden)**

You can also use the Terms and Connectors search method, which allows you to enter a query consisting of key terms from your issue and connectors specifying the relationship between those terms. For example, to search for the term *object, objection, objecting*, or *objected* in the same sentence as the term *discovery* and either the term *oppressive* or the phrase *"undue burden,"* type the following Terms and Connectors query: **object! /s discovery /s oppressive "undue burden"**

Use KeyCite® to Check Your Research

KeyCite is the citation research service available exclusively on Westlaw. Use KeyCite to see if your cases or statutes are good law and to retrieve cases, legislation, and articles that cite your cases and statutes.

For more information regarding searching on Westlaw, call the West Group Reference Attorneys at **1-800-REF-ATTY** (1-800-733-2889).

*

TABLE OF CASES

References are to Pages

TABLE OF CASES

*

TABLE OF STATUTES
AND RULES

UNITED STATES

UNITED STATES CODE ANNOTATED
15 U.S.C.A.—Commerce and Trade

28 U.S.C.A.—Judiciary and Judicial Procedure

TABLE OF STATUTES AND RULES

UNITED STATES CODE ANNOTATED
28 U.S.C.A.—Judiciary and Judicial Procedure

42 U.S.C.A.—The Public Health and Welfare

POPULAR NAME ACTS

CIVIL RIGHTS ACT OF 1964

FEDERAL RULES OF CIVIL PROCEDURE

TABLE OF STATUTES AND RULES

FEDERAL RULES OF CIVIL PROCEDURE

FEDERAL RULES OF CIVIL PROCEDURE

FEDERAL RULES OF CIVIL PROCEDURE

FEDERAL RULES OF CIVIL PROCEDURE

TABLE OF STATUTES AND RULES

FEDERAL RULES OF CIVIL PROCEDURE

FEDERAL RULES OF CIVIL PROCEDURE

TABLE OF STATUTES AND RULES

FEDERAL RULES OF CIVIL PROCEDURE

FEDERAL RULES OF CIVIL PROCEDURE

FEDERAL RULES OF CIVIL PROCEDURE

FEDERAL RULES OF CIVIL PROCEDURE

FEDERAL RULES OF CIVIL PROCEDURE

FEDERAL RULES OF CIVIL PROCEDURE

TABLE OF STATUTES AND RULES

FEDERAL RULES OF CIVIL PROCEDURE

TABLE OF STATUTES AND RULES

FEDERAL RULES OF CIVIL PROCEDURE

TABLE OF STATUTES AND RULES

FEDERAL RULES OF CIVIL PROCEDURE

TABLE OF STATUTES AND RULES

FEDERAL RULES OF CIVIL PROCEDURE

TABLE OF STATUTES AND RULES

FEDERAL RULES OF CIVIL PROCEDURE

*

PRETRIAL LITIGATION

IN A NUTSHELL

Third Edition

*

CHAPTER ONE

INTRODUCTION

I. AN OVERVIEW OF PRETRIAL LITIGATION

Encompassed within the area of pretrial litigation is everything that a lawyer does for a client prior to trial. No single volume can cover this field in great depth. The aim of this book is to discuss the primary law governing the civil pretrial process and the major lawyering skills necessary to represent a client prior to trial. The book should be helpful to law students in pretrial litigation, civil procedure, or clinical courses, to newly admitted attorneys who are embarking upon careers as civil litigators, and to other attorneys who have not regularly or recently handled litigation and may want a quick primer on pretrial law and practice.

The book progresses in the same chronological fashion as does most civil litigation. The next four chapters deal with client interviewing and the establishment of the attorney-client relationship, pretrial planning and investigation, and the pleadings. Chapters 6 through 10 concern disclosure and discovery. The final chapters of the book address pretrial motions, pretrial conferences and orders, and negotiation and settlement. While most civil litigation progresses in this fashion, this is not always the case. Pretrial investigation can continue throughout the course of the lawsuit, up to, and through, trial. Pretrial motions and conferences can engage counsel's attention before, during, and after the completion of discovery.

Whether or not the pretrial process in a particular case proceeds in the same sequence as the chapters in this book, counsel must be aware of the related nature of the various pretrial phases of a case. The manner in which a pleading is drafted can limit later opportunities for discovery, and a thorough pretrial investigation may uncover a witness upon whose affidavit a motion for summary judgment may turn.

Nor can pretrial litigation be divorced from trial. The pretrial phase of a case is crucial in preparing the case for trial, and pretrial decisions will bind the parties and limit counsel's options at trial. In the great majority of cases that are settled or otherwise resolved short of trial, the pretrial resolution usually is dependent upon counsel's pretrial litigation skills and decisions.

Some cases are resolved by the parties, and some cases are resolved by the court. Some cases are resolved prior to trial, some cases are resolved during trial, and some cases are resolved by the judge or jury after trial. In all cases, pretrial litigation is crucial to the ultimate case resolution.

II. THE LAW GOVERNING PRETRIAL LITIGATION

In law school, subjects are taught in discrete courses. In Torts, you study the substantive law of torts; in Civil Procedure, you study the procedural rules governing the adjudication of civil disputes; and in Professional Responsibility, you study the ethical proscriptions that regulate attorney conduct. In practice, legal problems do not come so neatly packaged.

While the focus of this book is on the procedural rules governing the pretrial process, counsel must constantly consider and reconsider the applicable substantive law and ethical proscriptions. Only if the substantive statutory or common law provides a cause of action is there any basis for drafting a complaint on behalf of a client. Rule 11 of the Federal Rules of Civil Procedure prohibits counsel from advancing claims or defenses that are not "warranted by existing law or by a nonfrivolous argument for the extension, modification, or reversal of existing law or the establishment of new law," and the ABA's Model Rules of Professional Conduct and Code of Professional Responsibility contain similar proscriptions. Such claims and defenses also run afoul of the codes of litigation conduct and creeds of professionalism adopted by many bar associations and some state and federal courts.

Having acknowledged the importance of substantive law and ethical rules, let's return to the procedural law that is the primary subject of this book.

Even restricting the inquiry to procedural law, there is still a lot of law that must be considered. Once the complaint is filed and a civil action has been initiated, the primary procedural law will be that contained in the applicable rules of civil procedure. While the rules of procedure vary from state to state, a majority of states have adopted rules very similar, if not identical, to the Federal Rules of Civil Procedure. The Federal Rules of Civil Procedure provide the basis for the discussions in this text.

While the Federal Rules of Civil Procedure govern most procedural questions in the United States District Courts, there are both higher-level and lower-level legal rules that govern specific procedural situations. In fact, Rule 82 provides: "These rules shall not be construed to extend or limit the jurisdiction of the United States district courts or the venue of actions therein." In addition, the Rules Enabling Act in part provides: "Such rules shall not abridge, enlarge or modify any substantive right." 28 U.S.C. § 2072(b). However, the supersession clause of the Rules Enabling Act, 28 U.S.C. § 2072(b), provides: "All laws in conflict with [the Federal Rules of Civil Procedure] shall be of no further force or effect after such rules have taken effect."

While the United States Constitution may not apply directly to many procedural situations, it acts as a constraint upon the procedural requirements imposed by statutes, rules, or orders of individual judges. For example, the due process clause of the fifth amendment may require that notice be given to a party before a judgment is entered against it or to an attorney before procedural sanctions are imposed.

One rung below the United States Constitution are the federal procedural statutes that are compiled primarily in Title 28 of the United States Code. It is these statutes that define the jurisdiction and venue of the federal courts and govern removal of cases from state to federal court, supplemental jurisdiction, and statutory interpleader.

Both a federal statute, 28 U.S.C. § 2071, and Rule 83 of the Federal Rules of Civil Procedure recognize the power of the ninety-four United States District Courts to promulgate local rules governing matters not covered in the Federal Rules of Civil Procedure. Acting pursuant to this authority, federal district courts have adopted rules governing the details of motion practice (such as the timing and length of motion briefs), disclosure and discovery (defining, for instance, common terms that parties often use in discovery requests), and pretrial conferences and orders (perhaps providing a standard pretrial order form).

Federal Rule of Civil Procedure 83(b) in part provides: "A judge may regulate practice in any manner consistent with federal law, rules adopted under 28 U.S.C. §§ 2072 and 2075, and local rules of the district." Acting pursuant to this authority, many federal district judges and magistrate judges have adopted standing orders detailing their individual practices concerning, for instance, pretrial conferences, oral argument procedures, and contact with the judge's chambers.

While standing orders express the general practices and predilections of district judges and magistrate judges, judges also issue numerous orders governing specific issues in particular cases. Although Rule 33(a) generally limits parties to twenty-five interrogatories, a judge might issue an order permitting a party to propound additional interrogatories in a specific case in which additional interrogatories are justified.

Finally, much pretrial litigation is governed by unwritten customs and practices. Rule 30(b)(1) of the Federal Rules of Civil Procedure requires that "reasonable notice" be given prior to a deposition, but does not specify what notice will be considered "reasonable." In many districts matters such as this are governed by local, unwritten practice. Counsel may have to ask other attorneys or perhaps clerk's office personnel to determine this unwritten procedural law.

There are thus numerous sources that must be consulted to answer questions of procedural law in any particular case.

III. THE LAWYER'S ROLE IN PRETRIAL LITIGATION

The fact that almost 98% of federal civil cases are resolved short of trial has important implications for the lawyers handling those cases. One study has found that, while the attorneys studied devoted 16.0% of their time to client conferences, 16.7% of their time to discovery, and 15.1% of their time to settlement negotiations, they only spent 9.5% of their time on trials, hearings, appeals, and enforcement of judgments. Trubek, Sarat, Felstiner, Kritzer & Grossman, "The Costs of Ordinary Litigation," 31 *UCLA L.Rev.* 72, 91 (Table 3) (1983).

Unfortunately, to the extent that it deals with these subjects, legal education does not stress the skills and governing law which the civil litigator continually encounters. Courses in pretrial litigation, and some civil procedure and clinical courses, have attempted to fill this void. This book has a similar mission: to acquaint the law student and lawyer with the law and skills that must be mastered to be an effective civil litigator.

Mastery cannot be gained merely from reading this or any other book. Mastery of any subject, whether it be pretrial litigation, musical performance, or throwing a curve ball, can only come from practice and experience. Complete mastery may never be achieved, but is an ideal that one strives for throughout a legal career. Nevertheless, even though reading a book such as this will not lead to mastery of pretrial litigation, it is a beginning.

Let's get started!

CHAPTER TWO

CLIENT INTERVIEWING AND THE ESTABLISHMENT OF THE ATTORNEY–CLIENT RELATIONSHIP

I. THE IMPORTANCE OF CLIENT INTERVIEWING

Attorneys spend a great deal of time talking with their clients, with approximately sixteen percent of their total litigation activity devoted to client conferences according to the study cited in Chapter 1, supra p. 7. There are several reasons why such a large amount of attorney time is devoted to client conferences and interviews.

Attorneys are ethically bound to represent the interests of their clients in litigation, and it is difficult to do this adequately without thorough client interviews. Attorneys need to obtain complete information from their clients so that (1) they will be able to achieve the clients' ultimate litigation goals and (2) they will have the factual information (about the parties' dispute, potential witnesses, and important documents) with which to litigate the case. If this were not enough incentive, Rule 11 of the Federal Rules of Civil Procedure requires that counsel conduct a reasonable inquiry to ensure that litigation documents have evidentiary support or are likely to have such support after a reasonable opportunity for further investigation or discovery.

Everything that counsel does during the pretrial process builds upon her client interviews. Attorneys first learn about actual and potential litigation from their clients, and factual and legal case theories are developed based upon client interviews. Just as importantly, attorneys often decide not to pursue certain legal research or factual leads because of what their clients tell them in client interviews.

Successful client interviews are a way to build good attorney-client rapport. Good rapport is important, because it encourages clients to provide the maximum amount of information to their attorneys and to otherwise assist in the litigation. In addition, losing a lawsuit and paying legal fees are stressful situations, and clients may handle such events better with counsel they trust.

Effective interviewing techniques can be useful even when not dealing with one's own client. A major task of counsel during the pretrial period is to motivate people to provide information. Some of the same techniques that motivate a client to share information may cause a third-party witness to provide informal discovery or an adverse party to volunteer information during a deposition.

II. THE STRUCTURE OF THE INITIAL ATTORNEY–CLIENT INTERVIEW

Client interviewing is crucial to litigation success. Counsel should use the client interview to maximize communication between client and counsel, facilitate client decision-making, and build rapport. One of the ways this can be done is to adopt an explicit structure for client interviews.

Whether they realize it or not, over their years of practice experienced attorneys have developed their own interview structures. The interview structure suggested here is one that eventually should become second nature, and it is not something to be posted on the office wall or printed on attorney flash cards. In fact, if counsel appears more interested in an interview form than in the client, effective client communication can be stifled. While a structure is necessary, counsel should remember that the purpose of any structure should be to facilitate client communication, decision-making, and rapport.

Counsel also should realize that no interview proceeds rigidly from step A, to step B, to step C. Human conversation is not that mechanical. Moreover, it is misleading to speak of a single client interview. In most cases, there are a series of client interviews and conferences throughout the course of a lawsuit. Nevertheless, attempting to structure initial client interviews can help attorneys maximize the benefits of this crucial pretrial litigation activity.

A. Introductions and Introductory Remarks

Most clients are nervous about visiting an attorney, particularly if they have never consulted an attorney before. One of the reasons for this anxiety may be the problem about which the client has sought counsel in the first place: the client has been injured in some manner and seeks legal recompense or has been named as a defendant in a lawsuit.

Because the unfamiliar terrain of a lawyer's office can make lay persons uncomfortable, introductory pleasantries often are quite important in putting a client at ease. Not only is a handshake and introduction in order, but counsel should give the client her undivided attention by informing her secretary to hold calls and other interruptions until after the interview.

After the initial pleasantries, counsel should explain to the client exactly what will happen during the initial interview. The attorney might give an explanation something like this:

> Well, Mr. Jones, I'm very glad to meet you. Let me first tell you how I'd like to proceed this morning, and then you can ask me any questions before we continue with the interview.
>
> I have asked my secretary to hold my calls, so we should have at least 30 minutes to talk. I'll take as much time as is necessary. As you know, the charge for this initial interview will be $50.00.
>
> When we get started, the first thing I'll want you to do is to explain the problem that has

brought you here and tell me how that problem came about. I'd then like to know from you what you'd like me to try to do for you.

After I've heard from you, I'm sure I will have some questions. But I want to hear from you first, and I'll try not to interrupt as you describe your problem.

At the end of the interview, we'll talk about your next step. You may want to retain me as your attorney, and we'll talk about that. You may not want to do anything. It's likely that I will need to do some legal research or factual investigation before I can offer you any definitive advice, and we'll talk about that, too.

You should know that, whether or not you decide to retain me to do further work for you, what you say to me today is protected by the attorney-client privilege. Because I'm required to keep confidential what you tell me, you should feel free to tell me all the facts—even if you aren't sure that a particular fact is even relevant.

Do you have any questions about what we'll try to do today?

If not, why don't you tell me why you've come to see me.

In the above introduction, counsel has explained how she hopes the interview will proceed. Just knowing what to expect should put the client a bit more at ease. Knowing the total cost of the initial interview session may do even more to relax the client. The client may not expect counsel to hold her questions until the client problem definition and narrative are complete. Alerting the client to this fact and the existence of the attorney-client privilege should make him more forthcoming in his narrative. The final portion of the introduction reminds the client that it is his decision whether or not to retain the attorney, and he must decide what legal action to take. The client also is alerted to the fact that the attorney may not be able to give definitive legal advice based only upon the initial client interview.

B. The Client's Problem Definition

Once any questions have been asked and answered about the initial interview and its structure, counsel should ask the client to briefly summarize why he has sought legal help. Such a summary should help the client in giving his more detailed narrative and counsel in following that narrative.

During the course of the interview, counsel may discover that the client has several legal problems, including some of which he may be unaware. However, it is best for the client initially to identify the problem that has brought him to seek legal help. In some situations, this problem definition will be both simple and obvious. The client may state, "I received this summons and complaint in the mail yesterday" or "My son was in a serious automobile accident, and we're wondering about suing the driver of the other car." In other situations, counsel may have to ask a few questions before the client fully defines the problem. This stage of the interview is analogous to the doctor's query, "Where does it hurt?"

C. The Client's Narrative

The client's narrative, which follows the client's problem definition, is the most important portion of the interview. This usually is the longest part of the interview, for it is the client's description of the events that triggered his resort to counsel. While a client can state in a single sentence that he has been sued, a narrative of the events leading up to suit may be quite long and involved.

Counsel should permit the client to provide his narrative in an uninterrupted fashion. From the moment a client begins his narrative, the attorney will begin to make tentative assumptions about the client's legal problems. These assumptions are necessary to bring order to the interview, to permit the attorney and client to maximize what they can accomplish in the limited interview time available, and to permit counsel to reach preliminary conclusions upon which to plot a future course of action. Extended client narratives take time, and for this reason both counsel and client may be inclined to curtail this part of the initial client interview. The client may be hesitant to mention matters that he believes are not relevant or that he would rather not reveal for personal reasons. Counsel may not want to hear an extended client narrative if she already has characterized the case as falling within a particular legal pigeonhole.

Counsel and client must fight these tendencies to curtail the client narrative. Counsel may never learn information that is not disclosed at the initial client interview. Premature diagnosis by the attorney based upon a partial factual narrative may mean that alternative legal and factual theories may never be explored. To avoid these problems, the widest possible net should be cast in the initial client interview or interviews. The major cost of an extended client narrative is the time that such a narrative takes. This is a cost well worth paying to ensure that all possibly relevant facts are elicited from the client at the very outset of the legal representation.

D.   The Relief Sought by the Client

By the end of the client narrative, counsel will have made certain assumptions about the relief sought by the client. Before verbalizing these assumptions, counsel should ask the client what relief he desires. The fact that a client may be entitled to monetary relief may not mean that he actually wants money damages.

Counsel should remember that the attorney's job is to seek to achieve the litigation objectives of her client. ABA Model Rule of Professional Conduct 1.2(a) provides that a lawyer generally is to abide by a client's decisions concerning the objectives of representation, while Disciplinary Rule 7–101(A)(1) of the ABA Model Code of Professional Responsibility similarly requires an attorney to seek the lawful objectives of her client.

Because counsel is to advance the client's objectives, a clear statement of those objectives and the relief the client seeks should be obtained at the very outset of the representation.

E. Attorney Follow–Up Questioning

Once the client has defined and explained his problem and told counsel the relief that he seeks, it's counsel's turn to do some talking. In particular, counsel should ask questions raised by the client's problem definition, narrative, and statement of relief desired.

As previously stated, it is important that the client initially define and explain his problem and the relief sought without major interruptions from counsel. Counsel should strive to facilitate a client narrative in which the client states all the facts, without holding back facts the client believes are unimportant or of no interest to counsel. Note-taking can be a barrier to full communication. Counsel should encourage a complete narrative by maintaining eye contact with the client rather than attempting to write down everything the client says in the first instance.

If the client has brought documents to the interview, counsel may want to review them before asking any questions. The follow-up questions may include requests for documents, corroborative physical evidence, or other information that the client cannot immediately furnish. Clients may be requested to supply the names of potential witnesses or others who can verify specific facts. Dates may need to be verified to ensure that there are no statute of limitations problems. Just as counsel may have to conduct legal research or factual investigation after the initial client interview, there may be further matters for the client to pursue before definitive legal advice can be rendered. If counsel is retained, the client should be asked to sign releases permitting counsel herself to obtain relevant documents on behalf of the client.

There is little to be gained from giving your client the third degree during the initial client interview. However, counsel should pursue aspects of the client narrative that are vague or that seem unlikely: "Could you tell me about your conversation with Alan Chen, again? I don't understand." Reference to other people and physical evidence can motivate clients to provide a complete narrative in the initial client interview: "I'll need to talk to Alan Chen about this. What will he tell me?" While attempting to engender client confidence, counsel should maintain a healthy skepticism concerning the client narrative. This can be a hard balance to strike.

Through her questions, counsel should elicit detailed, specific facts rather than being content with the generalities and conclusions that the client initially may offer. Do not be satisfied with statements that someone was "driving fast," or "threatened" the client, or was "drunk." After the client narrative is complete, ask for the specific facts upon which each conclusion or characterization is based.

Attorney questioning can be concluded with a question or two summarizing the narrative, so that there is no misunderstanding about important facts: "Let me see if I've got this right. The only time you saw Randy was on December 1, when he visited you at your office and told you he wanted to buy your house?"

F. Concluding Remarks

Just as it is important to tell the client at the outset what will happen during the interview, counsel should inform the client at the interview's conclusion what will happen next. While the client will want an indication as to his chances of prevailing in litigation or obtaining other legal objectives, it may be difficult to make such a prediction without conducting legal research and factual investigation. Even if counsel believes that a litigation assessment is feasible, she should stress that any predictions are tentative and are based upon the facts as related by the client at the interview. Clients should be made aware of the delays and costs inherent in civil litigation, the likely time frame for resolving the particular litigation, and the extent to which the client will have to participate in that litigation through discovery and testimony at trial. If the client's best interests will not be well served by resort to the legal process, alternative dispute resolution possibilities should be explored with the client.

Before further work is done on the case, the client will have to decide whether he wishes to retain this attorney. If the client decides to retain counsel at the initial attorney-client conference, he should be given a client retainer form. The terms of this contract should be explained to the client, and he should be encouraged to think about retaining counsel before he signs anything. However, counsel should stress that she will not begin work on this case until the client makes his decision.

If the statute of limitations is a potential problem, the client should be alerted to this fact. The attorney also should counsel the client not to talk about his situation except with other attorneys whom he may consult about legal representation. The client must understand that any statements he makes might be used against him by an opposing party. If the client already has made statements, counsel needs to know about them and obtain copies of any statements that were in writing.

Finally, a specific date should be set for either (1) the next meeting between client and counsel (if the client decides to retain counsel at the initial interview) or (2) the client to decide whether to retain this attorney. If counsel is retained, a follow-up appointment should be set, and the client should be clear as to what both he and counsel are to do before that next meeting.

III.   INTERVIEWING TECHNIQUES

Do you remember the first time you visited the doctor as a small child? These initial visits are frightening for most people, because we don't know what to expect, we may not understand what the doctor is doing or saying, and we may not really believe that the doctor is concerned about our own best interests. Similar barriers to full and effective communication often exist in the attorney-client interview.

While attorneys don't give out lollipops to facilitate client communication, there are interviewing techniques that can be used to ensure successful client interviews. Attorneys should seek "the truth, the whole truth, and nothing but the truth." The following techniques therefore are not to manufacture facts or in any sense distort the truth. Instead, they should be thought of as inducements to truth, as techniques to break down barriers to candid attorney-client communication.

A.   Traditional Techniques to Facilitate Communication

Counsel should consider the possible effect upon client communication of everything that she does in the initial client interview. Even office management decisions made well before a particular interview can influence the success of that interview.

A client's first contact with an attorney's office usually will be through office staff. Secretaries and receptionists can help prepare clients for their initial interviews by providing them with information about what to bring to the interview and what the initial consultation will cost. They also should answer client questions and be generally helpful in scheduling interviews. Office personnel usually gather information from prospective clients before arranging an interview, in order to confirm that counsel handles the type of problem presented by the client and perhaps to check potential conflicts of interest. Additional information gathered by office personnel concerning the client's background and problem may help counsel prepare a bit for the initial interview, perhaps permitting her to check a relevant statute or cursorily review other relevant law.

The physical office structure can encourage client confidence in counsel and thereby facilitate communication. Client confidence is not engendered by an office in which confidential documents from other cases are randomly strewn across the floor or in which clients are required to sit in an uncomfortable chair and face an attorney sitting directly behind a desk the size of a battleship. For this reason, many attorneys sit with clients around a small table, perhaps alongside the client.

The time that an attorney devotes to interviews can have a direct bearing on the information provided by clients. A client is more likely to provide a detailed narrative during a long, uninterrupted block of time than during a short interview with a hurried attorney who has many other, apparently more important, things to do.

There are several techniques attorneys can use to encourage clients to give complete narratives. One of the most effective motivators of communication is silence. Many people are uncomfortable with silence and will fill any silence by volunteering additional information. Counsel should not attempt to make clients uncomfortable by seeing who can best bear silence. On the other hand, counsel should be careful not to interrupt client narratives and should use interview pauses to encourage client communication.

If a client does not remember a particular fact, counsel should give the client time in which to try to remember. Counsel can inquire if there is anything that would help the client remember. This may lead to the identification of individuals, documents, or other physical objects about which counsel should be aware.

Paying attention to a person encourages that individual to continue talking. People are more ready to say things that they believe are of interest to an attorney. By maintaining eye contact with a client, and minimizing distractions, more effective communication can be ensured.

Counsel can verbally encourage clients in several ways. Open-ended questions tend to elicit longer, narrative answers. By responding to client narratives with phrases such as "That's helpful" or "That's what I need to know," useful narrative statements can be encouraged. Care should be taken, however, that such statements do not become verbal cues that the client follows to slant the substance of his narrative to please counsel. While "active listening" is discussed and recommended in the next subsection, counsel should be careful to avoid "overactive listening" in which attorney questioning leads a client to desired factual statements.

Counsel should explicitly tell the client that she only can represent him if she has all the facts, unfavorable as well as favorable. There is a natural tendency for clients to omit or gloss over facts that they consider harmful or embarrassing. In listening to a client narrative, counsel should consider both things the client does and does not say. The client should understand that unfavorable facts are either already known to the opposing party or are likely to become known through discovery. Revealing these facts to counsel sooner, rather than later, will ensure that counsel can best handle them during the litigation.

Maintaining eye contact with a client may provide counsel with important non-verbal cues concerning significant facts that the client has not yet volunteered. If the client looks at the floor, grows red in the face, or develops a nervous tic at a certain point in his narrative, there may be matters that counsel should pursue further. If counsel does not maintain eye contact with her client, these non-verbal cues will be missed.

Clients may have a difficult time talking about certain subjects, and counsel should be sensitive to this fact. If the client was involved in an accident in which he lost a family member, do not immediately ask him to relive the details of the accident. To put the client more at ease, it may make sense to talk initially about less sensitive matters such as the client's employment or place of residence.

When counsel decides to ask about a sensitive subject, she should acknowledge the sensitive nature of the information sought and explain why that information may be legally relevant: "You mentioned that you were with your secretary in the hotel penthouse when the fire broke out. I know that this may be uncomfortable for you, but I need to know more about your relationship with your secretary. This is something about which the hotel attorneys will question you, so we need to discuss it now."

Toward the end of the interview, counsel should explicitly ask the client for any facts that may not yet have been provided: "What else should I know?" A similarly open-ended question can be used to encourage the client to reveal unfavorable facts: "Is there anything else that the plaintiff is telling his attorney that you haven't yet told me?"

Many clients will remember facts after the interview, and clients should be asked to write them down so that they can be provided to counsel at the next interview. Some attorneys suggest that their clients carry a notepad, perhaps keeping it by their bedside at night, so they can preserve any facts that may come to them at odd hours.

B. Active Listening

In addition to techniques that traditionally have been used to encourage and facilitate communication, some attorneys attempt to stimulate client communication by "active listening." Active listening has been described as follows by Professors David Binder and Susan Price in their book *Legal Interviewing and Counseling: A Client–Centered Approach* 25 (1977):

Active listening is the process of picking up the client's message and sending it back in a *reflective statement which mirrors what the lawyer has heard.*

Client: "When I asked him for the money, he had the nerve to tell me not to be uptight."

Lawyer: "Rather than telling you about the money, he suggested you were somehow wrong for asking. I imagine that made you angry."

Note the lawyer does not simply repeat or "parrot" what was said. Rather, the lawyer's response is an affirmative effort to convey back the essence of what was heard. It is a response which, by mirroring what was said, affirmatively demonstrates understanding. Further, since the statement only mirrors, it does not in any way "judge" what has been said. In short, it is a completely empathetic response.

Active listening is not something that comes naturally to most people. Some attorneys have neither the time nor the patience for active listening. Some clients come to counsel seeking judgments, and they become impatient if the attorney does not simply "tell them what to do." In some situations there is simply no time for attorneys to engage in active listening or this technique is inappropriate for other reasons. The attorney preparing for a temporary restraining order hearing will not have time to mirror client statements but must obtain specific facts quite quickly. Even attorneys who practice active listening may not employ the technique to the same extent in uncontested proceedings as they do in other litigation.

Nevertheless, active listening can be an extremely useful interviewing technique. A client's legal problem may be intertwined with non-legal problems, and this may be difficult to ascertain if the client narrative is restricted to facts that have only legal significance. In order to be successful at active listening, counsel must actually listen. The attorney must focus on the client and listen to his real concerns, rather than think of how he, counsel, would react if placed in a similar situation.

Counsel must appreciate that it is not just "the facts" that drive a lawsuit, but that client feelings, aspirations, and emotions may determine how vigorously a case is litigated or whether a case can be settled or must be tried. In addition, active listening helps establish client rapport and encourages the client to take an active role in the litigation. Whether or not labeled as "active listening," empathy can go a long way in encouraging clients to share their problems with counsel.

IV. THE CLIENT'S RETAINER OF THE ATTORNEY

The legal agreement governing the attorney-client relationship is one of the important matters that should be discussed at the initial client interview. Many clients sign a retainer agreement during the initial client interview, while others do not do so until they have had a chance to reflect on the matter and consult with other attorneys.

There is no prescribed form for retainer agreements. Some attorneys send potential clients a letter in which they summarize the initial attorney-client conference and any preliminary advice and set forth the terms of the proposed retainer. The client is instructed that in order to retain the attorney, he should sign, date, and return the letter to the attorney's office by a specific date. Other attorneys ask clients to sign form representation agreements. No matter what form the agreement takes, both client and counsel should realize that the representation agreement is a legal contract. For this reason, all terms of the agreement should be in writing, and counsel should ensure that the client understands the agreement.

The substance of retainer agreements varies from attorney to attorney and from case to case. Typically these agreements set forth the promises of the attorney, the promises of the client, and miscellaneous terms of the representation (such as the manner in which disputes between counsel and client will be resolved and billing and payment schedules).

The major promise of counsel is to represent the client in a specific legal matter. The representation agreement should be explicit about the specific legal matter involved. If any legal advice is included in the agreement, it should be clear that this advice is preliminary and based upon the facts provided by the client at the initial client interview. Many lawyers include a statement in the agreement that litigation results cannot be guaranteed and, if the client is a plaintiff, the caveat that obtaining a judgment from the court is not the same as collecting that judgment from a defendant.

The agreement should be explicit concerning not just what counsel will do for the client, but also what tasks are not encompassed by the retainer. For instance, the retainer might state that it is only for work done at the trial level and counsel does not commit to handle any appeal.

In most retainer agreements, the client agrees to cooperate in the prosecution or defense of his action. Of even greater importance to counsel is the client's promise to pay the legal fees and costs of suit. Legal fees can take several forms. The client may agree to pay counsel on an hourly basis for time spent on his case, and this is the customary manner in which defense counsel are compensated. Both Model Rule of Professional Conduct 1.5 and Disciplinary Rule 2–106 require that an attorney's fee be reasonable. In determining reasonableness, these rules suggest consideration of factors such as the time and labor involved in the representation, customary local fees, the amount involved in the case and the results obtained, and the experience and ability of the lawyer.

The representation agreement should be explicit that the client will pay not only legal fees, but the costs of suit such as filing fees, copying charges, and the expense of court reporters, factual investigators, and expert witnesses. The client should understand that non-attorney costs can be quite expensive. However, counsel should not forget her duty to render public interest legal service, which may include the provision of legal representation for free or at reduced rates for clients unable to pay. See Model Rules of Professional Conduct Rule 6.1; Model Code of Professional Responsibility EC 2–25.

In personal injury actions, in particular, plaintiffs may retain counsel on a contingent fee basis, under which counsel will recover a set percentage (typically thirty to forty percent) of any judgment or settlement the plaintiff ultimately receives. Often the percentage of recovery that counsel receives will increase if the recovery comes at a more advanced stage of the case. Thus counsel may receive one-third of any recovery obtained prior to trial, forty percent of any recovery obtained after the commencement of trial, and forty-five percent of any recovery if an appeal is taken by any party.

Agreements by counsel to handle a particular matter for a fixed sum are less common in the litigation context than hourly rate or contingent fee agreements. Fixed fee agreements are most common in relatively simple matters such as uncontested divorces, where the attorney's time commitment can be predicted with a fair degree of certainty at the outset of the case.

Counsel should use plain English in the retainer agreement and take the time to explain the agreement to the client. Explanations at the outset of a lawsuit can prevent later misunderstandings between client and counsel that can sour the entire attorney-client relationship.

CHAPTER THREE

PRETRIAL PLANNING AND INVESTIGATION

I. THE NEED TO PLAN LITIGATION

You've conducted a good initial client interview. The client has decided to retain you as counsel, and a follow-up meeting has been scheduled. What next? Well, it depends. The options may range from filing suit and immediately seeking a temporary restraining order, to sending a demand letter to the opposing party, to closing the file and doing nothing. Regardless of the option that client and counsel select, counsel should carefully plan the anticipated course of the litigation at the very outset of the case.

Why plan litigation? There is so much else to do in a litigation practice, most of it quite time-consuming. Why worry about what may happen six months from now, when other cases require that several major motions must be briefed this week, a series of out-of-town depositions must be taken next week, and a trial is set for the end of the month? As a practical matter, the hectic nature and relentless pace of civil litigation preclude some attorneys from systematic litigation planning. As the saying goes, some attorneys are so busy chopping wood that they never take time to sharpen their axes.

The very pace and volume of a litigation practice are major reasons why litigation planning is imperative. As in much else in life, the urgent often displaces the important in a litigation practice. By planning litigation, counsel can set priorities: among litigation tasks within a particular case, among the cases counsel is handling at any given time, and among those cases and counsel's non-litigation needs and obligations.

Attorneys should plan litigation so that they can provide the best possible representation in each of their cases. Different phases of pretrial litigation are linked to one another, and there is a natural progression within the pretrial process. Discovery generally is limited to matters that are relevant to the claims or defenses of parties to the pending action, and the decision to plead a particular claim or defense therefore may determine the ability of the parties to obtain specific discovery. More generally, decisions made early in the pretrial process may restrict later pretrial and trial options.

Even when there is no requirement that pretrial litigation tasks be scheduled in a particular sequence, there may be tactical advantages or disadvantages to scheduling pretrial proceedings in a certain order. Interrogatory answers may provide the basis for later deposition questioning, although the interrogatories may alert opposing counsel to likely deposition questions. Litigation maneuvering by one party may stimulate litigation responses by other parties. The decision to take a deposition will not only require the expenditure of attorney time and client money in connection with that deposition, but may cause other parties to schedule depositions of their own.

Litigation is an increasingly costly undertaking. The transcript of a relatively short deposition may cost hundreds of dollars, in addition to the attorney time necessary to plan and take the deposition. Counsel therefore owe it to their clients to only take depositions, or engage in other pretrial litigation tasks, that will enhance the chances of litigation success. Because of the high cost of litigation, corporate clients are increasingly requiring counsel to prepare litigation budgets detailing anticipated litigation activity and expenses. Whether required to or not, counsel can use litigation plans and budgets to alert clients to the costs of litigation, including nonmonetary litigation costs such as client aggravation and business disruption.

Attorneys also should plan litigation so that they can provide all of their clients with the best possible representation. If litigation has not been planned, counsel may find herself with two trials scheduled for the same day. If one of the trial dates can't be moved, there will be pressure on counsel to settle a case merely to accommodate her own schedule. Cases that must be settled generally do not result in optimum results for the client.

A final reason for planning litigation is to minimize the wear and tear on counsel. While a hectic pace is endemic to most litigation practices, attorneys need to schedule occasional vacations and other breaks. Even the sternest judges usually are sympathetic to long-scheduled vacations and wedding anniversaries and will try to accommodate such special events.

A litigation plan is essential if one hopes to maintain litigation control. While time and effort are required to develop these plans, the alternative to not planning usually is not welcome. The choice may not be between following or not following a litigation plan. Instead, the choice may be whether to attempt to follow your own litigation plan or be required to adhere to a plan developed by the court or opposing counsel.

II. PREPARING THE LITIGATION PLAN

Now that you understand the need to plan litigation, how do you go about the actual planning? Before any plan can be constructed, counsel must ascertain the client's litigation objectives. Does the client want to recover damages, obtain an injunction, quickly settle out-of-court, or attempt to resolve the dispute by non-judicial means? The answers to these questions may depend upon the client's financial resources, need for a quick resolution of the dispute, or desire to avoid the publicity and disruption of internal and external relationships that may result from extended discovery or trial.

Once counsel determines the client's litigation objectives, she must plot the path that will achieve those goals. This may involve working backwards from the ultimate litigation goals. If counsel believes she can win the case on a motion for summary judgment, what discovery will be necessary prior to that motion? What motions or other litigation moves might the opposing party make prior to the court's ruling on the motion for summary judgment? What are the court's likely actions and reactions? What if the court denies the planned motion for summary judgment? Counsel always should have a "Plan B" to fall back on if things don't work out exactly as anticipated.

A litigation plan is essential. The plan may be encompassed in a memorandum to the file and generally should include matters such as the following:

  1. Counsel's current understanding of the governing facts and law, as well as factual and legal areas requiring further investigation and research.

  2. The potential witnesses and exhibits to be used during pretrial and trial.

  3. The pretrial litigation activities planned by counsel, including documents to be drafted and filed, disclosure and discovery to be undertaken, and motions to be prepared and argued.

4. The pretrial litigation activities that counsel anticipates the opposing party will undertake.

5. The judge's anticipated responses to the litigation initiatives of each party, including the likelihood that the court will grant each motion and request.

6. Any orders or requirements that will be imposed independently by the court, such as required pretrial conferences and discovery and motion deadlines.

7. A timetable for all of the above activity.

8. A litigation budget for all of the above activity.

The litigation plan should be developed as soon as possible in the litigation. Plaintiff's plan should be developed prior to filing suit. One of plaintiff's major litigation advantages is that he has initiated the litigation. In order to exploit that advantage, plaintiff should know exactly how he wants the litigation to develop and should attempt to keep the initiative. For example, plaintiff's counsel should have planned her discovery prior to commencing suit and, if not precluded by Rule 26(d) of the Federal Rules of Civil Procedure, may want to file discovery requests simultaneously with the complaint.

Rules 16 and 26(f) of the Federal Rules of Civil Procedure can be useful for counsel who have developed a litigation plan. Rule 16 provides for pretrial conferences, scheduling, and management, while

Rule 16(b) requires the court to enter scheduling orders in most cases. Rule 26(f) requires the parties in most actions to confer at least 21 days before a scheduling conference is held or a Rule 16(b) scheduling order is due; this is so that the parties will consider their claims and defenses, consider the possibility of settlement, make or arrange for Rule 26(a)(1) disclosures, and develop a proposed discovery plan for submission to the court. Having first developed her own litigation plan, counsel can attempt to reach agreement with opposing counsel on scheduling and other pretrial matters and incorporate those agreements into the proposed discovery plan submitted to the court.

Counsel also should think ahead to the final pretrial order that will be required in most districts. These Rule 16(e) orders control the course of trial. Thinking about what ideally should be included in such an order may help counsel plan a structure for the pretrial proceedings leading up to the entry of that order.

Whether dealing with opposing counsel or the court, counsel's aim should be to obtain an agreement or order adopting the pretrial litigation plan developed for her own client. However, before proposing that opposing counsel or the court adopt your litigation plan, be certain that the deadlines it contains are ones that you, yourself, can meet. The completion of pretrial litigation tasks often takes longer than counsel first anticipates. In setting pretrial deadlines, consider the pretrial activity that you plan to undertake, the probable pretrial initiatives of opposing counsel, and the likely responses to this activity by other parties and the court.

Having established the necessity of litigation planning, an important caveat is in order. There are some litigation events that cannot be anticipated and therefore cannot be scheduled. For instance, the case may be transferred to another judge or an opposing party may obtain new counsel.

Counsel must remain flexible during the pretrial process and remember that pretrial proceedings are merely one aspect of the total litigation process. The litigation plan should be continually updated to reflect ongoing litigation developments. Pretrial litigation activities not only should be consistent with one another but consistent with the litigation strategy counsel intends to employ at trial.

For this reason, counsel should adopt a case theory and theme early in the pretrial process. A litigation theory provides an organizational structure for the litigation plan. The case theory is the explanation of what, factually, happened between the parties and why, legally, the defendant is or is not liable for plaintiff's alleged injuries.

Early in a case, counsel may pursue multiple case theories. In an automobile accident case, the plaintiff may investigate case theories based upon speeding or reckless driving, the defendant's intoxication, and mere carelessness on the defendant's part. As discovery and informal investigation progress, some of these theories will appear stronger than others or there may be insufficient facts to support certain theories. Thus certain theories may be dropped as the case gets closer to trial.

Federal Rule of Civil Procedure 8(e)(2) permits a party to "state as many separate claims or defenses as the party has regardless of consistency." As a tactical matter, though, it's usually best to avoid inconsistent theories at trial. A defendant can argue both that he never hit the plaintiff and, if he did, the plaintiff was contributorily negligent. However, these arguments may suggest that the defendant has little confidence in either case theory.

In addition to a case theory, or explanation, counsel should develop a case theme. The case theme is a persuasive case summary developed to motivate the court or jury to find for a particular party. Counsel should be able to state the case theme in a single sentence. In a contract action, a possible theme for the plaintiff might be: "This is a case about a man who failed to keep his promises."

Case theories and themes not only help counsel organize pretrial case development, but they can strengthen the case that counsel ultimately presents to the judge or jury.

III.   LEGAL RESEARCH

Those of you reading this book undoubtedly know a fair amount about legal research; many of you may know more about legal research than you really want to. If so, brace yourself for some bad news:

legal research is very important in most civil litigation.

However, the legal research lawyers conduct in practice is quite different from those library exercises that students are assigned in the first year of law school. The research may concern different subjects, may require counsel to consult different sources, may have to be conducted much more rapidly, and may be more fragmentary than the research conducted in legal research and writing classes. Moreover, legal research in practice is much more fluid than in the classroom and must be coordinated with counsel's ongoing factual investigation.

A. Legal Research During the Pretrial Process

Just as in law school, legal research concerning the governing substantive law often will be necessary during the pretrial process. For instance, counsel may need to determine whether certain conduct constitutes a tort. However, pretrial legal research often concerns subjects different from those typically researched in law school classes. Important research may be required concerning procedural matters, conflict of laws, or statutes of limitations. The sources that are checked may be different as well. While many law school legal research exercises require extensive analysis of case law, research in practice may focus on statutes, administrative regulations, local rules of court, or standing orders of individual judges.

The depth of legal research undertaken in practice may not be as extensive as that done in law school. The key judicial decisions will be the cases decided in this circuit, this district, and, best of all, by this judge. In most cases, the focus is on how the presiding judge will decide a given issue, rather than on determining the "better" rule or finding statutes from other jurisdictions. Electronic data bases can be quite useful in quickly uncovering decisions within a particular district or by a particular judge. Many pretrial rulings are quite discretionary and are not reflected in reported decisions. Counsel should ask others about how the judge is likely to rule in pretrial situations that may arise in her case.

Pretrial legal research may have to be performed extremely quickly. While counsel may have several weeks in which to research the law concerning a planned motion to dismiss or for summary judgment, there will not be as much time if the research is needed to oppose motions filed by other parties. Some research must be conducted even more quickly. If unexpected legal questions arise during a pretrial conference or deposition, the research may have to be conducted during a short break in the proceeding. Even when there is no legal research deadline, there may be a tactical advantage in completing research quickly so that a motion or other legal paper can be filed as soon as possible.

Legal research in practice is much more fluid than in law school. Facts change over the course of a lawsuit, which may necessitate new research initiatives. Litigation research therefore may be continuous. As more facts are discovered, additional legal research may be necessary. This legal research may in turn cause counsel to search for additional facts to support new legal theories.

The litigation plan should anticipate motions and other pretrial positions that opposing counsel is likely to take. The assessment of these litigation moves may require at least preliminary legal research. This legal research can be essential in planning one's own litigation strategy, and it can permit a much faster and complete response when opposing counsel actually takes the anticipated position during pretrial.

Counsel should memorialize all legal research. That research may be useful at a latter time, in another case if not in the present lawsuit. A record should be made of the sources checked, rather than merely making a note that "nothing could be found" concerning a particular issue. If the research is put to one side and later resumed, counsel may have to retrace her steps if she has made no record of the research previously conducted. Legal research records also may come in handy in defending against a Rule 11 motion challenging the legal sufficiency of a complaint or other litigation document.

Pretrial litigation and, especially, pretrial discovery can be extremely wide-ranging. One of the ways in which pretrial litigation can be focused and issues can be narrowed is by conducting thorough legal research prior to taking positions in the pretrial process. Good legal research can save attorney time and client money, and it can increase the likelihood of litigation success in the pretrial process. If this weren't enough reason to conduct thorough legal research, Rule 11 of the Federal Rules of Civil Procedure provides that the attorney's signature on a litigation document is a certification that the document is "warranted by existing law or by a nonfrivolous argument for the extension, modification, or reversal of existing law or the establishment of new law."

B. The Litigation Grid

How should counsel actually organize her legal research? How should that research be coordinated with her ongoing factual investigation? One method used by many attorneys is the development of a litigation grid.

The starting point for a litigation grid is the creation of a check list of the elements of each claim asserted in the lawsuit. If counsel is unfamiliar with the legal theory underlying a claim, legal research may be necessary. If a more common legal theory is asserted, counsel may obtain a succinct listing of a claim's legal elements from a book of commercially prepared jury instructions or from pattern jury instructions applicable in a particular jurisdiction. The elements underlying specific causes of action also may be set forth in a controlling judicial precedent or governing statute.

Having obtained a statement of each element that must be proved, counsel must determine the particular evidence relevant to each element. If counsel represents the plaintiff, she must determine what evidence she must offer to establish every element of each of plaintiff's claims. Defense counsel's analysis may be a bit different, because the defendant can defeat a claim if plaintiff fails to prove even a single element of that claim. Therefore counsel may choose to concentrate the defense upon only some of the elements of plaintiff's claim.

Figure 3–1 shows a rudimentary litigation grid prepared by plaintiff's counsel in a negligence action stemming from an automobile accident. The first vertical column lists the elements in a negligence action: defendant's negligence (breach of legal duty), proximate or legal causation of injury, and resulting damages. The next vertical column lists the possible witnesses (both the parties and third persons) whose testimony can establish each element. The final column lists the possible exhibits concerning each element of plaintiff's negligence claim. In the brackets underneath each witness and exhibit is the manner in which counsel plans to obtain the evidence in question.

FIGURE 3–1

PLAINTIFF'S LITIGATION GRID

Element of Case	Possible Witnesses Concerning Element	Possible Exhibits Concerning Element
Defendant's Negligence	Plaintiff **[client interview]** Passenger in Defendant's Car **[witness interview]** Police Officer **[witness interview]** Defendant **[deposition]** Accident Eyewitnesses **[witness interviews/ depositions]**	Photographs **[taken by plaintiff's investigator]** Police Report **[informal request]** Car Maintenance Log **[document production request]**
Proximate or Legal Causation	Plaintiff **[client interview]** Eyewitnesses **[witness interviews/ depositions]**	Diagram of Accident **[prepared by plaintiff's investigator or expert witness]**
Resulting Damages	Plaintiff **[client interview]** Plaintiff's Spouse **[witness interview]** Plaintiff's Doctors **[witness interviews/ depositions]**	Drug Prescriptions Doctors' Bills Wage Statements Doctors' Reports

The structure of the litigation grid can be altered in many ways. The grid can be expanded to show the cost of developing certain proof, the dates for the completion of pretrial tasks, or sources of proof such as party stipulations, disclosure or discovery responses, and judicial notice.

The litigation grid can be used throughout the pretrial process. As initially constructed, the grid merely may list the witnesses to contact and documents and other possible exhibits to locate and examine. As pretrial proceedings continue, the grid should be refined so that, ultimately, it will list the actual witnesses and exhibits to be offered at trial. During the pretrial process counsel may decide that certain people will make poor trial witnesses, certain exhibits are unavailable, certain claims or defenses are not likely to be successful, or the legal elements of a particular claim have changed. Each of these decisions should be reflected in changes to the litigation grid.

IV.   FACTUAL INVESTIGATION

Factual investigation begins during the initial client interview and often continues through trial. While the governing law may be relatively easy to research, factual investigation may pose practical difficulties. Whether it poses difficulties in a given case or not, factual investigation is extremely important to ultimate litigation success and can be extremely costly. A major portion of any litigation plan therefore should focus on pretrial factual investigation.

A.   Investigative Structure and Strategy

As with litigation generally, there should be a structure and plan for pretrial factual investigation. In planning factual investigation, counsel should creatively speculate about the facts that she hopes are true (because they will help her client) and the facts that she hopes aren't true (because they will harm her client). The investigator's job then is to determine if those facts actually exist, search for all other relevant facts, and attempt to preserve helpful facts so that they can be used in the lawsuit. Investigative plans are necessary because of the alternative means of gathering facts, the manner in which early investigatory efforts may preclude or create later litigation opportunities, and the cost of factual investigation.

In planning a factual investigation, counsel should consider (1) what information to obtain; (2) how to obtain the information; (3) from whom to obtain the information; and (4) when to obtain the information.

In determining what information to seek, counsel first should ascertain the facts that must exist for plaintiff to prevail. The element check list should provide the answer to this question. If counsel represents the plaintiff, her job is to find facts establishing each element of plaintiff's claims. If counsel represents the defendant, her job is to find facts negating (or the absence of facts establishing) at least one element of each of plaintiff's claims.

The starting point for any factual investigation is the initial client interview. Numerous questions should be asked and answered by counsel after the client interview. What were the facts about which my client was unsure? If my client was correct about a certain fact, what other facts must be true? What is the weakest part, factually, of my client's case? What facts should be corroborated by other witnesses or physical evidence? After the client interview, a factual chronology of important events can be created to organize the facts already known and highlight those that still must be determined.

Pretrial investigation can seek to uncover facts, preserve facts, and create facts. Typically, the investigator will be seeking to uncover facts in order to either use those facts affirmatively or to rebut other facts in the litigation. However, if facts are to be used, they must be preserved. This may require that a photograph be taken before debris is cleared from the scene of an accident or that a witness statement or deposition be taken before a witness's memory fades. Facts can be created by asking an expert witness to construct a model, prepare a diagram, or simulate an accident or other relevant event.

Counsel should discuss with her client the scope of the anticipated investigation. Because factual investigation can become very expensive, very quickly, counsel must identify the facts that she *must* have to be successful and the additional facts that she *would like* to have if costs permit. The client may have useful resources, such as staff employees who can help in the investigation and thereby help to contain costs.

Once counsel determines what information to seek, she must decide how to obtain that information. Initially, counsel must decide whether to undertake the investigation herself or use a secretary, paralegal, law clerk, or investigator. A non-attorney investigator may be more experienced in factual investigation than counsel, and it may be more economical to use his services than for the attorney herself to investigate. In addition, Rule 3.7 of the Model Rules of Professional Conduct and Disciplinary Rule 5–102 of the Model Code of Professional Responsibility generally preclude a lawyer from representing a party to a lawsuit in which the lawyer is likely to be a necessary witness. For this reason, counsel should not conduct witness interviews or take photographs by herself if later trial testimony may be necessary.

Counsel must decide whether to employ formal or informal discovery methods to obtain information. Much of pretrial practice consists of making and responding to formal discovery requests. The Federal Rules of Civil Procedure have quite liberal provisions for formal discovery, and those rules permit parties to compel formal discovery responses from parties and non-parties alike. However, there are many advantages to informal discovery.

One of the major advantages of informal discovery is that it can be significantly cheaper than formal discovery. Expensive attorney time may be consumed in drafting formal discovery requests. Why prepare such requests when a simple telephone call to opposing counsel may produce the same response? Informal discovery may not only be the most expeditious means of obtaining information, but the informal discovery obtained may permit counsel to be more focused in her formal discovery requests.

Another major advantage of informal discovery is that information may be obtained informally without alerting opposing parties that discovery is being sought. Rule 30 of the Federal Rules of Civil Procedure permits parties to take the deposition of any person, but notice of the deposition must be provided to all parties. In contrast, counsel can interview a non-party and take a witness statement without notifying other parties. Investigative secrecy can be important, particularly before suit is filed.

Nevertheless, there are times when formal discovery should be employed, as well as situations in which formal discovery is the only option. If a person will not talk with counsel voluntarily, a formal deposition may be in order. Model Rule 4.2 and Disciplinary Rule 7–104(A)(1) prohibit an attorney from communicating with a person about a matter concerning which that person is represented by counsel. Accordingly, formal discovery requests generally are used when information is sought from parties to a lawsuit.

Formal discovery responses also may be more useful in the litigation than informal discovery. Formal discovery responses are either written or, in the case of a deposition, transcribed as a written record. These responses are signed by opposing counsel, the opposing party, or both. It is much easier to impeach a party with his sworn interrogatory answers than with an unsigned letter or notes of an oral conversation.

How specific information should be obtained is related to the next major investigative question: From whom should the information be requested? These questions are intertwined, because formal discovery requests for interrogatory answers, documents, and examinations only can be made to parties. Indeed, if information is sought from a party, there may be no alternative but to use formal discovery because of the ethical prohibitions against contacting persons represented by counsel.

Sources of informal discovery, however, should not be overlooked. Important information may be available from public records, such as accident reports, title and other property records, permits and licenses, filings with a state secretary of state, and judicial records. While this type of information generally is available for the asking, other governmental records may require a request under a state or federal freedom of information act.

The reference section of the library can provide useful information, perhaps contained in annual corporate reports, back issues of newspapers and periodicals, bibliographical directories, or out-of-town telephone directories. Research from public sources can help counsel prepare deposition questions and discovery requests, without alerting others to the investigatory work. In addition, such research may be much cheaper than formal discovery.

If certain information is available from a corporation or government agency, there may be several individuals or offices within the agency that can provide the information. A private investigator may have contacts with individuals within large corporations or agencies who can cut through red tape and expedite the production of documents or information. In some cases it may be faster to request information directly from corporate or agency headquarters, while in other situations the quickest response may come from local personnel.

Certain information should be sought from multiple sources. The client may have the most relevant information concerning many important issues, but it will be an easy matter for opposing counsel to charge him with bias. Client statements should be corroborated, ideally by neutral third parties or contemporaneously prepared documents.

An important fact in determining from whom to request information is whether the request will become known to other parties. A disadvantage of formal discovery requests is that the opposing party knows exactly what information you are after. Formal discovery requests may even educate opposing counsel about important facts on which she hasn't yet focused. While there is no requirement that opposing counsel be notified about informal discovery requests to third persons, some third persons are more likely than others to inform opposing parties about informal discovery requests. If investigative secrecy is important, counsel should carefully consider the sources from which information will be sought.

The timing of investigative initiatives also is important. Plaintiff's counsel is required by Rule 11 of the Federal Rules of Civil Procedure to conduct an "inquiry reasonable under the circumstances" to ensure sufficient evidentiary support for the factual allegations of the complaint. Apart from this requirement, there are major tactical advantages to conducting as much informal investigation prior to the filing of suit as possible.

As a general rule, the sooner discovery is conducted, the better. If the information obtained is favorable, counsel may want to make use of that information as soon as possible. If the information is not favorable, counsel will want as much time as possible to deal with that information before it is used against her client by opposing counsel. Some information simply won't be available if it is not obtained quickly. Memories fade, witnesses disappear, and the appearance of an accident scene may change with the seasons or after skid marks or oil stains have faded. Therefore the investigator's job is not only to discover, but to preserve, relevant evidence.

If plaintiff's counsel plans to file a motion for a temporary restraining order, preliminary injunction, or summary judgment, completion of informal investigation prior to filing suit may permit those motions to be heard at the very outset of the case. This should enable plaintiff to gain and retain the initiative in the litigation. If defense counsel are required to immediately respond to these motions, defendants may have difficulty filing any motions of their own or otherwise gaining control of the action.

Early informal discovery may enable counsel to conduct more effective formal discovery. If witnesses are willing to talk and are not represented by counsel, they should be interviewed informally before their depositions are scheduled. Informal interviews may permit counsel to focus her deposition questions on relevant matters and, in some cases, decide not to depose certain individuals. Witnesses may identify other sources of informal and formal discovery previously unknown to counsel. Informal discovery may permit plaintiff's counsel to file focused formal discovery requests at the very outset of the litigation.

Once suit is filed, counsel should carefully consider the sequence of formal discovery requests. Rule 26(d) of the Federal Rules of Civil Procedure provides that, except in categories of proceedings exempted from initial disclosure under Rule 26(a)(1)(E) or when authorized under the Federal

Rules or by order or agreement of the parties, discovery cannot be sought before the parties have conferred pursuant to Rule 26(f) to make or arrange for Rule 26(a)(1) disclosures and develop a discovery plan. However, Rule 26(d) also provides that, absent a court order to the contrary, "methods of discovery may be used in any sequence, and the fact that a party is conducting discovery, whether by deposition or otherwise, does not operate to delay any other party's discovery."

Most attorneys therefore use discovery devices in the order that makes the most tactical sense. Many attorneys commence formal discovery with interrogatories, using the interrogatories to obtain information about documents that should be requested and individuals who should be deposed. Requests for admission are used by some attorneys at the very outset of discovery, often with the hope that the admissions obtained may obviate the need for discovery concerning certain issues. Other attorneys use admission requests after other discovery has been completed, in order to nail down undisputed facts for trial. Some attorneys use admission requests at both the beginning and end of the discovery period.

Even once the decision is made to use a particular discovery device, consideration should be given to the timing of that discovery. In scheduling depositions, counsel should presume that the questions the first deponents are asked will become known to later deponents. If there is an advantage in catching certain individuals off guard at their depositions, those depositions should be taken first.

Most lawsuits turn on the facts uncovered during pretrial investigation, rather than on the law contained in appellate opinions. Pretrial factual investigation should be structured to obtain, as quickly and inexpensively as possible, the most relevant information for one's client while providing the least information to opposing counsel.

B.   Investigative Techniques

Once the factual investigation has been planned, that plan must be implemented by employing various investigative techniques. In some cases, expert analysis of a physical object may be essential. In many cases, evidence must be preserved by taking photographs or making a videotape recording. In all cases, the investigator must ask the right questions, at the right time, of the right people. Good investigators must maintain a healthy skepticism concerning the answers received and must know how to conduct an effective witness interview and memorialize the interview in a witness statement.

1.   Witness Interviews

Witness interviews are similar to client interviews in many respects. The interviewer's job is to obtain all relevant facts from the witness. However, because the witness is not the client, he may be less willing to cooperate. The most difficult aspect of witness interviews, therefore, is motivating the witness to talk.

The success of a witness interview may be determined by the circumstances under which the interview is conducted. Counsel should carefully select the time, place, and manner in which to approach the witness. Because it's so easy to hang up the phone or refuse to take a phone call, witnesses usually should be interviewed in person rather than over the telephone. Personal interviews also permit counsel to evaluate the credibility of the witness and have a witness statement signed on the spot.

Counsel must determine whether the witness will be more likely to be helpful if approached at work, at home, or at another locale. If the witness is a fellow employee of the plaintiff in an employment discrimination action, plaintiff's counsel may be wise to speak with the witness in the privacy of his home rather than at work.

Counsel should consider the best time to approach the witness. Will the witness have more time to talk on his lunch hour, during work, in the evening, or on the weekend? Counsel should attempt to interview third-party witnesses before they are approached by opposing counsel, in order to gain their confidence and enlist their support.

The success of a witness interview depends not only on the circumstances under which the interview is conducted, but on the actual conduct of the interview. Counsel should identify herself at the outset of the interview and tell the witness why she needs his help: "Hello. I'm Sarah Malloy, and I represent Lloyd Lester in his suit against the driver of the truck that hit him last August. You're listed as one of the witnesses on the police accident report, and I need to talk with you about just what you saw of the accident." While deception may motivate witnesses to talk ("I represent the estate of a deceased millionaire, and you're a very lucky man!"), misrepresentation is prohibited by Model Rule of Professional Conduct 8.4(c) and Disciplinary Rule 1–102(A)(4). In addition, a statement will be of little use if it's obvious that the witness was duped into giving it.

Efforts to personalize your client and create sympathy for him may help convince a witness to talk: "Lloyd is in the hospital right now, and his wife has gone back to work to help support the family. They really need your help." Reluctant witnesses can be reminded that their testimony can be subpoenaed: "I hope that if you talk with me now, I won't have to subpoena you to give a formal deposition. If that becomes necessary, I'll try to be cooperative in scheduling that testimony for a convenient time. But I need your cooperation now and would like to talk with you for just a few minutes." Witnesses who still refuse to be interviewed are reminded by some attorneys that "All I'm after is the truth." If this doesn't convince the witness to talk, the attorney has laid the foundation for later trial cross-examination: "Mr. Wright, isn't it true that you refused to talk with me before trial? Even though I told you that all I was after was the truth?"

Some witnesses will be more likely to talk with an investigator if other witnesses have done so: "Mrs. Jones, I've just talked with Marion Casey from the plant, and he suggested that I talk with you, too, about the accident." A client or particularly friendly witness might even be used to schedule an interview or introduce counsel to the new witness.

Counsel should consider scheduling witness interviews so that those people most likely to be cooperative are interviewed first. Hostile witnesses may be motivated to talk by the following reporter's technique: "Mr. Moore, I've spoken with Molly O'Neil about the accident. What I'd like to do now is give you a chance to tell me your side of the story." Witnesses always should be asked about contacts they have had with other investigators and about other persons with relevant knowledge.

Once the witness agrees to an interview, the interviewing techniques discussed in Chapter 2 should be utilized as appropriate. However, because the witness is not your client, the attorney-client privilege will not protect either statements made by counsel or by the witness. In addition, because the witness is not your client, you may have much less time for the interview. Counsel should never presume that she will have a second opportunity to speak with a witness, but should question the witness so that a statement can be taken at the interview's conclusion. Because there may be only a single chance to interview a witness, counsel should prepare thoroughly for witness interviews. In particular, counsel should learn as much as possible about the witness and his involvement in the case and have an interview plan.

2. Witness Statements

The major question concerning witness statements is whether to take them. Under Federal Rule of Civil Procedure 26(b)(3), a person is entitled to a copy of her own witness statement. Counsel should think twice before creating a document that eventually may reach an opposing party and be used against her own client.

On the other hand, there are important reasons why witness statements should be taken from most witnesses. If the witness has favorable testimony, the statement will preserve that testimony. The fact that the witness knows nothing about an event may be significant. If this is the case, or if the testimony of the witness is not favorable, counsel may wish to preserve the testimony to discourage the witness from offering even less favorable testimony in the future.

Witness statements can be taken in several ways. Audiotapes or videotapes can preserve a statement in a dramatic fashion, but they can be difficult to understand and awkward to use for trial impeachment. In addition, witnesses may feel uncomfortable being recorded in this manner.

Another possibility is to have the witness write out his statement in long-hand. Statements that are in both the own words and own handwriting of the witness can be highly credible evidence. However, the witness may not write as strong a statement as counsel could draft. While counsel should never prepare a witness statement that is factually misleading, by drafting the statement counsel can ensure that irrelevant information is not included and that the basic facts are presented in the most persuasive manner.

For this reason, many attorneys draft the witness statement and ask the witness to confirm the statement's accuracy. Counsel then typically have the statement typed and submitted to the witness for signature. If there is a chance that the witness may change his mind and not sign the statement at a later time, counsel may decide to write the statement on the spot and have the witness sign it at the conclusion of the interview.

Whether the statement initially is prepared by counsel or the witness, the substance of most witness statements is fairly standard. The initial paragraph of the statement should identify the witness, setting forth his qualifications to offer the statement and, perhaps, some general background information.

The heart of the statement is the factual narrative of the witness. The narrative should include specific facts, rather than generalizations or characterizations. While the facts should be related in as favorable a fashion as possible, the witness statement should not omit important, unfavorable facts. If it later appears that counsel and witness have attempted to cover up important facts, the credibility of the statement, the counsel, and the witness will be undermined if not destroyed.

Traditionally, witness statements were signed and notarized. In the federal courts, unsigned declarations under the penalty of perjury can be used instead of sworn affidavits. Section 1746 of Title 28 of the United States Code provides that unsworn declarations have the same effect as a sworn affidavit if executed within the United States and subscribed to by the witness in substantially the following form:

I declare (or certify, verify or state) under penalty of perjury that the foregoing is true and correct. Executed on (date).

(Signature)

Some attorneys might amend the first sentence of the above declaration to provide: "I, [witness name], have read the above statement consisting of ___ pages, and I declare under penalty of perjury that the foregoing is true and correct." To guard against a later charge that pages in a multiple-page statement have been switched, counsel can have the witness initial each page or have the statement typed so that no sentence ends at the bottom of a page but all sentences carry over to the next page.

Witnesses are entitled to copies of their statements under Rule 26(b)(3) of the Federal Rules of Civil Procedure, and it's a good practice to offer witnesses copies of their statements. Such an offer should make it clear that the attorney is dealing aboveboard with the witness and should engender confidence in the attorney. Counsel also should ask witnesses for copies of any statements they have given to other investigators. These prior statements should be obtained before taking a new witness statement, and the new witness statement can explain or otherwise address statements previously made.

CHAPTER FOUR

THE COMPLAINT

I. PREREQUISITES TO SUIT

The Federal Rules of Civil Procedure contain important requirements for pleading claims in the federal courts. Before even considering those requirements, though, counsel must be certain that the prerequisites for a federal action are met.

A useful check list of federal suit prerequisites is set forth in Rule 12(b) of the Federal Rules of Civil Procedure. The suit prerequisites listed in Rule 12 include subject matter jurisdiction (Rule 12(b)(1)), personal jurisdiction (Rule 12(b)(2)), venue (Rule 12(b)(3)), process and service of process (Rules 12(b)(4) and (5)), the statement of a claim upon which relief can be granted (Rule 12(b)(6)), and the joinder of persons needed for a just adjudication (Rule 12(b)(7)).

In contrast to state courts of general jurisdiction, which can hear all cases except those specifically excluded from their subject matter jurisdiction, federal district courts are courts of limited jurisdiction. This means that a statutory jurisdictional basis must be found for any federal civil action. Specific federal statutes provide grants of subject matter jurisdiction in discrete areas such as bankruptcy, civil rights, intellectual property, and admiralty. However, the two major categories of federal subject matter jurisdiction permit the district courts to hear cases involving federal questions and cases between citizens of different states.

Section 1331 of Title 28 of the United States Code is the general federal question statute, under which the federal district courts have jurisdiction over "civil actions arising under the Constitution, laws, or treaties of the United States." Section 1331's $10,000 amount in controversy requirement was repealed in 1980, so that federal question cases can be heard by the federal courts regardless of the amount in controversy.

Section 1332 of Title 28 provides for federal subject matter jurisdiction over actions between citizens of different states in which the matter in controversy, exclusive of interest and costs, exceeds $75,000. For a natural person to be a citizen under Section 1332, he or she must be a citizen of the United States and be domiciled within a particular state. State domicile is based upon residence within a state plus the intent to remain in that state indefinitely. Section 1332(c)(1) of Title 28 provides that a corporation is a citizen of both the state in which it is incorporated and the state in which it has its principal place of business.

If subject matter jurisdiction exists under one of the above statutes, a federal district court can exercise "supplemental jurisdiction" over related claims pursuant to 28 U.S.C. § 1367. Under the doctrine of pendent jurisdiction recognized in *United Mine Workers v. Gibbs* (S.Ct.1966), federal courts exercised nonstatutory jurisdiction over claims arising from the same "nucleus of operative fact" as claims over which there was a statutory basis for subject matter jurisdiction. Under the doctrine of ancillary jurisdiction, federal courts exercised jurisdiction over related claims that were an outgrowth of plaintiff's original claims: compulsory counterclaims, cross-claims, third-party claims, and intervention as a matter of right. Congress endorsed both variants of supplemental jurisdiction in 1990, providing in 28 U.S.C. § 1367 that, with certain specified exceptions, "the district courts shall have supplemental jurisdiction over all other claims that are so related to claims in the action within [the court's] original jurisdiction that they form part of the same case or controversy under Article III of the United States Constitution." Even if this test is met, however, counsel should confirm that the claim in question does not fall within the exceptions to supplemental jurisdiction contained in 28 U.S.C. § 1367(b) and is not a claim over which the court may decline to exercise supplemental jurisdiction under 28 U.S.C. § 1367(c).

In addition to jurisdiction over the subject matter of a case, the court must have personal or territorial jurisdiction over the parties. By filing suit, plaintiffs submit themselves to the personal jurisdiction of the court. Nor is there usually any difficulty obtaining personal jurisdiction over a defendant who is present within the forum state.

Achieving personal jurisdiction over defendants who are not physically present can be a bit more difficult. There must be a statute or rule permitting the court to exercise personal jurisdiction over an absent defendant. Most states have adopted long-arm statutes, permitting their courts to exercise jurisdiction over absent defendants who have contacts with the state. Rule 4(k)(1) of the Federal Rules of Civil Procedure permits district courts to exercise personal jurisdiction over defendants pursuant to federal statutes authorizing service upon out-of-state defendants in specific types of cases or by employing long-arm statutes or rules of the state in which the federal court sits. With respect to federal question claims, Rule 4(k)(2) authorizes service upon a defendant who is not subject to the personal jurisdiction of any state court so long as that defendant's aggregate contacts with the United States are sufficient to subject that defendant to the constitutional exercise of the federal judicial power.

Not only must there be a statute or rule authorizing the exercise of personal jurisdiction, but that exercise must be constitutional under the due process clause of the fifth or fourteenth amendment. Under the Supreme Court's decision in *International Shoe Co. v. Washington* (S.Ct.1945), personal jurisdiction can be asserted over an absent defendant if that defendant has minimum contacts with the forum state, the claim asserted arises from those contacts, and the maintenance of suit does not offend "traditional notions of fair play and substantial justice."

In addition to this general formulation of the due process test, the Supreme Court in *Burnham v. Superior Court* (S.Ct.1990) reaffirmed the doctrine of "transient jurisdiction." Under this doctrine personal jurisdiction can be asserted over a defendant who may not have minimum state contacts but who is physically present in the forum state when served with process. Moreover, under the doctrine of "general jurisdiction," personal jurisdiction has been upheld over defendants with substantial, rather than merely minimum, forum contacts even though the substantive claim asserted does not arise from those contacts.

Finally, a defendant who is not physically present within a forum may be subject to personal jurisdiction because he or she consented to the personal jurisdiction of the court. This consent may have been expressed in a contractual forum selection clause. These clauses have been upheld by the Supreme Court in *Carnival Cruise Lines, Inc. v. Shute* (S.Ct.1991) and *M/S Bremen v. Zapata Off–Shore Co.* (S.Ct.1972).

Venue requirements determine the specific court within a court system that will hear a case. Venue provisions are contained in many of the statutes that recognize federal causes of action. In addition, Section 1391 of Title 28 is a general venue statute allocating federal actions to specific federal district courts.

Under Section 1391(a), actions in which subject matter jurisdiction is based solely upon diversity of citizenship can be brought in (1) a federal judicial district in which any defendant resides (if all defendants reside in the same state), (2) a district where a substantial part of the events or omissions giving rise to the claim occurred or where a substantial part of the property that is the subject of the action is situated, or (3) if there is no other district in which the action may otherwise by brought, a district in which any defendant is subject to personal jurisdiction at the time the action is commenced. Under Section 1391(b), actions in which subject matter jurisdiction is not based solely on diversity of citizenship can be brought where the defendant resides, a substantial part of the events or omissions giving rise to the claim occurred, or the subject property is situated (just as under Section 1391(a)). In addition, non-diversity claims can be brought in "a judicial district in which any defendant may be found, if there is no district in which the action may otherwise be brought." Regardless of the basis of federal subject matter jurisdiction, there may be more than one judicial district in which suit can be brought under 28 U.S.C. § 1391.

Once the complaint has been drafted, it must be filed with the court clerk and served upon each defendant. Unless the plaintiff is authorized to file the action *in forma pauperis* under 28 U.S.C. § 1915 because he is unable to pay the costs of suit, the clerk will require the payment of a filing fee. In addition, plaintiff's counsel must complete a civil cover sheet providing basic information about the action. The federal civil cover sheet also asks if an action is related to any pending case, to permit possible assignment of the new action to the judge handling the pending case.

Traditionally, the complaint had to be formally served upon each defendant with a summons, but many jurisdictions now permit service by mail in order to avoid the expense of personal service. Under Rule 4(d)(2) of the Federal Rules of Civil Procedure, a plaintiff can request that competent adults, corporations, and associations waive formal service of process by sending such defendants a copy of the complaint and a written request that they waive formal service. As an inducement for a defendant to waive service of process, Rule 4(d)(2) provides that if a domestic defendant fails to comply with a waiver request that defendant typically must bear the cost of personal service. In addition, Rule 4(d)(3) provides that defendants who timely return requested waivers have 60 (90, if the defendant was addressed outside the United States) days after the date on which the request for waiver was sent to serve an answer to the complaint (rather than the 20 day response time otherwise provided for non-United States defendants). Waiver of service can save all parties the expense of formal, personal service. However, Rule 4(d)(4) provides that a summons and complaint are not considered to have been served until the completed waiver is filed with the court, so plaintiff's counsel should not seek a waiver if service of process must be effected in order to satisfy an impending statute of limitations or

Rule 4(m)'s 120 day time limit for service of process.

Rules 12(b)(6) and 12(b)(7) of the Federal Rules of Civil Procedure concern the legal sufficiency of the claim asserted. Rule 12(b)(6) provides for dismissal of pleadings that do not state a claim upon which relief can be granted. The essential elements of the claim should have been identified in the element check list that was prepared at the very outset of the case. In order to defeat a Rule 12(b)(7) motion to dismiss, plaintiff's counsel must be certain that all persons necessary for a just adjudication have been joined as parties. Rule 19 of the Federal Rules of Civil Procedure governs situations in which the inability to join an absent party may result in the dismissal of the action.

In addition to the seven requirements of Rule 12(b), the action must be filed within the applicable statute of limitations period. For certain causes of action, prefiling notice to a governmental defendant may be required or there may be administrative remedies that must be exhausted. For instance, prior to filing an employment discrimination claim under Title VII of the Civil Rights Act of 1964, an administrative complaint must be filed with the Equal Employment Opportunity Commission or a designated state agency. Even absent a statutory requirement that a prefiling demand be made upon the defendant, in many cases claimant's counsel may send a demand letter to the defendant (possibly with a draft of the complaint that will be filed if no settlement is reached). Some claims are easier to settle before the defendant has been accused of wrongdoing in a public lawsuit and the parties' positions have hardened.

The local rules of the district court always should be checked before filing an action. Clerk's office personnel may provide helpful guidance, and some clerk's offices provide check lists of local filing requirements.

II.   THE CLAIMS ASSERTED

Once counsel ensures that all suit prerequisites have been satisfied, she still must determine exactly what claims to assert in the action. Even though several claims can be asserted, there may be tactical reasons not to plead each of them in the complaint. Even though numerous persons can be sued, there may be tactical reasons not to name each of them as a defendant.

If there is a strong claim against a potential defendant, there may be little reason to assert additional, weaker, claims. The pleading of additional claims may make the best claim seem weaker than it otherwise would appear. The defendant may move to dismiss weaker claims, which will require the expenditure of time and resources even if the claims are not ultimately dismissed. In some cases, counsel may not be able to determine the strength of certain claims without the benefit of formal discovery. In such a situation, the plaintiff can plead alternative or hypothetical claims pursuant to Federal Rule of Civil Procedure 8(e)(2) and seek a Rule 41(a) voluntary dismissal of problematic claims after the completion of discovery.

Sometimes there will be no single forum in which all potential claims can be asserted against a defendant or several potential defendants. Counsel therefore will have to decide whether to withhold certain claims or file multiple suits in order to assert all potential claims.

There may be more than one federal district court in which venue is proper, thus permitting suit to be filed in the district that appears most favorable to the plaintiff. Cases can be won or lost due to the judge who will hear the case, the geographic area from which the jurors are selected, the geographic convenience of the alternative venues for counsel, the parties, and the witnesses, the probable delay in the alternative districts, and any difference in governing law in different judicial circuits.

The choice of claims asserted and defendants sued can either create or destroy potential judicial venues. Absent any other basis for federal subject matter jurisdiction, a potential federal forum can be destroyed if a citizen of the same state as the plaintiff is named as a defendant. Aside from its impact on potential judicial venues, the assertion of a particular claim may permit the court to entertain other claims that it otherwise could not. The assertion of a claim under 28 U.S.C. § 1331 may permit the court to exercise supplemental jurisdiction over related claims pursuant to 28 U.S.C. § 1367. Pursuant to the federal interpleader statute, 28 U.S.C. §§ 1335, 1397, and 2361, district courts can consider multiple property claims despite jurisdictional, venue, and service of process problems that otherwise would exist.

In choosing the claims to be asserted, counsel should not overlook defense counsel's likely response to those claims. The defendant may seek to have a case transferred to another district court pursuant to 28 U.S.C. § 1404, or, if the case originally was filed in state court, may seek to remove it to federal court pursuant to 28 U.S.C. § 1441. Another possible response to plaintiff's claim may be the filing of a counterclaim pursuant to Federal Rule of Civil Procedure 13(a) or (b). The defendant also might bring additional parties into the suit pursuant to Rule 14, while co-defendants may assert cross-claims against one another pursuant to Rule 13(g).

Apart from any particular claims or motions that they may file, some potential defendants may more aggressively defend an action and be less likely to settle than other potential defendants. Certain requests, such as for class certification under Rule 23 of the Federal Rules of Civil Procedure, may invite procedural skirmishing that will delay the ultimate resolution of the case on the merits. Thus both governing law and pretrial tactics should be considered in determining the claims to assert in the complaint.

III.　THE RELIEF REQUESTED

In addition to the considerations discussed in the prior section, an important factor in choosing the claims to assert in the complaint is the relief to which the plaintiff may be entitled under each claim. Statutes may provide for the award of treble damages, costs, and attorneys' fees to prevailing plaintiffs, while the relief available under common law causes of action may be significantly more limited. In the initial client interview, counsel should ascertain the relief the client desires. Her job then is to structure the complaint and resulting lawsuit to attempt to obtain that desired relief. Federal Rule of Civil Procedure 8(a) provides that relief "in the alternative or of several different types may be demanded."

The most common form of relief is legal relief, which primarily consists of monetary damages. Several types of monetary relief may be available in connection with any given claim. Compensatory damages are to make the injured plaintiff whole, and may be either special or general damages. Special damages are to compensate the plaintiff for injuries that are not the necessary consequence of defendant's actions, and Federal Rule of Civil Procedure 9(g) requires that they be specifically pled. Thus while general damages such as pain and suffering need not be pled with any greater specificity than other elements of a personal injury claim, special damages such as medical bills must be specifically set forth in the complaint.

Punitive damages may be assessed against a defendant who has acted in a wilful or reckless manner and are to deter similar conduct in the future. Punitive damages may be particularly important if plaintiff's injuries are minimal and there is little chance of obtaining significant compensatory damages.

When it is difficult to calculate damages precisely, liquidated damages may be recoverable. The amount of liquidated damages may be specified by statute or established by party agreement. For instance, a commercial or consumer contract may state that any breach of the contract entitles the injured party to recover damages in a set amount. If there is no statutory or contractual provision for liquidated damages, nominal damages may be awarded to plaintiffs whose monetary loss is difficult to measure.

In addition to legal damages, an injured party may be entitled to equitable relief. Rescission, specific performance, restitution, and reformation all are forms of equitable relief. However, the most notable type of equitable relief is the injunction. While a legal judgment requires the defendant to pay money to the prevailing plaintiff, an injunction is a court order requiring the defendant to take certain action or refrain from acting. The plaintiff might seek an injunction against the destruction of his house by defendant's bulldozers; in such a situation, it may be of little comfort to the plaintiff that he can recover damages at a later time if the house is wrongfully destroyed. As with all equitable relief, injunctions are only available if legal relief would be inadequate.

Sometimes even a permanent injunction will not be sufficient to protect a plaintiff from wrongful injury. If the plaintiff is about to be illegally evicted from his apartment, the issuance of a permanent injunction may not provide timely relief. In this situation, the plaintiff might seek a temporary injunction to preserve the status quo until the court can consider the merits of a request for a permanent injunction.

Rule 65 of the Federal Rules of Civil Procedure recognizes two types of temporary injunctions: preliminary injunctions and temporary restraining orders. A preliminary injunction cannot issue without notice to the adverse party, although the preliminary injunction proceedings may be more truncated than the full trial that may be held prior to issuance of a permanent injunction.

If time is truly of the essence, the plaintiff can seek a temporary restraining order. Federal courts can issue temporary restraining orders without notice to the party to be enjoined, although Rule 65(b) requires the moving party's counsel to certify the attempts that have been made to notify the adverse party. Temporary restraining orders cannot extend for a period of more than ten days. However, a single ten-day extension of the order is possible, as is a longer extension if the party against whom the order is directed consents. Unless the applicant is the United States or one of its officers or agencies, the court generally requires the party seeking a preliminary injunction or temporary restraining order to post a bond pursuant to Rule 65(c) before an injunction issues.

In addition to legal and equitable relief, 28 U.S.C. § 2201 authorizes the federal courts to grant declaratory judgments. Although an actual controversy must exist for declaratory relief to issue, such relief can be quite useful to parties desiring a judicial declaration of their legal rights before they embark on a particular course of conduct. A defendant might file a separate declaratory judgment action against its insurance carrier to obtain a declaration of the insurer's obligations to defend and indemnify the defendant in a prior suit.

The plaintiff may be entitled to incidental relief in addition to the primary relief he seeks. Under Federal Rule of Civil Procedure 54(d)(1), the costs of suit are generally awarded to the prevailing party unless the court otherwise directs. However, the costs recoverable under Rule 54 are narrowly defined in 28 U.S.C. § 1920 to include only such items as court filing and service fees and the cost of transcripts necessarily obtained for use in the case.

The most significant litigation cost—attorneys' fees—is not included within the costs recoverable as a matter of course under Rule 54(d). Nor are attorneys' fees recoverable as a matter of course under the "American Rule" on attorneys' fees that prevails in this country. However, increasing numbers of federal statutes explicitly provide for the award of attorneys' fees to prevailing plaintiffs. When a statute so provides, attorneys' fees can be recovered pursuant to the procedures set forth in Rule 54(d)(2).

An important factor in choosing the defendants to sue is the extent to which each potential defendant can satisfy any judgment that might be entered against it. In many cases this will depend upon insurance coverage, about which the plaintiff generally learns only after filing suit and receiving a Rule 26(a)(1)(D) initial disclosure or a response to a formal discovery request. If the same relief can be obtained from several defendants, counsel may decide to pursue claims only against those defendants who will appear the least sympathetic to the judge or jury at trial.

If a defendant refuses to satisfy a judgment, the plaintiff can execute on that judgment pursuant to Federal Rule of Civil Procedure 69(a). Rule 69(a) adopts the execution procedure of the state in which the federal district court sits, which typically provides for seizure of property or income of the judgment debtor pursuant to a writ of execution.

In addition to relief on the merits, there may be other "relief" that can be obtained by naming a person as a defendant or filing a particular claim. While non-parties with relevant information can be deposed or required to produce documents, only parties are subject to interrogatories and requests for admission. A request for a preliminary injunction may result in a faster resolution of the lawsuit, and a request for punitive damages may entitle the plaintiff to discovery concerning defendant's financial resources that otherwise would not be available.

Counsel should consider whether to request a jury trial on any legal claims. If a jury is likely to be more favorably disposed to plaintiff's claims than a judge, counsel should be certain to comply with Federal Rule of Civil Procedure 38(b) and demand a jury "not later than 10 days after the service of the last pleading directed to [the] issue" concerning which the jury is sought.

A federal magistrate judge may be available to hear the lawsuit if the parties consent. Counsel should be aware of the relative advantages of having plaintiff's claims heard by a magistrate judge or federal district judge. While this determination will hinge on the judicial proclivities and abilities of the district judges and magistrate judges available to hear the case, in many districts the parties can obtain a more expeditious trial date from a magistrate judge.

Nor should counsel ignore the possibility of obtaining relief apart from formal legal proceedings. Many attorneys send a demand letter to the defendant prior to filing the complaint, offering to settle the case on specified terms before the parties are put to the time and expense of contested litigation. Counsel always should remember that disputes usually can be resolved more expeditiously and inexpensively outside the formal judicial process. The parties also can exert greater control over dispute resolution techniques they have tailored to their own disputes. For these reasons, an area of increasing interest to attorneys and judges alike is alternative dispute resolution ("ADR").

Alternative dispute resolution techniques such as private judges, arbitration, mediation, and negotiation have been used successfully to resolve many disputes short of litigation. ADR techniques also have been used as an adjunct to formal adjudication to resolve claims that have been filed in the courts. Among the techniques that have been used by the courts are mini-trials and summary jury trials (in which greatly abbreviated case presentations are made to either a judge or jury and the resulting advisory verdict is used as a basis for settlement discussions), court-annexed arbitration and mediation, and court-facilitated settlement.

IV. MODERN PLEADING AND PRACTICE

Once counsel determines that the prerequisites to suit are satisfied and decides upon the specific claims to assert and relief to request, she must draft the complaint. Fortunately, the pleading requirements of the Federal Rules of Civil Procedure are very liberal in nature. In contrast to common law and code pleading systems, under which the pleadings played a much greater role in defining, and resolving, civil actions, the Federal Rules of Civil Procedure establish a very liberal system of "notice pleading." The Supreme Court observed in *Conley v. Gibson* (S.Ct.1957) that "all the Rules require is 'a short and plain statement of the claim' that will give the defendant fair notice of what the plaintiff's claim is and the grounds upon which it rests." Rather than requiring the parties to plead the detailed facts upon which they rely, the Federal Rules of Civil Procedure grant them a broad right to discovery by which to ascertain the relevant facts.

The pleadings recognized by the Federal Rules of Civil Procedure are quite limited in number. Rule 7(a) provides for a complaint and an answer, a reply to a counterclaim "denominated as such," an answer to a cross-claim, a third-party complaint, and a third-party answer. Rule 7(a) further provides: "No other pleading shall be allowed, except that the court may order a reply to an answer or a third-party answer."

Rule 10 of the Federal Rules of Civil Procedure governs the form of pleadings filed in the federal courts. Rule 10(a) requires that every pleading contain a caption setting forth the name of the court, the title and file number of the action, and the title of the pleading. Rule 10(b) requires that all "averments of claim or defense shall be made in numbered paragraphs, the contents of each of which shall be limited as far as practicable to a statement of a single set of circumstances." Rule 10(b) further permits reference to earlier paragraphs of the pleading to be made by paragraph number, and it requires that each claim "founded upon a separate transaction or occurrence and each defense other than denials shall be stated in a separate count or defense whenever a separation facilitates the clear presentation of the matters set forth." In addition, Rule 10(c) permits statements in a pleading to be adopted by reference in a different part of that pleading or in a different pleading or motion.

Counsel should be certain to comply with the more specific requirements governing the format of pleadings and other court papers that are contained in local rules of court. However, Rule 5(e) of the Federal Rules of Civil Procedure precludes clerks from refusing to accept for filing any paper "solely because it is not presented in proper form as required by these rules or any local rules or practices," and Rule 83(a)(2) provides that a local rule imposing a requirement of form shall not be "enforced in a manner that causes a party to lose rights because of a nonwillful failure to comply with the requirement." Nevertheless, all attorneys should be thoroughly familiar with applicable local rules and adhere to their precise requirements.

Rule 8 of the Federal Rules of Civil Procedure contains the general rules of pleading applicable in the federal courts. Rule 8(a) provides that a claim for relief (in the original complaint or asserted as a counterclaim, cross-claim, or third-party claim) shall contain:

(1) a short and plain statement of the grounds upon which the court's jurisdiction depends, unless the court already has jurisdiction and the claim needs no new grounds of jurisdiction to

support it, (2) a short and plain statement of the claim showing that the pleader is entitled to relief, and (3) a demand for judgment for the relief the pleader seeks.

The Appendix of Forms to the Federal Rules of Civil Procedure contains illustrative complaints sufficient to satisfy Rule 8. The allegation of jurisdiction required by Rule 8(a)(1) is shown in Form 2. The portion of Form 2 that follows is a jurisdictional allegation for a diversity claim; the "sum specified by 28 U.S.C. § 1332" is, after the amendment of that statutory provision in 1996, $75,000:

Plaintiff is a * * * corporation incorporated under the laws of the State of Connecticut having its principal place of business in the State of Connecticut and defendant is a corporation incorporated under the laws of the State of New York having its principal place of business in a State other than the State of Connecticut. The matter in controversy exceeds, exclusive of interest and costs, the sum specified by 28 U.S.C. § 1332.

Form 9 of the Appendix of Forms is an illustrative, and quite simple, complaint for negligence. What follows is a slightly modified version of Form 9, with the addition of the caption required by Rule 10(a) and signature line required by Rule 11. The amount in controversy is asserted to be more than seventy-five thousand dollars, and the date of the accident alleged in the complaint has been changed. The left-hand column cites the provision of the Federal Rules of Civil Procedure and the illustrative form that pertain to each portion of the complaint.

Rule 10(a)

Form 1

UNITED STATES DISTRICT COURT FOR THE DISTRICT OF MASSACHUSETTS

Civil Action No. ____–_____

A.B., Plaintiff   )
      v.   )
C.D., Defendant)

Rule 10(a)
Form 9

COMPLAINT FOR NEGLIGENCE

Rule 8(a)(1)
Forms 2 & 9

1. Plaintiff is a citizen of the State of Connecticut and defendant is a citizen of the State of New York. The matter in controversy exceeds, exclusive of interest and costs, the sum of seventy-five thousand dollars.

Rule 8(a)(2)
Form 9

2. On June 1, 1997, in a public highway called Boylston Street in Boston, Massachusetts, defendant negligently drove a motor vehicle against plaintiff who was then crossing said highway.

3. As a result plaintiff was thrown down and had his leg broken and was otherwise injured, was prevented from transacting his business, suffered great pain of body and mind, and incurred expenses for medical attention and hospitalization in the sum of one thousand dollars.

Rule 8(a)(3)
Form 9

Wherefore plaintiff demands judgment against defendant in the sum of _____ dollars and costs.

Rule 11   Signed: _____
Form 3   Attorney for Plaintiff

            Address: _____

Rule 9 of the Federal Rules of Civil Procedure governs the pleading of special matters. Despite the generally liberal nature of federal pleading requirements, Rule 9(b) provides: "In all averments of fraud or mistake, the circumstances constituting fraud or mistake shall be stated with particularity. Malice, intent, knowledge, and other condition of mind of a person may be averred generally." Rule 9(g) requires that items of special damage such as medical expenses in a personal injury case must be "specifically stated." In addition to these Rule 9 requirements, Congress has demanded greater specificity in certain federal securities fraud actions, requiring that complaints shall, "with respect to each act or omission alleged to violate [these federal provisions], state with particularity facts giving rise to a strong inference that the defendant acted with the required state of mind." 15 U.S.C. § 78u–4(b)(2).

Apart from the requirements of the Federal Rules, there may be strategic reasons for drafting a complaint in a particular manner. Rule 26(b)(1) provides that parties may obtain discovery "regarding any matter, not privileged, that is relevant to the claim or defense of any party," and further states that, for good cause, "the court may order discovery of any matter relevant to the subject matter involved in the action." The complaint thus establishes the outer boundaries for discovery for both the plaintiff and defendant. In addition, individuals and documents only need be disclosed pursuant to Rule 26(a)(1) insofar as "the disclosing party may use [them] to support its claims or defenses, unless solely for impeachment." A request for punitive damages may entitle the plaintiff to discovery concerning defendant's finances that otherwise would be unavailable.

The complaint not only governs discovery, but can become an actual discovery device. The defendant must respond to the specific allegations of the complaint, which therefore may result in early defense admissions. Meaningful admissions only will be obtained, though, if the complaint contains specific, factual allegations. If general allegations are made in the complaint, the defendant will be able to deny those allegations and helpful admissions will be lost. Plaintiff's counsel should presume that defense counsel will only admit those allegations that she in good faith must admit. The complaint therefore should be reviewed to ensure that there is no ambiguity that will permit evasion by the defendant.

While the complaint should be tightly drafted, counsel should realize that it provides the defendant with a form of discovery concerning plaintiff's claims. Particularly if a case is likely to settle, the complaint can be used to show the extensive legal research and factual investigation undertaken by plaintiff's counsel. If settlement is unlikely, plaintiff's counsel may decide to draft a barebones complaint closer to Form 9 in the Appendix of Forms to the Federal Rules of Civil Procedure.

Counsel should avoid making allegations in the complaint that she doesn't have a good chance of proving. To the extent that plaintiff is unable to establish even minor factual allegations of the complaint, the credibility of both plaintiff and plaintiff's counsel may be undermined. The complaint provides both opposing counsel and the judge with their first impression of an action. To ensure that this important first impression is a favorable one, counsel should carefully draft the complaint and should not overstate her case.

There should be a reason for every allegation contained in the complaint, and the complaint should be logically organized. Rule 10(b)'s requirement of numbered paragraphs limited to a single set of circumstances is an organizational help. Because Rule 10(c) permits adoption by reference within the complaint, the facts underlying all counts of the complaint typically are set forth at the outset of the complaint and then incorporated by reference in succeeding counts. The complaint may be more compact if important items and events are given a shortened name or title the first time they are mentioned in the complaint.

While the Rule 8(a)(2) statement of the claim often is organized chronologically, it need not be. The allegations can be organized by the elements of the claim. For example, the statement of a tort claim might proceed from duty to breach to proximate cause to injury. In lengthier complaints, an introductory paragraph might describe the litigation in a few sentences so that the later specific paragraphs of the complaint will be more easily understood by opposing counsel and the court. Counsel also can use headings to describe separate portions of the complaint. A typical heading in a multi-count complaint might be:

COUNT I

Breach of the May 16, 2001, Contract

The prayer for relief should indicate if more than one type of relief is sought. If there are multiple counts in the complaint, different relief may be sought in connection with different counts. If a jury trial is sought, the Rule 38(b) jury demand should be included in the complaint. Local rules may specify the precise placement of the jury demand.

V. RULE 11 PLEADING REQUIREMENTS

In addition to the pleading requirements discussed in the prior section, Rule 11(a) of the Federal Rules of Civil Procedure requires that every "pleading, written motion, and other paper" must be signed by at least one attorney of record or, if a party is not represented by counsel, by the party. Rule 11(b) provides that by "presenting" such a paper to the court (which may occur by signing, filing, submitting, or later advocating the paper) an attorney or unrepresented party certifies that, "to the best of the person's knowledge, information, and belief, formed after an inquiry reasonable under the circumstances":

(1) [the document] is not being presented for any improper purpose, such as to harass or to cause unnecessary delay or needless increase in the cost of litigation;

(2) the claims, defenses, and other legal contentions therein are warranted by existing law or by a nonfrivolous argument for the extension, modification, or reversal of existing law or the establishment of new law;

(3) the allegations and other factual contentions have evidentiary support or, if specifically so identified, are likely to have evidentiary support after a reasonable opportunity for further investigation or discovery; and

(4) the denials of factual contentions are warranted on the evidence or, if specifically so identified, are reasonably based on a lack of information or belief.

Those signing a court paper thereby certify not only that the paper is not being presented for an improper purpose, but that there are sufficient legal and factual bases to support the paper. Rule 11(b) applies an objective standard to attorney and party conduct. An affirmative duty rests upon lawyers to conduct an "inquiry reasonable under the circumstances" before presenting a paper to the court. It is no defense that the allegedly offending party acted in good faith, although this may be a relevant factor in the determination of what, if any, sanction should be imposed if a violation is found. Rule 11(d) provides that the Rule 11(b) requirements do not apply to disclosures, discovery requests, responses, objections, and motions that are subject to the comparable disclosure and discovery certification requirements of Rule 26(g).

Rule 11 is triggered by presenting a paper to the court, which typically occurs by the filing or submission of the court paper. However, Rule 11 imposes a continuing duty upon parties and counsel, and the fact that a paper complied with that Rule at the time of its filing does not mean that there cannot be a current Rule 11 violation due to advocacy based upon that paper. Rule 11(b)(3) and (4) recognize that there may be uncertainty about particular facts at the outset of litigation; factual contentions and denials without current evidentiary support may be made if they are "specifically so identified" and "are likely to have evidentiary support after a reasonable opportunity for further investigation or discovery" or, if denials, "are reasonably based on a lack of information or belief." However, if evidentiary support is not found for an allegation after a reasonable opportunity for further investigation or discovery, counsel should not persist in making the factual contention.

Rule 11(c) provides that, "after notice and a reasonable opportunity to respond," a court may impose an "appropriate sanction" for a Rule 11 violation "upon the attorneys, law firms, or parties" that have violated the Rule or are "responsible for the violation" (even if they, themselves, have not signed the offending paper). The Rule 11 sanctioning process can be initiated either by party motion or on the court's own initiative.

Rule 11(c)(1)(A) provides that sanction motions shall be made separately from other motions or requests and describe the specific conduct alleged to violate Rule 11(b). Such a motion is not to be filed with the court in the first instance; instead, Rule 11(c)(1)(A) provides that the sanction motion is to be served on the parties pursuant to Rule 5 but only is to be filed with or presented to the court in the event that the challenged paper is not withdrawn or corrected "within 21 days after service of the motion (or such other period as the court may prescribe)." During this 21 day "safe harbor" period, the alleged Rule 11 violator can reconsider the paper in question and, by correcting or withdrawing the paper, nullify the possibility of Rule 11 sanctions. A similar 21 day safe harbor period does not exist if it is the court, itself, that challenges a paper pursuant to Rule 11, although Rule 11(c)(1)(B) requires the court to enter a show cause order describing the specific conduct that appears to violate Rule 11(b) before sanctions can be imposed.

Rule 11(c)(2) lists the various sanctions that the court can impose upon finding that Rule 11 has been violated. Sanctions must be "limited to what is sufficient to deter repetition of such conduct or comparable conduct by others similarly situated" and may include "directives of a nonmonetary nature, an order to pay a penalty into court, or, if imposed on motion and warranted for effective deterrence, an order directing payment to the movant of some or all of the reasonable attorneys' fees and other expenses incurred as a direct result of the violation." As the United States Court of Appeals for the Fifth Circuit recognized in *Thomas v. Capital Security Services, Inc.* (5th Cir.1988) (*en banc*), potential Rule 11 sanctions can include "a warm friendly discussion on the record, a hard-nosed reprimand in open court, compulsory legal education, monetary sanctions, or other measures appropriate to the circumstances."

Once a Rule 11 violation has been found, it is within the court's discretion whether to impose any sanction and, if the court decides to impose a sanction, what particular sanction is most appropriate. The court also must determine just who should be sanctioned if a violation of Rule 11(b) is found. The final sentence of Rule 11(c)(1)(A) provides: "Absent exceptional circumstances, a law firm shall be held jointly responsible for violations committed by its partners, associates, and employees."

Rule 11(c)(2) contains two other significant limitations on the imposition of sanctions. Rule 11(c)(2)(A) provides that only nonmonetary sanctions can be awarded against a represented party for a violation of Rule 11(b)(2) due to an insufficient legal basis underlying a particular paper; there is no such proscription barring the imposition of monetary sanctions against either unrepresented parties or attorneys in such a situation. Rule 11(c)(2)(B) further provides that monetary sanctions cannot be awarded on the court's own initiative unless the court's Rule 11(c)(1)(B) show cause order is issued before a voluntary dismissal or settlement of the claims made by or against the party or attorneys to be sanctioned. Thus parties may negotiate a settlement that comprehensively resolves all claims and thereby preclude any independent judicial imposition of monetary sanctions after such a party settlement has been reached.

Although Rule 11 has been the subject of great debate within the courts, the Congress, and the profession in recent years, it simply requires good lawyering and reminds attorneys of their duties to the court. Thorough factual investigation and complete legal research is an ethical duty as well as a Rule 11 command. Counsel should not take their clients' word on important matters, but should talk to other witnesses and review documentary evidence to corroborate client statements. Positions taken in litigation should be reassessed as a case progresses. Factual investigation and legal research should be memorialized, so that a contemporaneous record can be offered in response to any later Rule 11 challenge.

VI. AMENDMENT OF THE PLEADINGS

What if counsel makes a mistake in drafting the complaint or learns that certain facts alleged in the complaint are not true? What if counsel obtains information in discovery suggesting an additional claim that was not included in the original complaint? In situations such as these, amendment of the pleadings may be in order.

Rule 15 of the Federal Rules of Civil Procedure governs amendment of the pleadings. As with pleading generally, the Federal Rules are quite liberal when it comes to amendments. Rule 15(a) provides that a party may amend a pleading "once as a matter of course at any time before a responsive pleading is served or, if the pleading is one to which no responsive pleading is permitted and the action has not been placed upon the trial calendar, the party may so amend it at any time within 20 days after it is served." Thus, until the defendant files an answer, the plaintiff can file an amended complaint without seeking leave of court or agreement of counsel.

If a responsive pleading has been filed or no responsive pleading is permitted and twenty days has passed, Rule 15(a) requires that leave of court or written consent of the adverse party must be obtained for the amendment. Rule 15(a) further states that in such situations "leave shall be freely given when justice so requires." In *Foman v. Davis* (S.Ct.1962), the Supreme Court stressed that "this mandate is to be heeded. * * * If the underlying facts or circumstances relied upon by a plaintiff may be a proper subject of relief, he ought to be afforded an opportunity to test his claim on the merits."

In addition to Rule 15(a)'s provision for the amendment of pleadings prior to trial, Rule 15(b) permits the amendment of pleadings to conform to the evidence offered at trial. If no objection is made to the trial of issues not raised by the pleadings, the issues are to be treated as if they had been raised in the pleadings. If an objection is made that evidence is not within the issues raised in the pleadings, the court can still permit amendment. In fact, Rule 15(b) provides that the court "shall do so freely when the presentation of the merits of the action will be subserved thereby and the objecting party fails to satisfy the court that the admission of such evidence would prejudice the party in maintaining the party's action or defense upon the merits."

In many cases, the most significant question is not whether a party can amend its pleading but the effect of the amendment. If the statute of limitations has run on a claim prior to the assertion of that claim in an amended complaint, the plaintiff will have to show that the new claim relates back to the date of the original complaint. An amendment relates back to the date of the original pleading if "relation back is permitted by the law that provides the statute of limitations applicable to the action," Rule 15(c)(1), or the claim or defense "arose out of the conduct, transaction, or occurrence set forth or attempted to be set forth in the original pleading." Rule 15(c)(2).

If the amendment changes the party or the naming of the party against whom a claim is asserted, the amendment relates back if Rule 15(c)(2) is satisfied and, within the period provided by Rule 4(m) for service of the summons and complaint, the party to be brought in by amendment "(A) has received such notice of the institution of the action that the party will not be prejudiced in maintaining a defense on the merits, and (B) knew or should have known that, but for a mistake concerning the identity of the proper party, the action would have been brought against the party." Rule 15(c)(3).

In addition to Rule 15(a) and (b) amendments, Rule 15(d) provides for supplemental pleadings. While amendments are to rectify errors or permit parties to change their minds concerning their claims and defenses, supplemental pleadings permit parties to assert events that have occurred since the filing of the original pleading. If the plaintiff dies after the filing of a personal injury complaint, plaintiff's counsel can seek permission under Rule 15(d) to file a supplemental complaint including a new claim for wrongful death.

Despite the liberal opportunity for amendment under the Federal Rules of Civil Procedure, counsel should plead properly in the first instance so that amendments will not be necessary.

CHAPTER FIVE

RESPONSES TO THE COMPLAINT

I. DEFENSES TO THE ACTION

Until now, the focus of this book has been upon drafting the complaint and initiating suit. The present chapter deals with responses to the complaint: preanswer motions, the answer, and affirmative claims for relief. Before any response to the complaint is filed, counsel must determine the defenses that should be pled on her client's behalf. Rule 12(a)(1)(A) of the Federal Rules of Civil Procedure only permits non-federal defendants twenty days in which to respond to a complaint that has been formally served. Even if service of summons has been waived pursuant to Rule 4(d) or the defendant is the United States or one of its officers or agencies, Rule 12(a)(1)(B) and (3) only permit sixty days for the defense response (unless the defendant was addressed outside the United States, in which event 90 days are permitted for the response). Defense counsel's research and case-planning therefore must be conducted quite efficiently.

Defenses fall into several categories. Initially, defense counsel should consider whether all prerequisites to suit have been satisfied. If not, one or more of the Rule 12(b) threshold defenses should be raised: lack of subject matter jurisdiction (Rule 12(b)(1)), lack of personal jurisdiction (Rule 12(b)(2)), improper venue (Rule 12(b)(3)), insufficiency of process (Rule 12(b)(4)), insufficiency of service of process (Rule 12(b)(5)), and failure to join a party under Rule 19 (Rule 12(b)(7)). While these are the major threshold defenses, defense counsel also should consider whether the complaint is sufficiently definite to withstand a Rule 12(e) motion for a more definite statement or is subject to a Rule 12(f) motion to strike. These threshold defenses can be characterized as "Just a minute!" defenses, because an action can't proceed unless these procedural prerequisites have been met.

In contrast to the other Rule 12(b) defenses, the Rule 12(b)(6) defense of failure to state a claim upon which relief can be granted tests the legal sufficiency of the complaint. In considering this defense, which is the modern equivalent of the common law demurrer, the court is to presume the truth of all facts alleged in the complaint. The Rule 12(b)(6) defense thus can be characterized as the "So What?" defense. By this defense, the defendant, in effect, asserts: "So what if every fact the plaintiff alleges is true, he still doesn't have a legal basis for suit!"

While Rule 12(b)(6) concerns the legal sufficiency of the facts alleged in the complaint, the defendant usually will contest the factual allegations of the complaint as well. Rule 8(b) governs factual denials, which are included in the answer and are just what they sound like: "No, No, No!" defenses.

In addition to Rule 12 defenses and Rule 8(b) denials, counsel should consider possible affirmative defenses. In contrast to Rule 8(b) denials, which refute facts alleged in the complaint, affirmative defenses raise new matter not contained in the complaint. For this reason, affirmative defenses can be considered "Yes, but * * * " defenses. Rule 8(c) contains a helpful check list of common affirmative defenses, such as assumption of risk, contributory negligence, duress, estoppel, fraud, laches, release, statute of frauds, and statute of limitations.

II.   CONSOLIDATION AND WAIVER OF DEFENSES

Rule 12(b) states: "No defense or objection is waived by being joined with one or more other defenses or objections in a responsive pleading or motion." Defenses therefore can be consolidated in the answer or in a preanswer motion. Rule 12(g) reiterates the defendant's ability to consolidate Rule 12 defenses in a preanswer motion: "A party who makes a motion under this rule may join with it any other motions herein provided for and then available to the party." Thus a preanswer motion could assert that an action should be dismissed because of lack of subject matter jurisdiction (Rule 12(b)(1)), improper venue (Rule 12(b)(3)), and failure to state a claim upon which relief can be granted (Rule 12(b)(6)).

Not only is consolidation of defenses permissible under Rule 12, in some cases it is mandatory. After explicitly permitting consolidation of Rule 12 defenses in a preanswer motion, Rule 12(g) continues: "If a party makes a motion under this rule but omits therefrom any defense or objection then available to the party which this rule permits to be raised by motion, the party shall not thereafter make a motion based on the defense or objection so omitted, except a motion as provided in [Rule 12(h)(2)] on any of the grounds there stated." Rule 12(g) therefore requires consolidation of Rule 12 defenses.

If a preanswer motion raising any Rule 12 defense is made or if the answer is filed, a later Rule 12(e) motion for more definite statement or Rule 12(f) motion to strike cannot be filed. Rule 12(h) contains separate rules governing the waiver of Rule 12(b) defenses that have been omitted from a preanswer motion or the answer. Rule 12(h) places the Rule 12(b) defenses into three categories for waiver purposes.

The first category of Rule 12(b) defenses includes lack of personal jurisdiction (Rule 12(b)(2)), improper venue (Rule 12(b)(3)), insufficiency of process (Rule 12(b)(4)), and insufficiency of service of process (Rule 12(b)(5)). These four defenses are considered personal to the defendant, and Rule 12(h)(1) provides that they are waived (1) if a preanswer motion is filed that does not include them or (2) if no preanswer motion is filed, by failing to include these defenses in a responsive pleading such as the answer or in an amendment "permitted by Rule 15(a) to be made as a matter of course."

The second category of Rule 12(b) defenses includes the Rule 12(b)(6) defense of failure to state a claim upon which relief can be granted and the Rule 12(b)(7) defense of failure to join an indispensable party. Rule 12(h)(2) provides that these defenses, as well as an objection of failure to state a legal defense, "may be made in any pleading permitted or ordered under Rule 7(a), or by motion for judgment on the pleadings, or at the trial on the merits." The defenses and objection falling within Rule 12(h)(2) bear directly on the merits of the action, and they are preserved until trial despite Rule 12(g)'s consolidation requirement.

The Rule 12(b)(1) defense of lack of subject matter jurisdiction is treated separately under Rule 12(h)(3), which provides: "Whenever it appears by suggestion of the parties or otherwise that the court lacks jurisdiction of the subject matter, the court shall dismiss the action." Lack of subject matter jurisdiction cannot be waived. If you fail to include a Rule 12(b) defense in a preanswer motion or in the answer, hope that it's the defense of lack of subject matter jurisdiction. Better yet, be thorough in your factual investigation and legal research so that all viable defenses are raised and determined as soon as possible.

III.   RULE 12 MOTIONS

Once counsel has determined what defenses to assert on behalf of her client, she must decide whether to assert those defenses in the answer or in a preanswer motion. The Rule 12(e) and 12(f) defenses only can be raised by preanswer motion. Factual denials cannot be raised by preanswer motion, but must be asserted in the answer and raised in a motion for summary judgment or at trial. The Rule 12(b) defenses either can be raised in a motion to dismiss or asserted in the answer.

If defense counsel has a choice whether to raise the Rule 12(b) defenses in a preanswer motion or in the answer, what should she do? Occasionally, defense counsel merely assert a Rule 12(b) defense in the answer, on the theory that the defense will be stronger if presented in connection with a summary judgment motion (perhaps buttressed by discovery obtained from the plaintiff). In other cases, defense counsel may not ask the court to resolve a defense raised in the answer until some time has passed and public sentiment or local news coverage has changed.

In most cases, though, the defendant is interested in the quickest, cheapest termination of the lawsuit. For this reason, the defendant will raise Rule 12(b) defenses in a preanswer motion to dismiss. If a motion to dismiss is granted, the case is dismissed and this is the end of trial court proceedings. The mere assertion of a defense in the answer does not ensure a pretrial determination of the sufficiency of that defense, although Rule 12(d) provides that Rule 12(b) defenses "shall be heard and determined before trial on application of any party, unless the court orders that the hearing and determination thereof be deferred until the trial."

A. The Motion to Dismiss

All of the Rule 12(b) defenses, whether to a claim, counterclaim, cross-claim, or third-party claim, can be asserted in a preanswer motion to dismiss. While such motions are commonly filed, they also are commonly denied. Even if a motion to dismiss is successful, the court may grant the motion without prejudice to the plaintiff filing an amended complaint.

Ruling on a motion to dismiss may be the judge's first contact with a case, and defense counsel should consider the risk that the judge will deny the motion. Against this possibility should be balanced the likelihood that a successful motion will terminate the litigation short of expensive and time-consuming discovery, pretrial proceedings, and trial. Sometimes a motion to dismiss can be targeted at selected claims within a complaint, rather than seeking the dismissal of an entire action. The motion to dismiss therefore should be carefully researched and considered within the context of defendant's comprehensive litigation plan.

Because the Rule 12(b) defenses involve the threshold prerequisites to suit, Rule 12(b) motions to dismiss usually are not accompanied by supporting evidentiary material. However, affidavits can be submitted with a motion to dismiss. Thus if a motion is based upon lack of jurisdiction, the defendant might offer an affidavit to introduce facts concerning the parties' citizenship or the defendant's lack of contacts with the forum state.

The Rule 12(b)(6) motion is to test the legal sufficiency of the complaint, and all facts alleged in the complaint are to be considered true for the purposes of the motion. The Supreme Court in *Conley v. Gibson* (S.Ct.1957) held that "a complaint should not be dismissed for failure to state a claim unless it appears beyond doubt that the plaintiff can prove no set of facts in support of his claim which would entitle him to relief."

Rule 12(b) specifically provides that if, in connection with a Rule 12(b)(6) motion, "matters outside the pleading are presented to and not excluded by the court, the motion shall be treated as one for summary judgment and disposed of as provided in Rule 56, and all parties shall be given reasonable opportunity to present all material made pertinent to such a motion by Rule 56." Thus a motion to dismiss for failure to state a claim can be converted into a motion for summary judgment.

The defendant can combine a motion to dismiss with a motion for summary judgment by filing a motion to dismiss or, in the alternative, for summary judgment. Such a motion may be advantageous if the defendant has a good, but technical, Rule 12 defense and the plaintiff has alleged sympathetic facts in the complaint. While the judge is asked to dismiss the case based upon the face of the complaint, the summary judgment affidavit may allay any concerns the judge may have about the merits. Regardless of the satisfaction of the legal prerequisites to suit, most judges don't like to dismiss lawsuits if they believe the plaintiff has a strong claim on the merits.

Although it was drafted prior to the increase in the jurisdictional minimum for diversity cases to $75,000 (see paragraph 4) and the revision of federal venue requirements (see paragraph 3), Form 19 of the Appendix of Forms to the Federal Rules of Civil Procedure is an illustrative motion to dismiss:

MOTION TO DISMISS, PRESENTING DEFENSES OF FAILURE TO STATE A CLAIM, OF LACK OF SERVICE OF PROCESS, OF IMPROPER VENUE, AND OF LACK OF JURISDICTION UNDER RULE 12(b)

The defendant moves the court as follows:

1. To dismiss the action because the complaint fails to state a claim against defendant upon which relief can be granted.

2. To dismiss the action or in lieu thereof to quash the return of service of summons on the grounds (a) that the defendant is a corporation organized under the laws of Delaware and was not and is not subject to service of process within the Southern District of New York, and (b) that

the defendant has not been properly served with process in this action, all of which more clearly appears in the affidavits of M.N. and X.Y. hereto annexed as Exhibit A and Exhibit B, respectively.

3.   To dismiss the action on the ground that it is in the wrong district because (a) the jurisdiction of this court is invoked solely on the ground that the action arises under the Constitution and laws of the United States and (b) the defendant is a corporation incorporated under the laws of the State of Delaware and is not licensed to do or doing business in the Southern District of New York, all of which more clearly appears in the affidavits of K.L. and V.W. hereto annexed as Exhibits C and D, respectively.

4.   To dismiss the action on the ground that the court lacks jurisdiction because the amount actually in controversy is less than ten thousand dollars exclusive of interest and costs.

Signed: _____
                    Attorney for Defendant.

Address: _____

In addition to the motion, a notice of motion may be required by local rules of court. Form 19 includes a sample notice of motion:

NOTICE OF MOTION

To: _____

    Attorney for Plaintiff.

_____

Please take notice, that the undersigned will bring the above motion on for hearing before this Court at room ___, United States Court House, Foley Square, City of New York, on the ___ day of _____, 19__, at 10 o'clock in the forenoon of that day or as soon thereafter as counsel can be heard.

    Signed: _____

                Attorney for Defendant.

    Address: _____

The motion to dismiss and the notice of motion are quite simple documents to draft. The accompanying brief or memorandum setting forth the defendant's argument as to why the complaint should be dismissed will take much more time to prepare than the written motion itself. The brief should contain the defendant's legal arguments and, if affidavits have been filed in support of the motion to dismiss, address the facts in those affidavits.

The motion to dismiss and supporting papers must include or be accompanied by a certificate of service. Such a certificate must be prepared for every court paper after the complaint that is required to be served upon a party. The certificate should be signed by the person who mailed or otherwise served the document and might look like this:

CERTIFICATE OF SERVICE

I, [insert name of person who served the document], hereby certify that on this ___ day of ___, 200_, I served the foregoing [insert title of document(s) served] upon [insert name of opposing counsel] by [usually either (1) first class mail, postage prepaid or (2) hand].

_____

[signature of person who served papers]

The local rules of court should be consulted concerning additional motion requirements. In some districts, counsel are required to submit a form order for the judge to sign in the event that the motion is granted.

B. The Other Rule 12 Motions

In addition to a Rule 12(b) motion to dismiss, possible defense motions can be filed pursuant to Rule 12(c), (e), and (f). While these motions play a much less significant role in pretrial litigation than motions to dismiss, defense counsel should be familiar with all of the Rule 12 motions.

Rule 12(e) provides that a preanswer motion for a more definite statement can be filed if the complaint is "so vague or ambiguous that a party cannot reasonably be required to frame a responsive pleading." If a Rule 12(e) motion is granted, the plaintiff is given ten days to file a more definite complaint. The motion for a more definite statement can be addressed to the complaint and to any other "pleading to which a responsive pleading is permitted." These motions thus can challenge not only complaints but also counterclaims denominated as such, cross-claims, and third-party complaints.

Motions for a more definite statement are rarely filed, and they are even more rarely granted. Rule 8(a)(2) of the Federal Rules of Civil Procedure requires only a "short and plain statement of the claim showing that the pleader is entitled to relief," and this notice pleading standard is not difficult to satisfy. If there is uncertainty about plaintiff's allegations, the defendant typically can obtain discovery addressed to the complaint. In some cases where a motion for a more definite statement may appear appropriate, the defendant might seek the dismissal of the complaint rather than an order granting plaintiff additional time in which to file a more definite complaint.

Another little-used preanswer motion is the Rule 12(f) motion to strike, which can be directed at any pleading that contains "redundant, immaterial, impertinent, or scandalous matter." There may be little to be gained from a request that the court parse the complaint to strike material of this nature. Indeed, to the extent that the complaint contains such matter, the court may look less favorably on plaintiff and his counsel. However, defense counsel might consider a motion to strike if the complaint will be read to the jury and contains material that might unfairly prejudice the defendant. A motion to strike also can be addressed to specific elements of the prayer for relief to which the plaintiff is not entitled as a matter of law.

While it may be of little utility to defense counsel, the motion to strike may prove useful to the plaintiff. Rule 12(f) concerns not only "redundant, immaterial, impertinent, or scandalous matter," but provides for the striking of "any insufficient defense." In some cases a pretrial ruling on the sufficiency of a defense may be important in order to help the parties plan pretrial and trial proceedings. In these situations, the motion to strike can be used to challenge a defense in the answer just as a Rule 12(b)(6) motion can be used to challenge a claim asserted in the complaint.

The final Rule 12 motion is the Rule 12(c) motion for judgment on the pleadings. While Rule 12(e) and 12(f) motions are to be filed prior to the answer, the motion for judgment on the pleadings is to be filed after "the pleadings are closed but within such time as not to delay the trial." Any party can move for judgment on the pleadings.

Because Rule 12(c) motions are to be decided on the pleadings (typically, the complaint and the answer), these motions usually raise legal, rather than factual, issues. For this reason, the motion is not commonly filed. In the event the defendant has a good legal defense, that defense usually is asserted in a preanswer motion to dismiss for failure to state a claim upon which relief can be granted. If, however, a motion to dismiss cannot be prepared within the Rule 12(a) response period, a motion for judgment on the pleadings might be filed after the answer. The filing of an answer also precludes the plaintiff from filing a Rule 41(a)(1) notice of voluntary dismissal, by which the plaintiff can dismiss without prejudice. If there are no factual issues in the case, the plaintiff himself might file a Rule 12(c) motion seeking an early judgment.

Sometimes factual matters are considered in connection with a motion for judgment on the pleadings. The final sentence of Rule 12(c) provides: "If, on a motion for judgment on the pleadings, matters outside the pleadings are presented to and not excluded by the court, the motion shall be treated as one for summary judgment and disposed of as provided in Rule 56, and all parties shall be given reasonable opportunity to present all material made pertinent to such a motion by Rule 56." This provision contemplates that a motion for judgment on the pleadings, like a Rule 12(b)(6) motion, can be converted to a motion for summary judgment if matters outside the pleadings are considered by the court. Just as with a motion to dismiss, there may be practical advantages in filing a motion for judgment on the pleadings or, in the alternative, for summary judgment.

IV. THE ANSWER

If a preanswer motion is not filed, or if a motion is filed but is denied, the defendant is required to file an answer to the complaint. The complaint and answer are the basic civil pleadings, delineating the boundaries for discovery and framing the issues for resolution by the court.

The time for service of the answer depends upon whether the defendant has waived service of the summons pursuant to Rule 4(d). If so, Rule 12(a)(1)(B) grants the defendant 60 days after the waiver request was sent to serve the answer, although a defendant addressed outside the United States is given 90 days. Rule 12(a)(3) gives the United States or an officer or agency thereof 60 days in which to answer, while the answer must be served within twenty days after service of the summons and complaint by all other defendants who do not waive formal service of the complaint. If a preanswer motion is filed, the defendant has until ten days after the court's refusal to grant the motion in which to file an answer. If a Rule 12(e) motion for a more definite statement or a Rule 12(f) motion to strike is granted, the answer must be filed within ten days after the filing of the more definite statement or the order striking a portion of the complaint.

Rule 8(b) governs the form of the answer. That rule in part provides: "A party shall state in short and plain terms the party's defenses to each claim asserted and shall admit or deny the averments upon which the adverse party relies." If the defendant fails to deny an averment of the complaint other than one as to the amount of alleged damage, Rule 8(d) considers the averment to have been admitted.

Counsel should consult with the defendant concerning the answer and be sure to conduct the reasonable inquiry required by Rule 11. But what if the truth of particular matters alleged in the complaint is still not clear? Rule 8(b) provides: "If a party is without knowledge or information sufficient to form a belief as to the truth of an averment, the party shall so state and this has the effect of a denial."

If the answer contains denials of plaintiff's allegations, Rule 8(b) requires those denials to "fairly meet the substance of the averments denied." The answer thus should admit those portions of specific averments that are true. While the possibility of general denials is recognized by Rule 8(b), there will be few cases in which a general denial can be pled in good faith consistently with Rule 11.

Attorneys have different styles for admissions and denials in the answer. Typically these are set forth in numbered paragraphs of the answer that track the paragraphs of the complaint. Defense counsel might respond to the allegations of the complaint set forth in Chapter 4, supra, p. 85, as follows:

1. Defendant admits that he is a citizen of the State of New York. Defendant denies that the

matter in controversy exceeds, exclusive of interest and costs, the sum of seventy-five thousand dollars. Defendant is without knowledge or information sufficient to form a belief as to the truth of the averment that plaintiff is a citizen of the State of Connecticut.

2.   Defendant denies the allegations of paragraph 2 of the complaint.

3.   Defendant is without knowledge or information sufficient to form a belief as to the truth of the averments of paragraph 3 of the complaint.

Ambiguity in the answer should be avoided, especially because of Rule 8(d)'s provision that averments that are not denied are considered to be admitted. Thus there should be no confusion as to exactly which allegations of the complaint are denied and which are admitted. Instead of the above sentence denying paragraph two of the complaint, some attorneys would merely state in the answer:

2.   Deny.

Rule 8(e)(2) permits the pleading of alternative, hypothetical, and inconsistent claims and defenses, so long as there is a good faith basis for so doing and Rule 11 is satisfied. Form 20 of the Appendix of Forms of the Federal Rules of Civil Procedure is an answer that not only contains admissions and denials, but that sets forth several other defenses and claims:

ANSWER PRESENTING DEFENSES
UNDER RULE 12(b)

First Defense

The complaint fails to state a claim against defendant upon which relief can be granted.

Second Defense

If defendant is indebted to plaintiffs for the goods mentioned in the complaint, he is indebted to them jointly with G.H. G.H. is alive; is a citizen of the State of New York and a resident of this district, is subject to the jurisdiction of this court, as to both service of process and venue; can be made a party without depriving this court of jurisdiction of the present parties, and has not been made a party.

Third Defense

Defendant admits the allegation contained in paragraphs 1 and 4 of the complaint; alleges that he is without knowledge or information sufficient to form a belief as to the truth of the allegations contained in paragraph 2 of the complaint; and denies each and every other allegation contained in the complaint.

Fourth Defense

The right of action set forth in the complaint did not accrue within six years next before the commencement of this action.

Counterclaim

(Here set forth any claim as a counterclaim in the manner in which a claim is pleaded in a complaint. No statement of the grounds on which the court's jurisdiction depends need be made unless the counterclaim requires independent grounds of jurisdiction.)

Cross–Claim Against Defendant M.N.

(Here set forth the claim constituting a cross-claim against defendant M.N. in the manner in which a claim is pleaded in a complaint. The statement of grounds upon which the court's jurisdiction depends need not be made unless the cross-claim requires independent grounds of jurisdiction.)

The first paragraph of the answer in Form 20 asserts the Rule 12(b)(6) defense of failure to state a claim upon which relief can be granted, while the second paragraph is the Rule 12(b)(7) defense of failure to join a party pursuant to Rule 19. The third defense addresses the merits of plaintiff's allegations and contains defendant's admissions and denials of the factual allegations of the complaint. To ensure that there is no question concerning which portions of the complaint have been admitted, defense counsel has admitted or stated lack of knowledge concerning specific portions of the complaint and then has denied "each and every other allegation contained in the complaint." Some attorneys might start such a paragraph with a general denial, followed by an admission of specific facts: "Paragraph 4 of the complaint is denied, except for the allegation that the defendant's home office is in Anchorage, Alaska."

Form 20's fourth defense raises the Rule 8(c) affirmative defense of statute of limitations. Rule 8(c) requires that affirmative defenses be set forth affirmatively, and, because they inject new issues into the lawsuit, such defenses are considered waived if they are not included in the answer. The final two paragraphs of the form answer are a counterclaim and cross-claim, both of which are discussed in the final section of this chapter.

A Rule 10(a) case caption should be at the top of the answer, and Rule 10(b) requires that "each defense other than denials shall be stated in a separate * * * defense whenever a separation facilitates the clear presentation of the matters set forth." Rule 10(c) authorizes adoption by reference in the answer, and the defense headings in Form 20 make that answer much easier to understand and use.

Although not required by the Federal Rules of Civil Procedure, many defense counsel conclude the answer with a final sentence demanding dismissal of the complaint and requesting an award of the costs of suit and defendant's attorneys' fees. If a jury is desired, the jury demand is typically included in the answer pursuant to Federal Rule of Civil

Procedure 38(b). Finally, the answer must be signed by counsel pursuant to Rule 11 and must be filed with the court and accompanied by a certificate of service showing service upon all parties.

While it usually is a fairly short document, the answer should include all of the defenses that will be raised in the lawsuit. The time-consuming aspect of preparing an answer therefore is not the drafting of that pleading but the factual investigation and legal research that must be undertaken to determine exactly what defenses to include in the answer.

V.   COUNTERCLAIMS, CROSS–CLAIMS, AND THIRD–PARTY CLAIMS

In litigation as in athletics, it's often true that "the best defense is a good offense." Whether contained in a preanswer motion or in the answer, successful assertion of the defenses discussed above can only result in the dismissal of a claim or, perhaps, the lawsuit. In certain cases, the defendant can not only seek to defeat plaintiff's claims but may be entitled to affirmative relief. Defense counsel therefore should consider whether to file counterclaims, cross-claims, and third-party claims, which are illustrated in Figure 5–1.

FIGURE 5–1

CLAIMS IN A CIVIL ACTION

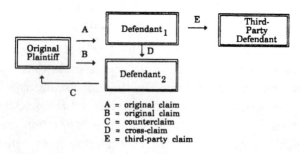

A = original claim
B = original claim
C = counterclaim
D = cross-claim
E = third-party claim

A. Counterclaims

In some cases, the defendant may have claims of his own against the plaintiff. Rule 13 of the Federal Rules of Civil Procedure permits, and, in some cases, requires, the defendant to assert those claims in the action that plaintiff has initiated. Claim "C" in Figure 5–1 is a counterclaim brought by defendant₂ against the plaintiff.

Defense counsel should be particularly aware of Rule 13(a), which provides for compulsory counterclaims. Rule 13(a) requires that an answer or other pleading "shall state as a counterclaim any claim which at the time of serving the pleading the pleader has against any opposing party, if it arises out of the transaction or occurrence that is the subject matter of the opposing party's claim and does not require for its adjudication the presence of third parties of whom the court cannot acquire jurisdiction." This transactional test for compulsory counterclaims is similar to the "same case or controversy" test for supplemental jurisdiction in 28 U.S.C. § 1367. For this reason, there need be no other jurisdictional basis for a district court to entertain compulsory counterclaims.

Presume, for instance, that the plaintiff filed a diversity claim for $85,000 seeking compensation for damages suffered in an automobile accident involving the plaintiff and defendant. If the defendant suffered injuries of $25,000 in that same accident, he would be required to assert his claim as a compulsory counterclaim in plaintiff's action because his injuries arise "out of the transaction or occurrence [the automobile accident] that is the subject matter of the opposing party's claim." Not only does defendant's claim fall within Rule 13(a), but, because both plaintiff's and defendant's claims "form part of the same case or controversy under Article III of the United States Constitution," the district court has supplemental jurisdiction to hear the counterclaim under 28 U.S.C. § 1367.

Because compulsory counterclaims that are not asserted are waived, they are routinely asserted. Rule 13(a), though, contains two exceptions to its compulsory counterclaim rule for situations in which "(1) at the time the action was commenced the [potential counterclaim] was the subject of another pending action, or (2) the opposing party brought suit upon the [original] claim by attachment or other process by which the court did not acquire jurisdiction to render a personal judgment on that claim, and the pleader is not stating any counterclaim under this Rule 13."

In addition to Rule 13(a) compulsory counterclaims, Rule 13(b) provides that a pleading *may* state as a counterclaim "any claim against an opposing party not arising out of the transaction or occurrence that is the subject matter of the opposing party's claim." Rule 13(b) thus permits a defendant to assert any claim he has against a plaintiff, whether or not the claim is related to plaintiff's original claim. However, in addition to satisfaction of Rule 13(b), there must be a separate jurisdictional basis for permissive counterclaims.

Presume, again, that plaintiff has asserted an $85,000 diversity claim for injuries stemming from an automobile accident. Rule 13(b) would provide a basis for the defendant to assert an unrelated $25,000 contract claim against plaintiff. However, because that claim is unrelated to plaintiff's original claim and thus does not "form part of the same case or controversy" under 28 U.S.C. § 1367, the court cannot exercise supplemental jurisdiction over the permissive counterclaim despite satisfaction of Rule 13(b). If the permissive counterclaim was for $80,000, the court could entertain the counterclaim under 28 U.S.C. § 1332.

Even if a permissive or compulsory counterclaim is entertained by the court, it may be tried separately from the plaintiff's original claim pursuant to Rule 42(b) of the Federal Rules of Civil Procedure. Moreover, Rule 13(c) provides that both compulsory and permissive counterclaims can seek relief "exceeding in amount or different in kind" from that sought in plaintiff's original claim or claims, while Rule 13(h) permits the Rule 19 or Rule 20 joinder of persons to a counterclaim who were not parties to the original action. However, a party cannot be added to a permissive counterclaim if the only jurisdictional basis for the counterclaim is diversity of citizenship and the new party's addition would destroy diversity.

In deciding whether to file a Rule 13(b) permissive counterclaim, defense counsel should be concerned primarily about the relative advantages of the forum in which plaintiff's original claim is pending and alternative forums in which the defendant could file an independent action asserting his claim against plaintiff. If the defendant is likely to obtain the dismissal of plaintiff's original claim by a pretrial motion, the defendant may not want to file a permissive counterclaim. To do so may merely prolong the original action and, perhaps, give some credence to plaintiff's claim. On the other hand, in many cases it will be more efficient to resolve both claims and counterclaims in a single action.

Defense counsel should consider whether the filing of a counterclaim will permit plaintiff to obtain discovery that otherwise would be unavailable. It also may be to defendant's advantage if the original claim and counterclaim are decided in two separate actions rather than risk confusion of the claims in a single action. Moreover, Rule 7(a) provides for a reply to a "counterclaim denominated as such," which reply itself might contain a new counterclaim.

Whether permissive or compulsory, the counterclaim must be included in the answer or other responsive pleading. Because Rule 7(a) only requires that a reply must be filed to a "counterclaim denominated as such," the portion of the answer containing the counterclaim should be labeled explicitly as a counterclaim.

B. Cross–Claims

The plaintiff may not be the only party against whom the defendant may want to assert a claim. Federal Rule of Civil Procedure 13(g) provides: "A pleading may state as a cross-claim any claim by one party against a co-party arising out of the transaction or occurrence that is the subject matter either of the original action or of a counterclaim therein or relating to any property that is the subject matter of the original action." Because Rule 13(g) employs a transaction or occurrence test similar to that for supplemental jurisdiction under 28 U.S.C. § 1367, supplemental jurisdiction exists to hear claims that satisfy Rule 13(g).

Claim "D" in Figure 5–1 is a cross-claim. Although this particular claim was filed by one of the original defendants against a co-defendant, cross-claims can be filed by any party against a co-party. If there is more than one plaintiff in an action, they can assert cross-claims against one another if Rule

13(g) is satisfied. Rule 13(h) also permits a cross-claim to name parties other than those who were parties to the original action. However, the requirements of Rules 19 or 20 must be satisfied and jurisdiction must exist under 28 U.S.C. § 1367 or another statute for a cross-claim against additional parties to be properly asserted.

Not only may a cross-claim seek relief from a co-party, but Rule 13(g) states that a cross-claim may assert "that the party against whom it is asserted is or may be liable to the cross-claimant for all or part of a claim asserted in the action against the cross-claimant." Rule 13(g) cross-claims therefore can seek indemnification from co-parties, just as Rule 14(a) third-party indemnification claims can be brought against persons not yet named as parties to the lawsuit.

One of the major advantages of cross-claims is that they permit several related claims to be resolved in a single lawsuit. This may result in not only judicial efficiency, but it may reduce pretrial delay and expense for the parties as well. However, cross-claims are not mandatory under Rule 13(g), and counsel should consider carefully both the advantages and disadvantages of these claims in any particular suit. The assertion of cross-claims may delay or confuse the resolution of the original claims and counterclaims, and there may be a more favorable forum in which counsel would prefer to litigate a potential cross-claim.

The litigation of a cross-claim also may shift the focus of the suit from the original claims to the new cross-claim. It is usually to plaintiff's advantage if the defendants can be pitted against one another, rather than presenting a unified front against plaintiff's claims. For this reason, defendants should try to informally resolve potential claims against one another, so that the defendants' full attention in the lawsuit can be focused on the plaintiff.

C. Third–Party Claims

The first sentence of Rule 14(a) states: "At any time after commencement of the action a defending party, as a third-party plaintiff, may cause a summons and complaint to be served upon a person not a party to the action who is or may be liable to the third-party plaintiff for all or part of the plaintiff's claim against the third-party plaintiff." Rule 14 third-party claims may be filed by a defendant to bring in (implead) a person who has not been named as a party, but who is or may be liable in contract or tort to indemnify the defendant if plaintiff recovers a judgment against him. A third-party claim for contribution might be filed against a joint tortfeasor who has not been named as a defendant or by a defendant employee seeking indemnification from his employer.

Claim "E" in Figure 5–1 is a third-party claim brought by an original defendant against a person who originally was not named as a party to the action. Once the third-party claim is filed, the defendant becomes the third-party plaintiff on that claim and the person newly named as a party becomes the third-party defendant.

Because of the nexus that Rule 14(a) requires between the original and any third-party claims, the federal courts entertain these claims pursuant to 28 U.S.C. § 1367. In contrast to counterclaims and cross-claims, which are asserted in the answer, third-party claims must be asserted in a separate third-party complaint. Unless the third-party complaint is filed within ten days after the original answer, leave of court must be obtained to file such a complaint. Even if leave is granted, the court may sever the third-party complaint pursuant to Rule 21 or hold a separate trial on that complaint pursuant to Rule 42(b).

The major question that must be answered in deciding whether a third-party claim can be asserted is whether, in the language of Rule 14(a), the potential third-party defendant "is or may be liable to the third-party plaintiff for all or part of the plaintiff's claim against the third-party plaintiff." This is generally a question of the substantive law of torts or contracts.

Because Rule 14 is permissive, counsel must decide whether to file a potential claim that satisfies the requirements of that rule. There are major advantages to third-party claims. For the court, third-party claims permit the efficient resolution of related claims in a single lawsuit rather than in the two separate lawsuits that otherwise would be necessary. Third-party claims may reduce litigation costs and delay for the parties. Absent a third-party claim, a defendant could be disadvantaged by the need to file a separate action for indemnification. The fact that a defendant loses an initial lawsuit and is ordered to pay a judgment is no assurance that the defendant will succeed in a second reimbursement action against the potential third-party defendant. Moreover, the defendant may be required to satisfy the initial judgment before he can obtain a judgment against the potential third-party defendant in a second lawsuit.

Nevertheless, there may be strategic reasons not to assert a third-party claim. In contrast to counterclaims and cross-claims, a third-party claim brings a new party, and new counsel, into the lawsuit. Whenever a new party enters a case, proceedings get a bit more complicated. Simple things like deposition scheduling become more complicated, because the schedule of an additional attorney now must be accommodated. In some cases, defense counsel may be able to use the threat of a third-party claim as leverage in discussions with the potential third-party defendant. For example, the nonparty might agree to provide the defendant with discovery voluntarily if he is not named as a third-party defendant.

CHAPTER SIX

DISCLOSURE AND THE SCOPE OF CIVIL DISCOVERY

I. DISCLOSURE UNDER RULE 26(a)

The broad discovery contemplated by the Federal Rules of Civil Procedure was one of the major innovations of those Rules. The exchange of information through the discovery process was expected to lead to more, and earlier, settlements and to result in better prepared and streamlined trials. Unfortunately, civil discovery took on a life of its own in all too many cases, and critics on the bench, in the profession, and among the general public called for a cheaper and more expeditious method of information exchange than that contemplated by the original discovery provisions of the federal and many state rules of civil procedure. As a result, the discovery provisions of the Federal Rules of Civil Procedure were amended in 1993 and 2000 to both restrict the information obtainable through formal discovery under Rules 26 through 37 and provide for automatic disclosure of relevant information without any formal discovery request.

As amended in 1993 and 2000, Rule 26(a) requires parties to disclose to other parties certain relevant, nonprivileged material without awaiting a formal discovery request. Rule 26(a) requires three different types of disclosures: (1) initial disclosures at the very outset of a case; (2) disclosures of expert testimony at a time and in the sequence set by the court; and (3) pretrial disclosures concerning the actual evidence to be presented at trial.

A. Initial Disclosures

Rule 26(a)(1) provides that, except in "categories of proceedings specified in Rule 26(a)(1)(E), or to the extent otherwise stipulated or directed by order," a party must provide to other parties basic information necessary to the prosecution or defense of most cases. The four categories of information that must be disclosed are specified in Rule 26(a)(1):

(A) the name and, if known, the address and telephone number of each individual likely to have discoverable information that the disclosing party may use to support its claims or defenses, unless solely for impeachment, identifying the subjects of the information;

(B) a copy of, or a description by category and location of, all documents, data compilations, and tangible things that are in the possession, custody, or control of the party and that the disclosing party may use to support its claims or defenses, unless solely for impeachment;

(C) a computation of any category of damages claimed by the disclosing party, making available for inspection and copying as under Rule 34 the documents or other evidentiary material, not privileged or protected from disclosure, on which such computation is based, including materials bearing on the nature and extent of injuries suffered; and

(D) for inspection and copying as under Rule 34 any insurance agreement under which any person carrying on an insurance business may be liable to satisfy part or all of a judgment which may be entered in the action or to indemnify or reimburse for payments made to satisfy the judgment.

The Rule 26(a)(1) initial disclosures should provide all parties with information concerning relevant witnesses, documents, and things. After disclosure of this basic information, parties may better plan discovery and prepare their cases for trial. While much of the information disclosed may itself be offered at trial, this is not the case with insurance agreements disclosed pursuant to Rule 26(a)(1)(D). Despite the disclosure requirement of Rule 26(a)(1)(D), Federal Rule of Evidence 411 and comparable state rules preclude the offering of evidence that a person was or was not insured upon the issue whether the person acted negligently or otherwise wrongly. Such evidence is inadmissible at trial because of a concern that a jury might return an unjustified verdict if it knew that an insurance company, rather than the defendant, must satisfy any judgment. Rule 26(a)(1)(D) requires that insurance information be disclosed, though, because of the significant role that insurance coverage plays in the settlement of civil litigation.

Rule 26(a)(1) requires that initial disclosures are to be provided automatically, "without awaiting a discovery request," and, unless otherwise stipulated or directed by the court, the disclosures are to be made at or within 14 days after the pretrial conference required by Rule 26(f). Except in categories of proceedings exempted from initial disclosure under Rule 26(a)(1)(E) or when otherwise ordered, parties are to hold such a conference as soon as practicable (and at least 21 days before a Rule 16 scheduling conference or a Rule 16 scheduling order is due) in order to consider their claims and defenses, the possibility of settlement, and discovery, as well as to make or arrange for the Rule 26(a)(1) initial disclosures. Rule 26(f) also provides that, within 14 days after their conference, the parties are to submit to the court a written report outlining the discovery plan upon which they have agreed. Rule 26(a)(1) provides that initial disclosures are to be made based upon the information then reasonably available and that a party is not excused from making its disclosures because it has not completed its case investigation or due to concerns about the sufficiency of another party's disclosures.

Counsel should consider the initial disclosure requirements in drafting the pleadings, for both the identification of individuals under Rule 26(a)(1)(A) and copies of documents and other things under Rule 26(a)(1)(B) only must be provided if "the disclosing party may use [them] to support its claims or defenses, unless solely for impeachment." Thus parties only are required to disclose information that they, themselves, may use to support the claims or defenses that they, themselves, have pled in the lawsuit.

While Rule 26(a)(1) is quite specific in its requirements, these requirements may not apply to the parties in a particular case for several reasons. While the 1993 amendments to Rule 26(a)(1) authorized individual district courts to promulgate local rules to exclude categories of cases from initial disclosure, such a local rule "opt-out" from the initial disclosure provisions is no longer possible as a result of the 2000 amendments to Rule 26(a)(1). Instead, Rule 26(a)(1)(E) itself exempts from initial disclosure eight specific categories of proceedings, including petitions for habeas corpus, subpoena enforcement actions, student loan collection actions, and actions to enforce arbitration awards. In addition, the Rule 26(a)(1) initial disclosure requirements may be superseded by court order in a specific case. Finally, Rule 26(a)(1) permits the parties to themselves circumvent or modify the initial disclosure requirements by stipulation. Thus, at a Rule 26(f) conference or otherwise, the parties may agree upon initial disclosure provisions that are most appropriate to their particular case.

B. Expert Disclosures

In addition to these initial disclosures, Rule 26(a)(2) requires the disclosure of information concerning expert witnesses. Parties are required not only to disclose the identity of any expert who will present testimony at trial, but, "with respect to a witness who is retained or specially employed to provide expert testimony in the case or whose duties as an employee of the party regularly involve giving expert testimony," to provide the other parties with a written report prepared and signed by the expert. Rule 26(a)(2)(B) is quite specific concerning the required expert witness report, which is to contain a complete statement of all opinions to be expressed and the basis and reasons therefor, information considered in forming the opinions, any exhibits to be used by the expert, the qualifications of the expert, compensation to be paid to the expert, and a listing of other cases in which the witness has testified as an expert at trial or by deposition within the preceding four years.

These expert disclosures are to be made at the times and in the sequence directed by the court. However, Rule 26(a)(2)(C) provides that, if a schedule is not set by court order or party stipulation, expert disclosures are to be made at least 90 days before the trial date or the date the case is to be ready for trial (unless the evidence is to contradict or rebut expert evidence identified pursuant to Rule 26(a)(2)(B), in which case the rebuttal evidence shall be identified within 30 days after the disclosure made by the other party).

As with Rule 26(a)(1) initial disclosures, the disclosure of expert testimony pursuant to Rule 26(a)(2) is not dependent upon a request for such information by another party. While experts must be identified in all cases, the parties by stipulation or the court by order may modify Rule 26(a)(2)'s requirement concerning the creation and disclosure of a written expert report.

C. Pretrial Disclosures

The final disclosure category is contained in Rule 26(a)(3), which requires pretrial disclosure of the following information that may be presented at trial other than solely for impeachment:

(A) the name and, if not previously provided, the address and telephone number of each witness, separately identifying those whom the party expects to present and those whom the party may call if the need arises;

(B) the designation of those witnesses whose testimony is expected to be presented by means of a deposition and, if not taken stenographically, a transcript of the pertinent portions of the deposition testimony; and

(C) an appropriate identification of each document or other exhibit, including summaries of other evidence, separately identifying those which the party expects to offer and those which the party may offer if the need arises.

Prior to the Rule 26(a)(3) requirement that this information be exchanged, parties typically were required by local rules or standing orders to exchange such information. Unless the court otherwise directs, Rule 26(a)(3) requires that these disclosures be made at least 30 days before trial and that objections to deposition testimony and exhibits be made within 14 days after the disclosure to which objection is made.

II. THE GENERAL SCOPE OF DISCOVERY UNDER RULE 26(b)

In addition to the three categories of Rule 26(a) required disclosures, Rule 26 also recognizes a party's right to obtain relevant and nonprivileged information pursuant to the discovery provisions of the Federal Rules of Civil Procedure. Rule 26(d), though, provides that parties generally are not entitled to seek discovery from any other source before they have conferred concerning initial disclosures and the other matters covered by Rule 26(f).

Rule 26(b) establishes the scope of civil discovery. Rule 26(b)(1) initially provides: "Parties may obtain discovery regarding any matter, not privileged, that is relevant to the claim or defense of any party * * * ." Not only are all parties entitled to nonprivileged information relevant to the specific claims and defenses asserted in the action, but Rule 26(b)(1) also provides: "For good cause, the court may order discovery of any matter relevant to the subject matter involved in the action." Prior to 2000, this broader scope of discovery applied in all cases, but the 2000 amendment to Rule 26(b)(1) restricted that section so that parties are only entitled to discovery relevant to the "subject matter involved in the action" upon a showing of good cause.

Rule 26(b)(1) further provides: "Relevant information need not be admissible at the trial if the discovery appears reasonably calculated to lead to the discovery of admissible evidence." Thus counsel might ask the witness at a deposition if she "has heard" who was responsible for a particular action. An answer to this question would most likely be hearsay that is inadmissible at trial. Nevertheless, if the hearsay identification is "reasonably calculated to lead to the discovery of admissible evidence" (perhaps from the person identified), the question would be proper in a discovery deposition.

Rule 26(a)(5) lists the methods by which discovery within the scope of Rule 26(b) can be obtained. The discovery devices listed include depositions upon oral examination or written questions, written interrogatories, production of documents or things or permission to enter upon land, physical and mental examinations, and requests for admission. Figure 6–1 shows these discovery devices that can be used to obtain information falling within the scope of Rule 26(b).

FIGURE 6–1

DISCOVERY UNDER THE FEDERAL RULES OF CIVIL PROCEDURE

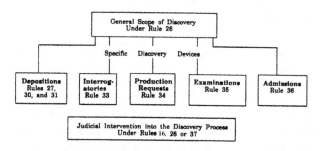

Discovery under the Federal Rules of Civil Procedure traditionally was conducted by the parties without a great deal of judicial oversight, although 1993 and 2000 amendments to Rules 16 and 26 have resulted in an increasing role for the courts in establishing discovery schedules and limitations. If, during discovery, counsel cannot resolve disputes concerning the discoverability of certain information, judicial intervention into the discovery process also may be necessary. This intervention may take the form of a Rule 26(c) order protecting certain information from discovery or a Rule 37(a) order compelling discovery. The specific discovery devices are discussed in Chapters 7 through 9 of this book, and Chapter 10 considers the court's intervention into the discovery process pursuant to Rule 26 and Rule 37.

Counsel engaged in civil discovery must be familiar with not only Federal Rules of Civil Procedure 26 through 37, but with local rules of court and the standing orders of individual judges concerning discovery. Counsel also should be aware of Rule 29 of the Federal Rules of Civil Procedure. This rule permits counsel, unless otherwise directed by the court, to modify by written stipulation the discovery procedures of the Federal Rules of Civil Procedure. Counsel therefore could agree that a non-party will answer written interrogatories rather than submit to deposition questioning or that depositions will be taken with less notice than otherwise required. However, Rule 29 provides that stipulations extending the time to respond to interrogatories and document and admission requests require court approval if the extension would interfere with any time set for completion of discovery, for hearing of a motion, or for trial.

A. Relevance

The major restriction on civil discovery is Rule 26(b)(1)'s requirement that information sought must be "relevant to the claim or defense of any party," or, if the court so orders upon a showing of good cause, "relevant to the subject matter involved in the pending action."

Liberal discovery was one of the most significant innovations of the Federal Rules of Civil Procedure. In *Oppenheimer Fund, Inc. v. Sanders* (S.Ct.1978), the Supreme Court interpreted discovery "relevant to the subject matter involved in the pending action" to encompass "any matter that bears on, or that reasonably could lead to other matter that could bear on, any issue that is or may be in the case." Such liberal discovery was to lead to better trials, at which all relevant evidence would be efficiently presented. The proponents of the Rules also hoped that liberal discovery would facilitate settlements. Counsel, knowing the evidence likely to be presented at trial, could predict the probable trial outcome and use that prediction as a basis for settlement short of trial.

In recent years, however, discovery and its broad scope have been blamed for increasing litigation cost and delay. These concerns led to a narrowing of the Rule 26(b)(1) scope of discovery in 2000, so that parties now are only entitled to discovery concerning nonprivileged matters relevant to "the claim or defense of any party." While parties still may seek discovery relevant to the "subject matter involved in the action" (the scope of discovery that previously applied in all cases), they only can obtain this broader discovery pursuant to a court order upon a showing of good cause.

Even before this limitation of the scope of discovery in 2000, Rule 26 was amended in other ways to involve the court in overseeing, and limiting, discovery. In 1983 Rule 26(b) was amended and its heading was changed from "Scope of Discovery" to "Discovery Scope and Limits." A 1993 amendment to Rule 26(b)(2) recognized the power of a court to alter the limits on numbers of depositions and interrogatories and to limit the length of depositions and number of admission requests. Rule 26(b)(2) also provides that a court *shall* limit discovery if it determines that:

(i) the discovery sought is unreasonably cumulative or duplicative, or is obtainable from some other source that is more convenient, less burdensome, or less expensive; (ii) the party seeking discovery has had ample opportunity by discovery in the action to obtain the information sought; or (iii) the burden or expense of the proposed discovery outweighs its likely benefit, taking into account the needs of the case, the amount in controversy, the parties' resources, the importance of the issues at stake in the litigation, and the importance of the proposed discovery in resolving the issues.

Under Rule 26(b)(2), the district court must consider not only whether requested discovery is relevant. Once the relevance determination is made, the court must consider the other Rule 26(b)(2) factors and balance the need for the discovery and the importance of that information against the burden and expense of obtaining the information through formal discovery. The greater the expense of production, the more important the information must be for it to be discoverable.

Even if not required to do so by Rule 26(b)(2), good client representation demands that counsel weigh the burden and expense of any proposed discovery against its likely benefit. Discovery can become very expensive, very quickly, and it can delay pretrial proceedings and the ultimate trial. One party's discovery initiatives can lead other parties to undertake their own discovery. Discovery therefore should be discussed with the client and a discovery plan constructed that considers both the costs and likely benefits of contemplated discovery.

B. Privilege

Not only must information be relevant to be a proper subject of civil discovery, but Rule 26(b)(1) explicitly precludes the discovery of privileged information. Unfortunately, neither the Federal Rules of Civil Procedure nor the Federal Rules of Evidence define what information is, and is not, privileged. Federal Rule of Evidence 501 provides:

> Except as otherwise required by the Constitution of the United States or provided by Act of Congress or in rules prescribed by the Supreme Court pursuant to statutory authority, * * * privilege[s] * * * shall be governed by the principles of the common law as they may be interpreted by the courts of the United States in the light of reason and experience. However, in civil actions and proceedings, with respect to an element of a claim or defense as to which State law supplies the rule of decision, * * * privilege[s] * * * shall be determined in accordance with State law.

Thus the federal courts fashion applicable federal privileges in most cases, but adopt state law privileges in federal diversity actions.

Among the privileges recognized by at least some federal courts or applied in diversity cases are those protecting attorney-client, husband-wife, psychotherapist-patient, and priest-penitent communications, as well as privileges for trade and official secrets. The most important privilege for counsel is the attorney-client privilege. This privilege applies to confidential communications between attorney and client for the purpose of securing legal advice. The privilege is to encourage full and frank communication between attorney and client, so that the attorney can provide the best possible client representation.

In *Upjohn Co. v. United States* (S.Ct.1981), the Supreme Court considered the application of the attorney-client privilege to corporate clients. At the request of the corporation's chairman, mid-level corporate employees had completed questionnaires prepared by the corporate general counsel seeking information about matters within the scope of the employees' employment. These questionnaires were returned to the corporate general counsel and were treated confidentially. The Court held that, on these facts, the attorney-client privilege extended to corporate managers without regard to whether they were within the corporate "control group."

In order to protect client communications from discovery, counsel should take precautions similar to those in *Upjohn*. Client interviews should be conducted outside the presence of third parties by the attorney herself or someone, such as a legal investigator, working under the direction of counsel. Written client correspondence can be headed "privileged attorney-client communication," and all such communications should be treated confidentially and protected from inadvertent disclosure. Prior to producing documents in discovery, they should be carefully reviewed to prevent production of privileged documents and the possible resulting waiver of the privilege.

The attorney-client privilege does not shield from disclosure the underlying facts communicated to counsel, but merely attorney-client communications. Counsel cannot ask in a deposition, "What did you tell your attorney about why you left the scene of the accident?" However, counsel might ask, "Why did you leave the scene of the accident?"

III.   THE WORK–PRODUCT DOCTRINE

The work-product doctrine was recognized by the Supreme Court in *Hickman v. Taylor* (S.Ct.1947). The plaintiff in *Hickman* sought to obtain witness statements from a defense attorney who had taken the statements from third persons who had survived an accident in which the plaintiff's decedent died. The Court held that, although the statements were relevant and not protected by the attorney-client privilege, they were covered by a qualified discovery protection for material prepared by counsel in anticipation of litigation.

The *Hickman* Court concluded that an attorney work-product protection was essential to ensure the proper, and private, functioning of counsel in our adversary system. The Court was concerned that if counsel's litigation preparations were not protected from discovery, attorneys might be hesitant to take witness statements or commit their mental thought-processes and legal strategies to writing. As Justice Jackson stated in his concurrence, "Discovery was hardly intended to enable a learned profession to perform its functions either without wits or on wits borrowed from the adversary."

The Supreme Court noted that not all attorney litigation materials are protected from discovery in all cases: "Where relevant and non-privileged facts remain hidden in an attorney's file and where production of those facts is essential to the preparation of one's case, discovery may properly be had." However, the witness statements sought in *Hickman* were from individuals who had given public testimony concerning the accident and who were still available to plaintiff's counsel. The Court also differentiated these written statements, which were in the witnesses' own words, from any attempt to require counsel to recollect what the witnesses had told him. According to the Court, an after-the-fact reconstruction of the witnesses' testimony not only might prove untrustworthy, but would improperly invade the mental impressions and thought-process-es of counsel.

Rule 26(b)(3), added to the Federal Rules of Civil Procedure in 1970, explicitly recognizes the work-product doctrine. Rule 26(b)(3) begins:

> Subject to the provisions of [Rule 26(b)(4) con-cerning expert witness discovery], a party may obtain discovery of documents and tangible things otherwise discoverable under [Rule 26(b)(1)] and prepared in anticipation of litigation or for trial by or for another party or by or for that other party's representative (including the other party's attorney, consultant, surety, indemnitor, insurer, or agent) only upon a showing that the party seeking discovery has substantial need of the materials in the preparation of the party's case and that the party is unable without undue hard-ship to obtain the substantial equivalent of the materials by other means.

The witness statements sought in *Hickman* would not have been discoverable under Rule 26(b)(3), because the witnesses had given public testimony and it is unclear whether the plaintiff had substan-tial need of the statements. In addition, the plaintiff could have obtained the substantial equivalent of the statements by contacting the witnesses directly. Rule 26(b)(3) explicitly protects not only attorney work-product materials, but documents and tangi-ble things prepared in anticipation of litigation by any party representative, including consultants, sureties, indemnitors, insurers, and agents.

Even if the requirements for disclosure are met, Rule 26(b)(3) admonishes the court to "protect against disclosure of the mental impressions, conclusions, opinions, or legal theories of an attorney or other representative of a party concerning the litigation." If substantial need and inability to obtain the information by other means can be established, a party might be able to obtain strictly factual data contained in an attorney memorandum. However, the discovering party would not be entitled to attorney impressions, conclusions, opinions or legal theories contained in that same memorandum, and such opinion work product should be excised from the memorandum before it is produced to the discovering party.

Rule 26(b)(3) provides that witnesses are entitled to a copy of their own witness statements. The statements covered by this provision are written statements signed or otherwise adopted or approved by the witness or contemporaneous recordings that are a substantially verbatim recital of an oral witness statement. Had Rule 26(b)(3) existed at that time, plaintiff's counsel in *Hickman* could have attempted to obtain the witness statements he sought by merely asking the witnesses to request copies of their statements from defense counsel and then provide them to plaintiff.

While Rule 26(b)(3) explicitly protects only "documents and tangible things," unwritten attorney work product is still protected under the work-product doctrine as recognized in *Hickman*. As with the attorney-client privilege, the attorney work-product doctrine does not necessarily protect underlying facts from discovery nor does it preclude asking witnesses directly about relevant facts. Instead, the attorney work-product doctrine protects counsel's own oral and written thoughts and impressions.

In planning their investigations, counsel should be cognizant of Rule 26(b)(3) and structure their investigations to fall within the work-product protections. Investigations should be conducted so that it is clear they were undertaken in anticipation of litigation by or on behalf of a client, and any resulting documents should be kept confidential.

In gathering information, counsel may have to balance the desire to obtain work-product protections for the information obtained against the need to collect information so that it will be most useful during later pretrial and trial proceedings. For example, if a signed witness statement is taken, the witness will be entitled to a copy of the statement and it eventually may end up in the hands of opposing counsel. However, a statement in the witness's own words may be necessary to impeach the witness effectively at trial.

IV. DISCOVERY CONCERNING EXPERTS

Under Federal Rule of Evidence 702, "If scientific, technical, or other specialized knowledge will assist the trier of fact to understand the evidence or to determine a fact in issue, a witness qualified as an expert by knowledge, skill, experience, training, or education, may testify thereto in the form of an opinion or otherwise, if (1) the testimony is based upon sufficient facts or data, (2) the testimony is the product of reliable principles and methods, and (3) the witness has applied the principles and methods reliably to the facts of the case." The latter portion of Rule 702 was added in 2000 in response to *Daubert v. Merrell Dow Pharmaceuticals, Inc.* (S.Ct.1993) and *Kumho Tire Co. v. Carmichael* (S.Ct.1999), which stressed that federal trial courts are to act as gatekeepers to exclude unreliable expert testimony. Nevertheless, expert testimony offered pursuant to Federal Rule of Evidence 702 has become increasingly common and important in modern civil litigation.

As amended in 1993, Rule 26(a)(2) requires the pretrial disclosure of experts and, except as otherwise stipulated or directed by the court, the provision of a written report prepared and signed by the expert. Rule 26(a)(2)(B) requires that this report contain a complete statement of all opinions to be expressed and the basis and reasons therefor, information considered in forming the opinions, any exhibits to be used by the expert, the qualifications of the expert, compensation to be paid to the expert, and a listing of other cases in which the witness has testified as an expert within the preceding four years. Unless the failure is harmless, failure to disclose this or other information pursuant to Rule 26(a) may result in the court invoking Rule 37(c)(1) to preclude the use of such information as evidence at trial, at a hearing, or on a motion.

Once an expert report has been provided under Rule 26(a)(2)(B), Rule 26(b)(4)(A) permits the deposition of any expert whose opinions may be presented at trial. Rule 26(b)(4)(B) provides that retained or specially employed experts who are not expected to testify at trial may be required to reveal facts or opinions only pursuant to Rule 35(b) (concerning physical or mental examinations) or "upon a showing of exceptional circumstances under which it is impracticable for the party seeking discovery to obtain facts or opinions on the same subject by other means." Unless manifest injustice would result, the party seeking expert discovery under Rule 26(b)(4) is to pay the expert a reasonable fee for time spent in responding to the discovery and, if the expert is not expected to testify at trial, to pay the other party a "fair portion of the fees and expenses reasonably incurred" by that party in obtaining facts and opinions from the expert.

In retaining and working with experts, counsel should keep in mind Rule 26(b)(4)'s categorization of experts. If an expert is merely used as a pretrial consultant and will not testify at trial, counsel should be able to preclude discovery concerning that expert. Some courts have held that if a non-testifying expert is a party's regular employee, and thus has not been "retained or specially employed * * * in anticipation of litigation or preparation for trial" within the meaning of Rule 26(b)(4)(B), the Rule

26(b)(4) discovery provisions do not apply. However, an expert such as an emergency room physician whose information was not acquired in anticipation of litigation but who was an actor or observer with respect to transactions or occurrences that are relevant to claims or defenses in the lawsuit is treated as an ordinary witness subject to Rule 26(b)(1) discovery.

Counsel working with experts also should be aware of Federal Rules of Evidence 612 and 705. Federal Rule of Evidence 612 generally provides:

> [I]f a witness uses a writing to refresh memory for the purpose of testifying, either (1) while testifying, or (2) before testifying, if the court in its discretion determines it is necessary in the interests of justice, an adverse party is entitled to have the writing produced at the hearing, to inspect it, to cross-examine the witness thereon, and to introduce in evidence those portions which relate to the testimony of the witness.

Acting pursuant to Rule 612, federal courts have required the production of documents that an expert has reviewed prior to her testimony.

Federal Rule of Evidence 705 provides that, although an expert may give opinion testimony without disclosing the facts or data upon which her opinions rest, the expert "may in any event be required to disclose the underlying facts or data on cross-examination." Counsel therefore should not give information to their experts that they do not want to produce to opposing parties.

V. DISCOVERY PLANNING

Not only is the scope of permissible discovery quite broad under the Federal Rules of Civil Procedure, but counsel have many options concerning the timing, sequence, and techniques of civil discovery. Rule 26(d) provides that, unless the court orders otherwise, "methods of discovery may be used in any sequence, and the fact that a party is conducting discovery, whether by deposition or otherwise, does not operate to delay any other party's discovery." However, in most cases counsel will not be able to unilaterally structure discovery. Except in categories of proceedings exempted from initial disclosure or when otherwise ordered, Rule 26(f) requires that the parties confer to develop a proposed discovery plan for presentation to the court, which plan, if approved by the court, will govern pretrial discovery.

Discovery planning should be a major aspect of the litigation plan that is developed at the very outset of the case. Because discovery can be so expensive and cause major case delays, the client should be consulted concerning the general scope of the discovery plan. Plaintiff's counsel should develop the discovery plan before filing suit, and defense counsel should have such a plan before the Rule 26(f) conference (which is to be held at least 21 days before a scheduling conference is held or a scheduling order is due under Rule 16(b)). Among the matters the parties are to address in their Rule 26(f) plan are (1) the timing, form, and types of disclosures to be made under Rule 26(a); (2) the subjects for discovery, a proposed discovery schedule, and whether discovery should be conducted in phases or focused on particular issues; (3) what limitations should be imposed on discovery; and (4) whether any Rule 26(c) protective orders or Rule 16(b) or (c) orders should be entered. Rule 16(b) provides that, except in "categories of actions exempted by district court rule as inappropriate," the court shall, "after receiving the report from the parties under Rule 26(f) or after consulting with the attorneys for the parties and any unrepresented parties," enter a scheduling order governing discovery and other pretrial proceedings.

In formulating a discovery plan, counsel must consider the information that can be gained through informal discovery and anticipate the likely discovery that opposing counsel will seek. While it usually is advantageous to begin discovery as soon as possible, no discovery should be undertaken until a plan has been developed for all discovery. There will not be a second chance to depose most witnesses, and the Federal Rules contain limitations on the number of depositions that can be taken and interrogatories that can be served without leave of court or party stipulation. Discovery timing, as well as substance, is quite important.

Although Rule 26(d) provides that there is no standard discovery sequence, counsel should consider the relative advantages of different discovery devices in different situations. Often the same information can be obtained in more than one way, and counsel should build discovery requests upon information previously obtained.

For this reason, many attorneys use interrogatories to begin discovery. Interrogatories are generally the least expensive discovery device, and they can be used to obtain basic information that was not provided in the initial disclosures. After requesting and reviewing documents identified in the initial disclosures and interrogatory answers, depositions can be taken of the witnesses identified in response to the interrogatories or initial disclosures. After the completion of these discovery stages, admission requests can be used to pin down opposing parties concerning important facts for trial.

While such an approach uses each layer of discovery to lay the foundation for the next round of discovery requests, it may reveal to opposing counsel where the discovery is headed. For instance, the initial interrogatories may alert opposing counsel to likely deposition questions and give that attorney a chance to prepare her witnesses accordingly.

As a result, attorneys sometimes begin discovery by deposing an important official of the opposing party. The disadvantage of this approach is that Rule 30(a)(2)(B) generally precludes more than one deposition of an individual in a lawsuit, and, if depositions are conducted too early in a case, there may be lines of inquiry that are not pursued because other important discovery has not yet been obtained. Counsel should consider these factors not only in scheduling different discovery devices, but in deciding the order in which depositions will be taken. Always presume that deponents will know the questions that were asked of individuals who were deposed before them.

Different attorneys adopt different approaches to discovery planning, and there is usually more than one approach that can be taken in any given case. Counsel should think through her discovery options in each case and adopt a discovery plan that is consistent with her overall litigation plan.

VI.   DISCOVERY AND DISCLOSURE SUPPLEMENTATION AND CERTIFICATION

Supplementation of discovery and disclosures is covered by Federal Rule of Civil Procedure 26(e). Rule 26(e)(1) provides:

> A party is under a duty to supplement at appropriate intervals its disclosures under [Rule 26(a)] if the party learns that in some material respect the information disclosed is incomplete or incorrect and if the additional or corrective information has not otherwise been made known to the other parties during the discovery process or in writing.

In addition to this general duty to supplement Rule 26(a) disclosures, Rule 26(e)(1) further provides that, with respect to experts, a duty to supplement extends to both expert reports and information provided in expert depositions.

Rule 26(e)(2) imposes a similar duty to supplement with respect to written discovery responses, providing:

> A party is under a duty seasonably to amend a prior response to an interrogatory, request for production, or request for admission if the party learns that the response is in some material respect incomplete or incorrect and if the additional or corrective information has not otherwise been made known to the other parties during the discovery process or in writing.

The Rule 26(e)(2) duty to supplement is addressed to written discovery responses, and, with the exception of expert depositions (which must be supplemented pursuant to Rule 26(e)(1)), there is no duty to supplement deposition responses.

Under Rule 26(e)(1) or (2), a party need only supplement *materially* incomplete or incorrect disclosures or discovery responses, and only if additional or corrective information has not otherwise been disclosed during the formal discovery process or in writing. Thus, while a telephone call to opposing counsel cannot satisfy the Rule 26(e) duty of supplementation, this duty can be satisfied by a letter to opposing counsel or witness testimony during a deposition.

In addition to the Rule 26(e) duty to supplement, Rule 26(g) requires that all disclosures and discovery requests, responses, and objections must be signed by counsel. Rule 26(g)(1) treats counsel's signature as a certification that a disclosure is "complete and correct as of the time it is made," while Rule 26(g)(2) provides that a signature on a discovery document constitutes a certification that the document is:

(A) consistent with [the Federal Rules of Civil Procedure] and warranted by existing law or a good faith argument for the extension, modification, or reversal of existing law;

(B) not interposed for any improper purpose, such as to harass or to cause unnecessary delay or needless increase in the cost of litigation; and

(C) not unreasonable or unduly burdensome or expensive, given the needs of the case, the discovery already had in the case, the amount in controversy, and the importance of the issues at stake in the litigation.

The first two of these certification requirements parallel the requirements of Rule 11, while the third requirement specifically addresses the problem of discovery abuse and overuse. In addition, Model Rule of Professional Conduct 3.4(d) forbids counsel from making frivolous discovery requests or failing to make reasonably diligent efforts to comply with legally proper discovery requests, while Model Rule 4.4 and Disciplinary Rule 7–102(A)(1) more generally prohibit actions to harass or injure a third person.

Rule 26(g)(3) provides that if, without substantial justification, a certification is made in violation of Rule 26(g), the court shall impose appropriate sanctions. In addition, Rule 37(c)(1) provides that if a party without substantial justification fails to disclose information required by Rule 26(a) or (e)(1) that party shall not, unless the failure is harmless, be permitted to use that information at trial, at a hearing, or on a motion and may be subject to other sanctions as well. Counsel therefore should ensure that discovery disclosures and responses are complete when made and, if for some reason they are not, be sure to supplement them pursuant to Rule 26(e).

CHAPTER SEVEN

INTERROGATORIES

I. THE RULE 33 INTERROGATORY

Rule 33 of the Federal Rules of Civil Procedure governs interrogatories. That rule provides that any party may serve interrogatories upon any other party. Unlike depositions, interrogatories only can be used to obtain information from other parties to the lawsuit—either opposing parties or co-parties.

Rule 33(a) provides that, absent leave of court or a written stipulation to the contrary, interrogatories cannot be served before the time specified in Rule 26(d), which generally prohibits parties from seeking discovery before they have held their Rule 26(f) conference to plan discovery. Interrogatories are to be addressed in the parties' discovery plan, unless the case is exempted from the Rule 26(f) discovery plan requirement by court order or because it is a category of proceeding exempted from initial disclosure by Rule 26(a)(1)(E). In another attempt to control the indiscriminate use of interrogatories, Rule 33(a) limits a party to 25 interrogatories, "including all discrete subparts," without leave of court or a written stipulation permitting the service of additional interrogatories.

Interrogatories may seek any information within the scope of Rule 26(b)(1). Rule 33(c) in part provides: "An interrogatory otherwise proper is not necessarily objectionable merely because an answer to the interrogatory involves an opinion or contention that relates to fact or the application of law to fact * * * ." Despite the protection of trial preparation materials in Federal Rule of Civil Procedure 26(b)(3), Rule 33(c) contention interrogatories can be used to elicit interrogatory answers concerning a party's contentions and theories in a lawsuit.

Rather than merely eliciting a factual response, the following contention interrogatory might help to narrow the parties' legal dispute: "Does the defendant contend that the plaintiff was contributorily negligent because he did not blow his horn before the parties' cars collided?" Contention interrogatories also can be used to determine the specific factual basis of claims or defenses asserted in the pleadings: "Upon what specific facts does the defendant rely in contending in paragraph 9 of the answer that the plaintiff was contributorily negligent?"

While Rule 33(c) permits interrogatories involving opinions or contentions relating to fact or the application of law to fact, it does not authorize interrogatories extending to legal issues unrelated to the facts of the case. Because relevant opinions and contentions may not be fully formulated at the outset of a lawsuit, Rule 33(c) provides that "the court may order that [a contention] interrogatory need not be answered until after designated discovery has been completed or until a pre-trial conference or other later time."

Rule 33(b)(1) requires that each interrogatory "shall be answered separately and fully in writing under oath, unless it is objected to, in which event the objecting party shall state the reasons for objection and shall answer to the extent the interrogatory is not objectionable." Interrogatory responses must be served within thirty days after service of the interrogatories, although Rule 33(b)(3) permits the court to direct a different time or, absent such an order, the parties to agree in writing to a different response time pursuant to Rule 29.

Interrogatories are the least expensive discovery device and, as a result, are one of the most commonly used devices by which discovery within the scope of Rule 26(b)(1) is obtained. However, interrogatories also can be quite easily abused. There is a great imbalance between the time and expense needed to draft and to respond to most interrogatories; an attorney may be able to dictate a set of interrogatories in thirty minutes that will take another party months to answer. For this reason, even prior to the 1993 amendment to Rule 33(a) limiting each party to 25 interrogatories without leave of court or written stipulation to the contrary, a majority of the federal district courts limited interrogatories by local rules of court. As amended in 2000, Rule 26(b)(2) no longer permits courts to use local rules to alter the limits on interrogatories, but the number of interrogatories still can be varied by specific orders in individual cases.

Local rules and standing orders of individual judges may restrict the types of interrogatories that can be used at different stages of a case. Initial interrogatories may be limited to questions concerning the identification of witnesses with relevant information, while contention interrogatories may not be permitted until other discovery has been completed.

The permissible number or types of interrogatories often are the subject of a Rule 26(f) discovery plan or a Rule 16(b) pretrial order. Regardless of governing local rules, Model Rule of Professional Conduct 3.4(d) prohibits frivolous discovery requests and Disciplinary Rule 7–102(A)(1) prohibits action merely to harass or injure. Counsel also should consider if interrogatories are the most practical means of obtaining the information desired.

Rule 33(c) provides that any interrogatory answers obtained "may be used to the extent permitted by the rules of evidence." Rule 33(a) requires that interrogatories must be answered by the party served or an officer or agent of that party, while Rule 33(b)(2) requires interrogatory answers to be signed by the party making them. Thus, under Federal Rule of Evidence 801(d)(2), interrogatory answers that are offered against a party are not hearsay. Presuming there is no other evidentiary objection, a party's interrogatory answers generally can be offered against that party. While a party can attempt to disown his interrogatory answers, this presents practical difficulties when those answers were given under oath in the very legal proceeding in question. In certain circumstances, a party can offer his own interrogatory answers pursuant to Federal Rule of Evidence 801(d)(1) as prior consistent statements to rebut a charge of recent fabrication or improper influence or motive.

II. USING AND DRAFTING INTERROGATORIES

Before considering how interrogatories should be drafted, the decision whether to even employ interrogatories must be made. While they are extremely inexpensive, interrogatories are not suitable for all purposes. In addition, interrogatories may provide opposing counsel with significant information concerning your case or alert opposing counsel to certain aspects of her case upon which she had not previously focused. When judiciously used, however, interrogatories can be an important part of a comprehensive discovery plan.

Interrogatories are perhaps most useful in obtaining basic background information, which may lay the groundwork for other discovery requests. Early interrogatory answers may reveal the organizational structure of a company or agency, dates of important meetings or conversations, the identity of important documents, the names, addresses, and telephone numbers of persons with relevant information, and a listing of another party's trial witnesses. Having received such information, the discovering party can formulate document requests, interview persons identified in the interrogatory answers, and depose important witnesses. In fact, a party might serve a Rule 34 document production request simultaneously with a set of interrogatories seeking "all documents described in response to interrogatories ___, ___, and ___."

Rule 33(a) requires the party answering interrogatories to furnish "such information as is available to the party." Thus the interrogatory answers of a corporate party must be based upon the collective knowledge of the corporation, rather than upon the mere knowledge of any single corporate official or employee. While an individual legitimately may answer "I don't know" to important deposition questions, posing those same questions in a set of interrogatories may elicit useful responses.

While interrogatories are effective in obtaining basic "name, rank, and serial number" information, they are of little use in procuring helpful characterizations or admissions. Parties have thirty days to respond to interrogatories, and interrogatory answers typically are reviewed by counsel. Counsel cannot ethically change the substance of interrogatory answers ("Just say the light was green, not red."). However, they should ensure that their clients provide no information beyond that actually called for by opposing interrogatories. Spontaneous admissions against interest sometimes occur in depositions, particularly if the deponent has not been well prepared by his attorney ("Yes, I guess I was driving pretty fast."). Rarely, if ever, do such spontaneous admissions occur in interrogatory answers. Counsel should save questions seeking descriptions, characterizations, or explanations for depositions.

Another major disadvantage of interrogatories is that an entire set of interrogatories must be drafted before the answers are known to any particular interrogatory. There is no opportunity for immediate follow-up questioning as there is in a deposition. Counsel therefore must draft interrogatories that anticipate likely interrogatory answers and that include follow-up questions based upon those likely responses. A follow-up interrogatory might state: "If your answer to interrogatory number ___ is 'Yes,' state the following: * * * ." If a truly unexpected interrogatory answer is given, the only chance to pursue that answer may come in a later set of interrogatories or during a deposition.

Counsel should be sure to "close-up" all of her interrogatory sequences. Personal injury plaintiffs should be asked not only about any personal injuries and personal and real property losses, but to list "any other damages that have not been described in answer to [preceding] interrogatories ___, ___, and ___." This should prevent an opposing party from offering a new fact or theory after the close of discovery and arguing that "you never asked me about that in the interrogatories."

The key to drafting useful interrogatories is to avoid ambiguity. Ambiguous interrogatories will be interpreted by opposing counsel in the manner that is most favorable to her client. Thus less information, and less useful information, will be provided than actually was sought. To prevent this from occurring, counsel should review all interrogatories for possibly ambiguous words or phrases.

Interrogatories also should be tightened to preclude any objection that they are overbroad. Interrogatories may have to be qualified by time period, geographic area, or particular subject matter. Rather than asking for the identification of "all correspondence" between particular individuals, an interrogatory might ask only for the identity of correspondence within the last five years concerning a particular subject.

Some attorneys find it helpful to consult interrogatories that have been used in other lawsuits. Eventually, counsel will develop a stock of interrogatories that she or other counsel have used successfully in other cases. Before that time, she might ask colleagues for sample interrogatories or consult commercial form books. Some state and federal courts have promulgated form interrogatories for use in certain common types of cases.

Form interrogatories can provide a helpful check list of important areas to probe in particular types of cases and suggest possible formats for certain questions. To be effective, though, interrogatories must be tailored to the facts of a specific case. Form interrogatories only should be used as a starting point for drafting one's own interrogatories. In order to target interrogatories effectively in a particular case, counsel must have conducted at least preliminary factual and legal research and devised an appropriate role for her interrogatories within a comprehensive litigation plan. Counsel, rather than a paralegal or someone without full knowledge of the case, ultimately should approve all interrogatories.

Interrogatory definitions and instructions may help reduce ambiguity and redundancy. Important terms in the litigation can be defined in a preface to the interrogatories in order to reduce potential ambiguity and save paper. In addition to terms that are specifically relevant to a particular case, words such as "document," "communication," "identify," and "parties" can be defined at the outset of the interrogatories. Counsel may want to use the definition of the word "document" contained in Rule 34(a) of the Federal Rules of Civil Procedure.

Instructions or rules of construction sometimes are included in an interrogatory preface. Such instructions might state that, as used in the interrogatories, singular words are intended to include the plural and masculine words are intended to include the feminine, and vice versa. Some attorneys use the preface to their interrogatories to remind the answering party that the interrogatories are continuing in nature, that interrogatory responses should divulge all information in the possession of the responding party, its attorneys and other agents, and that nonobjectionable portions of an interrogatory should be answered even if an objection is raised to other portions of the interrogatory.

In lengthy sets of interrogatories, headings can be used to categorize the interrogatories by specific topics. Such categorization should not only make the final interrogatories more readable but should focus the drafter upon the subjects to be probed and the relationship of the interrogatories to one another. Limiting interrogatories to discrete matters or breaking them into subparts may help avoid ambiguity and ensure at least partial interrogatory answers if an objection is raised to one portion of an interrogatory. However, before breaking down questions into a greater number of interrogatories, counsel should consider the impact of Rule 33(a) and any court order or party agreement restricting the number of interrogatories that can be asked without leave of court.

Form 9 of the Appendix of Forms to the Federal Rules of Civil Procedure is an illustrative complaint in a negligence action stemming from an automobile accident. What follows is a short set of interrogatories that might be filed by the defendant in an action based upon the modified version of Form 9 set forth in Chapter 4, supra, p. 85.

UNITED STATES DISTRICT COURT FOR THE DISTRICT OF MASSACHUSETTS

Civil Action No. __-_____

A.B., Plaintiff)
      v.)
C.D., Defendant)

DEFENDANT'S FIRST SET OF INTERROGATORIES TO PLAINTIFF

Pursuant to Rule 33 of the Federal Rules of Civil Procedure, the plaintiff is to fully answer under oath the following interrogatories within thirty days. The plaintiff also is required to supplement his answers pursuant to Federal Rule of Civil Procedure 26(e).

Definitions and Instructions

1. As used in these interrogatories, the phrase "the accident of June 1, 2001" refers to the collision between defendant's car and the plaintiff on June 1, 2001, on Boylston Street in Boston, Massachusetts.

2. The use of the singular form of any word in these interrogatories includes the plural and the use of the plural form of any word includes the singular.

3. If any interrogatory cannot be answered fully, the plaintiff shall answer to the extent possible and set forth all reasons for his inability to provide a complete answer.

Interrogatories

1. Please identify yourself by stating:

a. your name, including any nickname(s) by which you are commonly known;

b. your current residence address;

c. any addresses other than the address listed in answer to interrogatory 1(b) at which you have resided in the last five years;

d. your date of birth.

2. Please state:

a. the name and address of your current employer;

b. the date on which your employment began with the employer listed in response to interrogatory 2(a);

c. a description of your job duties while employed by the employer listed in response to interrogatory 2(a);

d. any employers other than the employer listed in response to interrogatory 2(a) for whom you have worked within the last five years.

3. Upon what specific facts do you base your contention in paragraph 2 of the complaint that the defendant was negligent in connection with the accident of June 1, 2001?

4. Describe all injuries—physical, mental, emotional, economic, and other—that you allegedly suffered as a result of the accident of June 1, 2001.

5. Describe any medical treatment that you have received in connection with the injuries described in answer to interrogatory 4. Include in your answer:

a. the names, business addresses, and business telephone numbers of any doctors or other medical personnel whom you consulted in connection with your injuries;

b. the dates upon which the persons listed in response to interrogatory 5(a) treated or examined you;

c. the nature of the treatment received on the dates listed in response to interrogatory 5(b);

d. an itemized listing of all expenses incurred as a result of the medical treatment stemming from the accident of June 1, 2001, including expenses for medical care and consultation, hospitalization, and prescription and non-prescription drugs;

e. your medical condition as of the date you answer these interrogatories;

f. the amount of damages that you claim in this lawsuit due to injuries that you allegedly received in the accident of June 1, 2001.

6. Describe any other damages that you contend you suffered as a result of the accident of June 1, 2001, that you have not described in answer to interrogatories 4 and 5.

7. Identify all persons with any knowledge concerning the accident of June 1, 2001, the damages that you allegedly suffered as a result of that accident, or any other matters relevant to the subject matter of this action. In addition to

the name of each person, state that person's home and business addresses, home and business telephone numbers, and summarize the information that the person possesses.

8.   Identify all persons whom you intend to call as witnesses at trial. In addition to the name of each person, state that person's home and business addresses, home and business telephone numbers, and a summary of the testimony that you anticipate the person will offer at trial.

9.   With respect to all persons whom you intend to call as expert witnesses at trial:

   a.   identify and set forth the qualifications of each expert witness;

   b.   state the subject matter on which each expert is expected to testify;

   c.   state the substance of the facts and opinions to which the expert is expected to testify and a summary of the grounds for each opinion.

10.   Identify any person who was consulted in preparing the answers to these interrogatories. Include in your answer the name, position, and business address and telephone number of each person consulted and the specific interrogatories concerning which each person was consulted.

> Respectfully submitted,
>
> [attorney signature lines]

III. RESPONDING TO INTERROGATORIES

Rule 33(b)(1) states that a party served with interrogatories shall either object to the interrogatories or furnish answers signed under oath. Rule 33(a) in turn requires that interrogatory answers contain "such information as is available to the party." Counsel for the responding party should carefully select the person who will sign interrogatories upon behalf of a corporation, partnership, association, or agency, because this individual will be a natural target for Rule 30 depositions.

Many attorneys ask their clients to prepare initial answers to interrogatories and then review those answers. Counsel's job is to ensure that the interrogatory answers are clear and to-the-point. While interrogatory answers should be drafted in good faith, there is no reason to volunteer information that is not explicitly sought. Definitional sections can be used in interrogatory answers, just as in interrogatories themselves. Such prefatory sections sometimes will note that the answers that follow have been drafted in the same fashion as answers of interrogatories of the opposing party. At oth times, statements at the beginning of the answ or within individual answers can explain how ambiguous interrogatory was interpreted b responding party.

Local rules of court may govern the fo interrogatory answers. These rules ofter that each interrogatory answer must be p the interrogatory to which the answer

This makes the interrogatory answers more understandable to the parties and to the judge and jury if the answers are offered at trial or the court is required to resolve a dispute concerning a particular answer or objection.

A different type of interrogatory response is recognized by Rule 33(d). The first sentence of Rule 33(d) states:

> Where the answer to an interrogatory may be derived or ascertained from the business records of the party upon whom the interrogatory has been served or from an examination, audit or inspection of such business records, including a compilation, abstract or summary thereof and the burden of deriving or ascertaining the answer is substantially the same for the party serving the interrogatory as for the party served, it is a sufficient answer to such interrogatory to specify the records from which the answer may be derived or ascertained and to afford to the party serving the interrogatory reasonable opportunity to examine, audit or inspect such records and to make copies, compilations, abstracts or summaries.

In 1980, the following sentence was added to the above provision: "A specification shall be in sufficient detail to permit the interrogating party to locate and to identify, as readily as can the party served, the records from which the answer may be ascertained." The Advisory Committee Note to this 1980 amendment observed:

The Committee is advised that parties upon whom interrogatories are served have occasionally responded by directing the interrogating party to a mass of business records or by offering to make all of their records available, justifying the response by the option provided by this subdivision. Such practices are an abuse of the option. A party who is permitted by the terms of this subdivision to offer records for inspection in lieu of answering an interrogatory should offer them in a manner that permits the same direct and economical access that is available to the party.

Even as amended in 1980, there are both advantages and disadvantages to utilizing the Rule 33(d) option to produce business records. The major advantage of the option is that the responding party can throw much of the work otherwise required by interrogatory responses back onto the inquiring party.

This savings, though, comes at the cost of permitting another party to search through one's records. Even if responding counsel is certain that the records contain no privileged or confidential information, it is helpful to know exactly what information the inquiring party has obtained. If the Rule 33(d) option is used, the responding party should (1) carefully screen all documents before their production to be certain that they do not contain harmful matter that goes beyond what has been requested and (2) have a representative present to maintain the order and integrity of the documents during their inspection and observe the other party's document inspection.

If some or all of a series of interrogatories are objectionable, objections, rather than answers, can be filed. Rule 33(b)(1) requires that the objecting party "shall state the reasons for objection and shall answer to the extent the interrogatory is not objectionable," while Rule 33(b)(2) requires that counsel sign the objections. The same thirty day period for serving answers to interrogatories also applies to interrogatory objections.

Rule 26(b)(1), governing the scope of discovery, and Rule 26(b)(2), establishing discovery limitations, provide useful check lists of common interrogatory objections. Thus interrogatories seeking privileged or irrelevant information are objectionable, as are interrogatories that are "unreasonably cumulative or duplicative," that seek information "obtainable from some other source that is more convenient, less burdensome, or less expensive," that impose a "burden or expense * * * [that] outweighs its likely benefit," or that seek discovery that the inquiring party already has had ample opportunity to obtain.

The attorney's signature required by Rule 33(b)(2) constitutes a certification under Rule 26(g)(2) that the objections are "(A) consistent with [the Federal Rules of Civil Procedure] and warranted by existing law or a good faith argument for the extension, modification, or reversal of existing law; (B) not interposed for any improper purpose * * * ;

and (C) not unreasonable or unduly burdensome or expensive, given the needs of the case, the discovery already had in the case, the amount in controversy, and the importance of the issues at stake in the litigation." The court is to impose an appropriate sanction if a certification is made in violation of Rule 26(g) without substantial justification.

Even if a potential objection poses no problem under Rule 26(g), there may be reasons not to assert a valid objection. If an interrogatory is ambiguous or unduly burdensome, counsel for the responding party might informally contact the attorney who drafted the interrogatory to seek clarification or might simply answer the interrogatory as most reasonably interpreted. If the interrogating party is entitled to the information sought and clearly intends to pursue its discovery, there is little to be gained from objecting except delay (with its concomitant expense to all parties).

In some situations, counsel may decide to raise an objection for the record, but nevertheless answer the interrogatory. This is to preserve the objection in the event that similarly objectionable interrogatories are served in the future, yet save the time otherwise necessary for rephrasing the technically improper interrogatory. Attorneys often take their cues concerning objections from opposing counsel. If an attorney raises picky objections to the interrogatories of other parties, she can't expect them to be generous in their responses to her interrogatories.

The actual interrogatory objection should be brief but should state "the reasons for objection" as required by Rule 33(b)(1). While a separate memorandum probably will be filed if the validity of an objection is raised with the court, the basic reason for the objection should be set forth in the objection. Not only may this prove helpful if the matter is contested, but a well constructed interrogatory objection may dissuade opposing counsel from even bringing the matter before the court. Counsel also should be aware of Rule 33(b)(4), which requires that interrogatory objections be stated with specificity and provides: "Any ground not stated in a timely objection is waived unless the party's failure to object is excused by the court for good cause shown."

An objection might look something like this:

Objection. The interrogatory is objectionable under Federal Rule of Civil Procedure 26(b)(2) because the burden and expense of providing the discovery sought outweighs its likely benefit. A response would require the manual search of 531 file cabinets located in the fifteen regional offices of the defendant company, and the information sought is only marginally relevant to the remaining issues in this case.

Because the party making interrogatory answers is required to sign the answers under oath and the attorney is to sign any objections, dual signature lines usually are necessary at the end of the interrogatory responses. In the following example, an unsworn declaration pursuant to 28 U.S.C. § 1746 has been used in lieu of the sworn signature otherwise required by Rule 33(b):

As to the answers herein:

Pursuant to 28 U.S.C. § 1746, I, [party's name], declare this ___ day of _____ 200__ under penalty of perjury that the above answers are true and correct.

[party's signature]

As to the objections herein:

[regular attorney
signature lines]

If a party objects to interrogatories or fails to answer them, the discovering party may decide to file a motion to compel interrogatory answers pursuant to Federal Rule of Civil Procedure 37(a). If an entire set of interrogatories has not been answered, the full range of discovery sanctions provided by Rule 37(d) is available. Rather than merely objecting to interrogatories, the party from whom discovery is sought may decide to file a Rule 26(c) motion for a protective order. As is more fully discussed in Chapter 10, infra p. 242, a protective order may be sought when the responding party wants to obtain a ruling on objectionable discovery rather than wait for the party seeking discovery to bring the issue before the court pursuant to a motion to compel.

CHAPTER EIGHT

DEPOSITIONS

I. DEPOSITIONS UNDER THE FEDERAL RULES OF CIVIL PROCEDURE

In contrast to interrogatories, which are inexpensive but may be of limited utility in obtaining certain types of discovery, depositions are among the most expensive yet effective discovery devices. Because of their effectiveness, all litigators should know how to take and defend depositions.

Deposition testimony may be taken from any person, so long as the testimony sought is within the scope of Rule 26(b)(1). Rules 27 through 32 concern depositions, although some of these rules are not frequently used. For example, Rule 31 concerns depositions upon written questions.

Rule 31 written deposition questions may be served, within the time limits of Rule 26(d), upon the person to be deposed and all parties to the lawsuit. Other parties then can serve cross questions, which may be followed by written redirect and recross questions. All of these questions ultimately are read to the deposition witness by a court reporter, who prepares a transcript of the witness's responses. Revealing questions to the witness and other counsel in advance of the deposition reduces the chance of spontaneous responses that otherwise might occur at a deposition upon oral examination. Nor is there an opportunity for follow-up questioning at the deposition. Because of the cost of the court reporter, Rule 31 depositions can be just as expensive as oral depositions but are significantly less effective. Rule 31 depositions upon written questions therefore are rarely used in practice.

Virtually all depositions are taken upon oral examination pursuant to Rule 30 of the Federal Rules of Civil Procedure. Any person's deposition can be taken pursuant to Rule 30, although a Rule 45 deposition subpoena must be used to compel the attendance of a non-party witness. Under Rule 45(a)(3), these subpoenas can be obtained from the clerk's office in blank or issued directly by an attorney as an officer of the court.

Depositions should be part of a comprehensive discovery plan. Rule 30(a)(2) provides that leave of court must be granted in order to depose an individual confined in prison or if, without written party stipulation,

    (A) a proposed deposition would result in more than ten depositions being taken by the plaintiffs, by the defendants, or by third-party defendants;

    (B) the person to be examined already has been deposed in the case; or

    (C) the deposition is sought before the time specified in Rule 26(d) unless the deposition notice certifies that the person to be deposed otherwise will not be available for deposition within the United States.

Despite these provisions of Rule 30(a)(2), these limitations do not apply if the parties have altered them by written stipulation or they have been modified by a court order to the contrary. However, even if the parties are not required to address the timing and number of depositions in a Rule 26(f) discovery plan, depositions generally are scheduled by agreement of counsel. Rather than merely sending a deposition notice, attorneys consult with one another in order to arrive at a deposition time that is convenient for all counsel and the person who will be deposed. A deposition that is scheduled without advance consultation is likely to result in a request to reschedule or, if the request is rebuffed, a Rule 26(c) motion for an order that the deposition not be held at the time set in the notice.

Rule 45(c)(3)(A)(ii) provides that the court on timely motion shall quash or modify a deposition subpoena that requires a non-party witness to "travel to a place more than 100 miles from the place where that person resides, is employed or regularly transacts business in person." There is no similar geographic restriction on party depositions (for which subpoenas are not necessary), although a party can seek a Rule 26(c) protective order from the court if the deposition locale is oppressive or unduly burdensome or expensive.

Rule 45(a)(1) provides that a subpoena can command the production of "designated books, documents or tangible things" and that a "command to produce evidence or to permit inspection may be joined with a command to appear * * * at deposition." Similarly, Rule 30(b)(5) permits the notice to a party deponent to be accompanied by a Rule 34 request for the production of documents and tangible things at the deposition.

Because a party generally has thirty days to respond to a Rule 34 request, combined deposition notices and production requests should be served at least thirty days before the deposition date to ensure that the requested documents and tangible things are produced at the deposition. An even better idea is to agree with other counsel that documents requested in connection with a deposition will be produced prior to the deposition. This should give counsel more time, in advance of the deposition, to review the documents and save everyone's time at the deposition.

While both a deposition notice and a Rule 45 subpoena are required to take the deposition of a non-party, Rule 30(b)(1) merely requires a notice of deposition to take a party deposition. Rule 30(b)(1) requires that the deposition notice be given to all parties, provide "reasonable notice" of the deposition, and state the time and place of the deposition and the name and address of the person to be examined. Rule 30(b)(2) additionally requires that the notice state the method by which the testimony will be recorded (stenographically or by audiotape or videotape).

The Federal Rules of Civil Procedure do not define the "reasonable notice" required for a deposition, but local rules of court or local practice often prescribe a notice period of five or ten days. Unless a local rule or court order provides to the contrary, Rule 26(f) requires the parties to prepare a proposed discovery plan for submission to the court. Such plans typically set forth all anticipated depositions and the dates by which they are to be completed. Rule 26(d) provides that depositions and other discovery are not to be sought until the parties have conferred pursuant to Rule 26(f), except in categories of proceedings exempted from initial disclosure under Rule 26(a)(1)(E) or when authorized under a Federal Rule, court order, or party agreement.

Rule 27(a) of the Federal Rules of Civil Procedure provides that depositions can be taken before an action is filed, while Rule 27(b) permits depositions pending appeal. In order to take a deposition before an action is commenced, a verified petition must be filed setting forth the exigency that necessitates a deposition even before suit has been filed. Such an exigency might exist, for example, if the deponent was gravely ill or about to embark on a long trip. If the court is satisfied that a deposition "may prevent a failure or delay of justice" within the meaning of Rule 27(a)(3), it shall enter an order permitting the deposition. An order of court is also necessary to obtain deposition testimony pending appeal. Rule 27(b) provides that the court can permit the taking of depositions to perpetuate testimony for use in the event of further proceedings in the district court.

If the person to be deposed is a corporation, partnership, association, or government agency, Rule 30(b)(6) requires the deposition notice to "describe with reasonable particularity the matters on which examination is requested." This designation is to permit the entity to designate one or more representatives with relevant information to provide the requested deposition testimony. Without the Rule 30(b)(6) deposition procedure, several depositions might be necessary before the examining party obtained the information that it sought. Despite the advantages of Rule 30(b)(6) depositions, a party still can serve a deposition notice seeking testimony from a particular corporate or governmental official. Not only are Rule 30(b)(6) deponents designated by the corporate or governmental body, but the examining party may not wish to provide advance notice of the particular matters that will be covered in the deposition.

A typical deposition notice looks something like this:

UNITED STATES DISTRICT COURT FOR THE DISTRICT OF MASSACHUSETTS

Civil Action No. __-_____

John Smith, Plaintiff	)
	)
v.	)
	)
Francis Thomas, Defendant	)

NOTICE OF DEPOSITION

To: Jane Q. Barrister

    1234 Barristers' Building

    Cambridge, Massachusetts 02138

Please take notice that at 9:00 a.m. on the 25th day of August, 2002, in Room 1313 of the Law and Accounting Building, 1999 Commonwealth Avenue, Boston, Massachusetts, the defendant in the above-captioned action will take the deposition of the plaintiff John Smith, 3501 Main Street, Hartford, Connecticut 06120. This deposition will be taken upon oral examination and recorded stenographically pursuant to the Federal Rules of Civil Procedure before a notary public or other person authorized to administer oaths. The examination will continue from day to day until testimony is completed. You are invited to attend and present cross-examination.

                Respectfully
                submitted,

                [attorney
                signature lines]

A court reporter typically transcribes the deposition, although Federal Rule of Civil Procedure 30(b)(2) permits depositions to be preserved by audiotape or videotape recording unless the court orders to the contrary. Rule 30(b)(3) permits a party to designate a method of recording the deponent's testimony other than the one specified by the person taking the deposition, but the additional record or transcript must be made at that party's expense unless the court otherwise orders. Rule 30(b)(4) requires that certain statements be made at the beginning and conclusion of the deposition and precludes the distortion of the appearance or demeanor of deponents or attorneys through camera or sound-recording techniques. Local rules of court may contain additional requirements for videotaped depositions, such as a requirement that the deposition be timed by a clock that is shown on camera. While Rule 30(d)(2) limits depositions to "one day of seven hours," that Rule also permits this limitation to be altered by court order or party stipulation.

In addition to audiotaped and videotaped depositions, Federal Rule of Civil Procedure 30(b)(7) permits the parties to stipulate to, or the court to order, depositions by telephone "or other remote electronic means." The practical difficulty with telephone depositions is that the examining attorney usually is not in the same room with the witness and other counsel. A telephone deposition can be a quite efficient discovery device, though, for obtaining straightforward deposition testimony from collateral witnesses.

Rule 32 of the Federal Rules of Civil Procedure governs the use of depositions in court proceedings. Rule 32(a)(1) provides that properly noticed depositions can be used to contradict or impeach the testimony of the deponent or "for any other purpose permitted by the Federal Rules of Evidence." Falling within this latter category is the use of deposition testimony as a prior consistent statement offered pursuant to Federal Rule of Evidence 801(d)(1)(B) "to rebut an express or implied charge against the declarant of recent fabrication or improper influence or motive."

Federal Rule of Civil Procedure 32(a)(2) provides that the depositions of parties "may be used by an adverse party for any purpose." In addition, the depositions of even non-parties may be used by any party for any purpose if the witness is dead or unavailable within the meaning of Rule 32(a)(3). However, Rule 32(a) provides that depositions only can be used against parties who were "present or represented at the taking of the deposition or who had reasonable notice thereof."

II. THE DECISION TO TAKE A DEPOSITION

The question an attorney must answer even before she considers how to take a particular deposition is whether or not that deposition should be taken. In order to answer this question, counsel must consider both the advantages and disadvantages of oral depositions.

A deposition is a wonderful discovery device because it permits counsel to ask questions of a party or non-party witness and receive direct answers from that person. The responses are not screened by counsel, as are interrogatory answers. If the examining attorney is skillful and well prepared for the deposition, valuable spontaneous admissions may be obtained from the deponent. A verbatim transcript of the witness's own statements can be a powerful cross-examination tool, as well as a helpful lever in settlement discussions.

The examining attorney can pursue answers given by the deponent immediately. When drafting interrogatories, counsel must structure questions based upon her best guess as to the manner in which a party will respond to those interrogatories. At a deposition, unexpected answers can be pursued on the spot.

Deposition "answers" are not limited to actual witness statements. Examining counsel can see the witness answer her questions, and the manner in which a witness answers questions can be just as significant as the actual answers. Witnesses may blush, stutter, pause, change the intonation of their voice, drum their fingers on the table, or look down when answering important questions, all of which may provide attorneys with important data about the witness and his testimony.

Even the manner in which a deponent dresses or walks can be important in some cases. If the defendant truck driver in a tort case appears at the deposition wearing a shirt with the nickname "Speedy," a favorable plaintiff's settlement may not be far in the offing. Similarly, defense counsel will be pleasantly surprised if the plaintiff who has claimed serious injuries in a personal injury action runs into the deposition room and exclaims, "Sorry I'm late, but my karate class ran over."

During the deposition, all counsel will have the opportunity to evaluate the witness's likely trial testimony. Counsel should ask themselves if the witness is someone who will create a favorable impression with the judge or jury. This question is even more important if the witness is a party to the action. Many lawsuits settle after the parties have been deposed.

Despite the many advantages of depositions, Rule 30(a)(2)(A) limits parties to ten depositions without leave of court or written stipulation to the contrary. In addition, unless there is a court order or stipulation to the contrary, Rule 30(d)(2) limits depositions to one day of seven hours. Indeed, there are disadvantages, as well as advantages, to depositions. The major disadvantage of depositions is their cost. Typically there will be at least two attorneys, a court reporter, and a witness at a deposition. Deposition transcripts are not cheap, particularly if the transcript is expedited. Videotaped depositions are even more expensive. In addition to the costs of reporters and attorneys, depositions require that the witness be present for what can be an extended question and answer session.

While counsel may not be particularly concerned with deposition burdens if the deponent is an adverse witness, a decision to depose an opponent's witnesses may trigger a decision by that party's counsel to conduct depositions of her own. In addition, deposition questioning may alert opposing parties to the details of both your case and their own. Even if a deposition is taken, certain lines of questioning may be saved for trial cross-examination so that an opposing party will not be able to prepare a response in advance of trial.

The manner in which depositions lock a witness into a particular version of the facts can be either a deposition advantage or disadvantage. Depositions of opposing parties and witnesses typically are taken to commit those individuals to a story. If the individual offers different testimony at trial, the deposition can be used to impeach that trial testimony. In some situations, though, counsel may not want to perpetuate the unfavorable testimony of an opponent's witnesses. If there is a good chance that a witness will not appear at trial, counsel should think twice before creating a deposition transcript that can be offered at trial pursuant to Federal Rule of Civil Procedure 32(a)(3). On the other hand, if one of your witnesses may not be available for trial, you may want to conduct a trial deposition of that witness to create a transcript that can be offered at trial in lieu of live testimony.

Deposition advantages and disadvantages vary from case to case and witness to witness. Both potential advantages and disadvantages should be considered before a deposition is taken.

III. PREPARING TO TAKE A DEPOSITION

Once the decision is made to take a deposition, agreement must be reached with other counsel concerning a suitable time and place for the deposition testimony. The deposition notice then should be prepared and served and arrangements made for a court reporter. If a party notices but fails to attend a deposition or fails to properly subpoena a nonparty witness who as a result does not attend the deposition, Federal Rule of Civil Procedure 30(g) permits the court to award expenses to those parties who appeared in response to the deposition notice.

Counsel should consider not only which individuals to depose, but in what order depositions should be taken. Many lawyers initially depose lower-ranking individuals within an organization or corporation, and only then depose the person at the top of the organizational hierarchy. This permits counsel to use information gained in early depositions as a basis for questions at later depositions. However, opposing counsel also will gain information from the initial depositions and can use that information to prepare later deponents for anticipated questions. For this reason, attorneys sometimes begin a series of depositions with an examination of people at the top, rather than at the bottom, of an organization.

If a decision is made to take a particular deposition, counsel should carefully prepare for that deposition. If possible, counsel should interview potential witnesses before their depositions. This can help counsel determine whether to actually conduct a deposition, what questions to ask at any deposition, and the most convenient deposition time and location for the deponent. If a witness is represented by counsel, the consent of his attorney is required prior to such an interview by Rule 4.2 of the Model Rules of Professional Conduct. See also Disciplinary Rule 7–104(A)(1) of the Model Code of Professional Responsibility.

In addition to talking to the witness before his deposition, counsel should review all documents pertaining to that witness prior to the deposition. Of particular importance are documents signed or adopted by the witness, correspondence that the witness sent or received, and pleadings, discovery responses, and other papers filed in the lawsuit. If counsel does not have all these documents, the deposition notice can be combined with a document production request to a party pursuant to Rule 30(b)(5) or a Rule 45 subpoena can be used to obtain documents from a third-party witness.

Consideration should be given to the location of the deposition. For reasons of personal convenience, many attorneys hold depositions in their own offices. Nevertheless, there may be advantages to be gained from accommodating a witness by holding a deposition at his office or place of work. Valuable information may be learned about a witness merely by observing him in his natural surroundings, and the deponent's fellow employees may provide helpful tidbits about a case. In addition, a witness will find it difficult to refuse an informal request for a document described during a deposition if that document is in a filing cabinet at the deposition site. Wherever the deposition is held, counsel should ensure that it proceeds free from interruptions and that the witness realizes that the deposition will demand his undivided attention.

Examining counsel should arrive early for the deposition. This may permit her to speak again with the deponent (if that person is unrepresented by counsel) and will provide an opportunity to confirm arrangements with the court reporter. The reporter will appreciate a copy of the deposition notice, from which the case caption can be taken, as well as the names of all those who will attend the deposition and the spelling of any unusual words that are likely to be used during the deposition. Unless there is a reason to withhold them until the deposition, counsel can give the court reporter copies of any documents that she intends to use as deposition exhibits and permit them to be marked as exhibits prior to the deposition.

IV. THE TAKING OF DEPOSITION TESTIMONY

Once everyone has arrived at the deposition room, it's time to begin the deposition. Before deposition questioning begins, the court reporter puts the witness under oath. At the outset of some depositions, counsel ask whether the "usual stipulations" apply. Typical deposition stipulations concern the witness's right to examine and sign the transcript, the filing of the deposition transcript, and the preservation of objections to deposition testimony until the time of trial. These matters are covered in Federal Rules of Civil Procedure 30(e), 30(f) and 32(d), and there may be no need for party stipulations. If there is a desire to stipulate to particular matters, the complete stipulation should be specified in the deposition record rather than alluded to by a cursory and possibly ambiguous agreement to the "usual stipulations."

After the reporter's statement required by Rule 30(b)(4) and any preliminary statement by counsel, the reporter records the examining attorney's questions, the answers of the witness, and any objections or other statements of counsel. The first sentence of Federal Rule of Civil Procedure 30(c) states: "Examination and cross-examination of witnesses may proceed as permitted at the trial under the provisions of the Federal Rules of Evidence except Rules 103 and 615." Because no judge is present at the deposition, Federal Rule of Evidence 103, dealing with trial objections, is not applicable during deposition questioning. The judge's absence also means that there is no way in which to resolve any objections that may be made by counsel. For this reason, deposition objections are recorded by the court reporter, but the witness usually will be required to answer all questions subject to a later ruling on counsel's objections. Nor can a party invoke Federal Rule of Evidence 615 to automatically exclude other potential deponents from a deposition. If the exclusion of another witness is desired, a court order excluding that witness from the deposition must be sought pursuant to Federal Rule of Civil Procedure 26(c)(5).

Federal Rule of Civil Procedure 32(d) concerns deposition objections and their waiver. This rule provides that objections as to the deposition notice must be promptly served and objections to the qualifications of the reporter must be made before the deposition begins or as soon thereafter as the disqualification becomes known or could have been discovered with reasonable diligence. Rule 32(d)(3)(A) provides: "Objections to the competency of a witness or to the competency, relevancy, or materiality of testimony are not waived by failure to make them before or during the taking of the deposition, unless the ground of the objection is one which might have been obviated or removed if presented at that time." However, Rule 32(d)(3)(B) provides that objections as to the manner of taking the deposition, the form of questions or answers, the oath or affirmation, the conduct of parties, or "errors of any kind which might be obviated, removed, or cured if promptly presented" are waived unless made at the deposition.

Thus there is no requirement for an objection to a deposition question calling for hearsay testimony; Rule 32(b) provides that, in most cases, "objection may be made at the trial or hearing to receiving in evidence any deposition or part thereof for any reason which would require the exclusion of the evidence if the witness were then present and testifying." However, if an attorney is improperly leading the witness, an objection must be made during the deposition so that examining counsel can ask her questions in a non-leading fashion and thereby obviate the ground for the objection.

Presuming that one of the parties has requested that the deposition testimony be transcribed, the reporter will prepare a transcript of the deposition questions, statements of counsel, and testimony of the deponent. If requested by the deponent or a party during the deposition, Rule 30(e) gives the witness the right to review the deposition transcript and sign a statement reciting changes in the form or substance of the transcript and the reasons for those changes.

V. DEPOSITION QUESTIONING TECHNIQUES

Federal Rule of Civil Procedure 30(b)(4) requires that the court reporter initially identify himself, the deponent, and all others present at the deposition, recite the date, time, and place of the deposition, and administer the oath or affirmation to the deponent. Many attorneys then begin the deposition with an exchange similar to the following.

Examining Attorney: Mr. Smith, my name is Sandra Ronnoc and I represent the defendant Sam Rogers in this case. We're here today to take your deposition pursuant to the Federal Rules of Civil Procedure and Federal Rules of Evidence. With me today is co-counsel, Lucy Baldwin, and plaintiff's counsel, Charles Lumpkin.

Have you ever had your deposition taken before?

Witness: No.

Examining Attorney: Well, then, let me explain that this deposition is for us to learn any relevant information that you may have concerning this lawsuit between Mr. Rogers and the plaintiff Eddie Mathers. I'll be asking you questions during the deposition, and the court reporter will record both my questions and your answers.

I'll try to make my questions as straightforward as possible and give you plenty of time to answer each question. Will you agree to let me know if you don't understand any question or if you haven't had enough time to answer?

Witness: Yes.

Examining Attorney: Good. Let's begin. * * *

Such a deposition opening establishes the authority of the examining attorney in the deposition. The introduction also should put the deponent at ease and make him more forthcoming in his deposition answers. By committing the witness to ask about unclear questions and for adequate time to answer all questions, the witness cannot later credibly disown a deposition answer by arguing that he didn't understand the question or wasn't given sufficient time to respond.

The deposition questions that follow the opening statement will depend upon the deposition strategy adopted by counsel, the purpose of the deposition, and the proclivities of counsel. Most depositions are discovery depositions. The usual strategy in discovery depositions is to ask open-ended questions to elicit all relevant information that the witness possesses. Trial depositions, in contrast, are usually taken of a party's own witnesses, in order to create a transcript that can be offered in lieu of live witness testimony at trial. For this reason, the questions, answers, and objections in a trial deposition should approximate those contained in a witness examination at trial. If you decide to take the deposition of a witness who may not be available at trial, realize that the deposition transcript later may be offered pursuant to Federal Rule of Civil Procedure 32(a)(3) and question accordingly.

There are some general examination strategies applicable to virtually all depositions. Most deposition witnesses are nervous about being deposed, and this nervousness often results in short, circumspect deposition answers. One of examining counsel's major jobs in a discovery deposition is to get the witness to drop his guard and provide more complete, and thus more helpful, answers to the deposition questions. One way to accomplish this task is to begin the deposition with questions about the witness's background and other non-threatening matters. If the initial deposition questions are confrontational or concern embarrassing matters, the witness may never sufficiently relax to provide anything more than monosyllabic deposition responses. Complete responses also can be encouraged by asking open-ended questions, treating the witness courteously, allowing plenty of time for the witness to answer each question, and following the active listening techniques discussed in connection with client interviews in Chapter 2, supra, p. 25.

Prior to the deposition, counsel should prepare an outline to guide deposition questioning. An outline that is too detailed and contains every deposition question can become the sole focus of counsel's attention in the deposition room. This can prevent counsel from establishing eye contact with the witness, cause her to neglect the witness's verbal and non-verbal responses, and become a barrier to spontaneous questioning. For this reason, many attorneys prepare a deposition outline that contains each of the topics to be covered in the deposition rather than every individual question.

A deposition outline, and subsequent deposition questioning, can be arranged logically by topic or, in some cases, chronologically. By structuring the deposition in such a fashion, counsel is less likely to forget to ask about an important matter. In addition, structured deposition questioning should produce a deposition transcript that will be easier to use in connection with a pretrial motion or at trial. The major disadvantage of questioning in a structured fashion is that it may be obvious to the witness and opposing counsel exactly where the deposition is heading. If a spontaneous answer is desired to a particularly important question, counsel might ask that question out of sequence at a time when it won't be anticipated by other counsel and the witness.

One of the major advantages of depositions is the opportunity they present to pursue witness answers, and counsel should make full use of this opportunity. After asking an initial open-ended question to elicit a narrative response, counsel can take the witness back through the narrative and pose specific follow-up questions. While a witness might initially state that he has "no idea" how fast a car was going or how long a conversation lasted, in response to follow-up questions he may be able to estimate that the car was going faster than fifty miles per hour or that the conversation lasted more than ten but less than thirty minutes.

To effectively pursue witness testimony, the examining attorney must listen to all answers and closely observe the witness. Counsel should pin the witness down rather than accept qualified or evasive answers. If a witness "can't remember" a particular matter, counsel should give the witness plenty of time to think about the question and should note this fact on the record. Counsel also should ask whether there is anything, such as a document, that would help the witness remember. These techniques should make the witness less credible if his memory is refreshed after the deposition and he attempts to offer new, damaging, testimony in a later proceeding or at trial. For this reason, some attorneys end a sequence of deposition questions by asking if there is any additional information about a particular subject that the witness has not yet provided or about which the witness might testify at trial.

In order to create a deposition transcript that can be used most effectively for trial cross-examination or with pretrial motions, counsel should "close-up" each segment of the deposition by summarizing testimony that otherwise might lay scattered over several pages of the deposition transcript. For example, counsel might ask: "So the only two times that you saw the plaintiff were on August 25, 2000, and December 2, 2001?"

Counsel's deposition goal should be a complete, self-contained deposition transcript. She therefore should insist on verbal responses to her questions rather than head shakes or other non-verbal gestures. Questions should be kept simple and to-the-point in order to avoid ambiguities in the deposition transcript. Any documents discussed during the de-

position should be identified in an unambiguous
fashion, and a record should be made of the documents that are produced in response to a deposition
production request or subpoena. One way in which
to prevent later confusion concerning documents is
to make them deposition exhibits and refer to them
during the deposition by their deposition exhibit
numbers.

VI. EXPERT DEPOSITIONS

The first sentence of Federal Rule of Civil Procedure 26(b)(4)(A) provides: "A party may depose any
person who has been identified as an expert whose
opinions may be presented at trial." Because of the
increasingly important and technical nature of expert testimony, depositions are essential to permit
counsel to cross-examine experts and otherwise
counter their testimony at trial.

Preparation for the expert deposition is especially
important. Rule 26(b)(4)(A) provides that if an expert report is required pursuant to Rule 26(a)(2)(B)
(as it will be in most cases involving experts), the
deposition is not to be conducted until after the
report is provided. In the event that such a report is
not provided, the deposition subpoena should include a request for the items to be included in an
expert report pursuant to Rule 26(a)(2)(B) and copies of the expert's prior relevant writings that are
not otherwise available to examining counsel.
Agreement should be reached with other counsel to
produce requested documents prior to the deposi-

tion, so that examining counsel can become familiar with the expert's field of expertise and his writings. The examining attorney can use her own expert to help in the educational process, and counsel sometimes agree that each party's expert can attend the deposition of the opposing expert.

The initial portion of many expert depositions is spent exploring the expert's qualifications. The expert's vita should have been obtained prior to the deposition or should be requested by a deposition subpoena. The vita can be marked as a deposition exhibit, and the witness should be asked if it is current in all respects.

Counsel then can inquire about aspects of the expert's background that are particularly important to the present case. Counsel should ask the expert about relevant matters that don't appear on the vita, probing for gaps in the expert's knowledge, skill, education, and other qualifications. The expert should be asked whom he considers to be the authorities in his field and what he recognizes to be the authoritative treatises. Additionally, he should be asked about the expertise of those who have been retained as experts by other parties to the case.

Counsel should question the expert about testimony he has given in other cases. Sufficient information should be elicited so that any transcripts of prior testimony can be obtained and the attorneys involved in prior cases can be contacted. The expert's specific role in the present case also should be confirmed, as well as the fee that he is being paid to serve as an expert.

Copies of any expert reports or studies should have been disclosed pursuant to Rule 26(a)(2)(B) or otherwise requested prior to the deposition. The expert's conclusions and opinions, whether or not contained in a written report, should be probed during the deposition. While expert opinions often can be summarized in a sentence or two, the facts and reasoning underlying those opinions will probably be the subject of extended deposition questioning. Counsel should ask about all material the expert relied upon or reviewed in reaching his opinions. Experts, as well as other deponents, can be asked to draw diagrams or perform simple calculations that then can be attached as exhibits to the deposition transcript.

Counsel should be sure to ask the expert if he anticipates performing further work in connection with the case, in order to avoid being surprised at trial by expert opinions that had not been formulated at the time of the deposition. If the expert says that he intends to do significant additional work, counsel should state on the deposition record that she reserves the right to continue the deposition after the expert's work has been completed.

VII. PREPARING WITNESSES FOR THEIR DEPOSITIONS

Examining counsel is not the only attorney who must prepare for a deposition. While defending a deposition is covered in the next section of this chapter, the most important work in defending any deposition is conducted outside the deposition room. The preparation of the deponent prior to the deposition is generally much more important than anything done by counsel during the deposition. Deposition testimony often limits the later testimony that a witness credibly can offer, and many cases are settled or otherwise resolved during the pretrial process based upon the deposition performance of a party or other important witness. Careful preparation of deposition witnesses therefore is essential.

Both your own client and your non-party witnesses should be prepared concerning deposition procedure and likely deposition questioning. A good starting point for any deposition preparation session is an explanation of exactly what a deposition is. Witnesses should understand that there will be no judge present at the deposition and that counsel's role in defending the deposition is likely to be quite limited. Witnesses should appreciate that, while deposition procedures are more relaxed than those at trial, their sworn deposition testimony may be vitally important in the ultimate case resolution. However, witnesses also should realize that a discovery deposition is usually not the forum in which to offer affirmative evidence. Instead, the witness should merely answer the questions of other counsel, realizing that there will be an opportunity to develop the witness's testimony fully in a later pretrial or trial proceeding.

In addition to explaining deposition procedure, counsel should prepare witnesses for the substance of the questions that they are likely to be asked. Counsel should never attempt to alter the substance of a witness's testimony. For this reason, witnesses should be prepared individually concerning the substance of their deposition testimony so that there can be no contention that counsel attempted to conform deposition testimony to a single version of the facts.

While counsel should not attempt to alter substantive testimony, witnesses should be alerted to likely deposition questions so that they can think through appropriate responses prior to the deposition. Depositions can be unnerving experiences for even experienced witnesses, and deposition preparation can help witnesses avoid making spontaneous guesses about matters beyond their personal knowledge. Explaining to a witness how his expected testimony fits within a case may help him better deal with the free-flowing nature of many depositions.

Witnesses should be shown any documents about which they are likely to be questioned at the deposition, especially interrogatories, witness statements, or other documents that they have authored or signed. While opposing counsel may make a request pursuant to Federal Rule of Evidence 612 for documents the witness has been shown, deposition misstatements may result if the witness has not recently reviewed important documents.

Some attorneys use deposition preparation sessions to play the role of examining counsel and question their witness as they believe he will be questioned in the actual deposition. Videotape is sometimes used to show witnesses the manner in which they respond in a simulated deposition setting. Many attorneys, however, quite successfully prepare their witnesses by merely talking with them about deposition substance and procedure.

Some attorneys give witnesses a deposition preparation sheet summarizing deposition "dos" and "don'ts." These sheets can be sent to witnesses prior to the deposition preparation session, and a witness may appreciate having the sheet to review the evening before the deposition. If a witness preparation sheet is used, counsel should be prepared to turn over a copy of the sheet to opposing counsel pursuant to Federal Rule of Evidence 612. What follows is a deposition preparation sheet used by the author during his service with the United States Department of Justice. This sheet contains much of the advice that should be given to witnesses either verbally or in writing prior to their depositions.

DEPOSITIONS

[CASE NAME]

WHEN: [TIME OF DEPOSITION]

WHERE: [PLACE OF DEPOSITION]

ATTORNEYS: [NAMES AND PHONE NUMBERS OF ATTORNEYS]

GENERAL INFORMATION:

You are about to have your deposition taken. A deposition is a discovery procedure in which an individual is asked to respond under oath to questions asked by an attorney for one of the parties to a lawsuit. There are several purposes of a deposition: (1) to provide the attorney with information that can be used to establish various aspects of the case; (2) to fix the testimony of a party or a potential witness so that it is available if that person is later unable to attend the trial; (3) to impeach or discredit the testimony of a party or witness who changes his or her story at the time of trial. Therefore, it is very important that you not guess at answers or think that mistakes can easily be corrected later.

The procedure for a deposition is that you will be in a room with your attorneys [list attorney names], plaintiff's [or defendant's] attorneys [list attorney names], and a court reporter. The court reporter will put you under oath and will record the proceedings. Plaintiff's [or defendant's] attorneys will question you first; when they are done, your attorneys will have the opportunity to ask you questions if there is a need for that. We will request that you be given the opportunity to read the typed transcript of the deposition before it is filed with the court.

Your attorneys will discuss the deposition with you before you are deposed. At that time, they will answer any questions that you might have. Please review this paper and the discovery responses with which you have been supplied before that meeting so that you will be prepared to discuss this matter with your attorneys.

HELPFUL HINTS:

1.   Set your own pace. You're under no obligation to respond immediately or quickly. Take sufficient time to understand the question and to formulate a responsive answer. You are entitled to plenty of time to think before you answer.

2.   Don't begin a response before the question is completed. As a rule, allow at least 2–3 seconds (longer, if you wish) between question and answer. This allows time for your attorney to decide whether to pose an objection to the question.

3.   If an objection is made, do not answer the question until your attorney tells you to do so.

4.   Answer only the question that is asked. It is very important that you listen carefully and understand the question. Do not answer the ques-

tion you want asked; answer the question that is asked.

5. If a question can be answered with a "yes" or "no," you should answer it that way. Do not volunteer information. For example, if the question is "Did you speak with Mr. X?" and the answer is "Yes," then say "Yes," not "Yes, I spoke with him several times" or "Yes, I spoke with him at the meeting with Y."

6. If you don't understand a question, say so. Do not try to answer a question if you don't understand what's being asked.

7. Do not be evasive. However, if you honestly can't remember, don't be afraid to say so.

8. You are to testify from your own knowledge, not from what someone else says may have happened or from what you think could have happened. Do not guess. If the answer to a question is not known to you, say so.

9. While you should not bring any documents to the deposition, you may be asked about documents by the examining attorney. Before responding to a question about a document, ask to see the document. Read it carefully before answering.

10. You may be asked if you spoke with your attorneys about your testimony or about matters that might be raised during the deposition. Since you will have discussed the deposition with your attorneys, your answer will be "Yes." Do not be

embarrassed or nervous by this question. While it is unethical for an attorney to tell you what to say, it is proper and part of a lawyer's duty to explain the nature of the matters involved and to prepare you for what to expect.

11.   Be courteous to the questioner. Do not under any circumstances argue with the questioning attorney. Resist the temptation to get "cute," angry, or defensive. Do your best to remain calm and polite.

12.   Do not look at your attorneys when asked a question. You are to answer the question. It is improper for your attorneys to "coach" a witness, so they will be maintaining an impassive expression during your testimony. You should not interpret this as a sign of disinterest or a sign that you are not doing well.

13.   Try to keep your voice loud, clear, and distinct so that your testimony can be taken down by the court reporter. Do not respond by head shakes or nods.

14.   The most important thing to remember in answering questions is: *Tell the truth.*

15.   If you have any questions, please call your attorneys before the deposition begins. If you have a question for your attorneys during the deposition, request permission to go off the record to ask your attorneys the question.

VIII.   DEFENDING DEPOSITIONS

While the most important aspect of defending a deposition is witness preparation, there is important work to be done in the deposition room. Defending counsel usually make few objections or other statements during the deposition. The greatest challenge during the deposition may be to stay alert. This requires attention to attorney questions, witness answers, and the condition of the deponent. One way to protect a witness from making incorrect statements or volunteering damaging information is to ask for a short break after long stretches of deposition questioning or if the witness appears to be tiring.

Most reporters take down everything said in the deposition room. Prior to the deposition, the examining attorney should confirm with the reporter that everything said will be recorded unless the attorney states to the contrary. There should be explicit agreement among all counsel and the court reporter before statements are made that are not intended to be part of the deposition transcript. Deposition transcripts are expensive, and there generally is no reason to record discussions concerning such matters as when or where to resume a deposition. Once agreement has been reached off the record, a simple statement can be made on the record summarizing the agreement.

Even though most deposition objections will not be waived if they are not raised during the deposition, there may be tactical reasons to raise deposition objections. There is no requirement that counsel object to irrelevant deposition testimony or testimony that is not within the scope of discovery under Rule 26(b). However, depositions can be lengthy enough when only relevant testimony is given. For this reason, objections may be noted to encourage examining counsel to move the deposition along. Rule 30(d)(1) requires that evidentiary objections be stated "concisely and in a non-argumentative and non-suggestive manner." If examining counsel persists, the testimony is taken subject to the objection pursuant to Rule 30(c).

There is one very important situation in which the attorney defending the deposition should not permit her client to answer an objectionable question. If a deposition question calls for privileged information, the privilege will be breached if the question is answered. For this reason, defending counsel must not only object but should instruct her client not to answer the question. While a similar instruction not to answer should not be made to non-party witnesses, an attorney can suggest that these individuals consult their own counsel before revealing obviously privileged information.

If privileged information is sought during a deposition, the following type of colloquy generally ensues.

Examining Attorney: What did you tell your attorney about your reasons for wanting to sue Mr. Jones?

Defending Attorney: I object because any answer to that question would violate the attorney-client privilege.

Examining Attorney: Any privilege that may have existed has been waived by your client's prior testimony. Mrs. Smith, will you answer my question?

Defending Attorney: Because any answer would reveal information within the attorney-client privilege, I instruct my client not to answer the question.

Examining Attorney: Mrs. Smith, do you refuse to answer my question?

Deponent: Yes, on the advice of my counsel.

Examining Attorney: Mr. Court Reporter, would you please mark my question and the witness's refusal to answer in your notes so that I can raise this matter with the court?

If counsel remain at an impasse and the deponent continues to refuse to provide the requested testimony, the examining attorney has several options. She can complete the deposition, obtain a deposition transcript, and file a motion to compel the testimony pursuant to Rule 37(a). She need not wait for the transcription of the entire deposition before filing a motion to compel, but can request that the reporter merely transcribe her question, the refusal to answer, and any other relevant testimony. If time is of the essence, counsel can seek leave to make an oral motion to the district judge or magistrate judge and perhaps bring the court reporter to the courtroom to read the deposition question and response from her notes.

In addition to situations involving privilege, Rule 30(d)(4) permits any party or the deponent to seek an order to halt or limit a deposition that is being conducted in "bad faith or in such manner as unreasonably to annoy, embarrass, or oppress the deponent or party." If such conduct occurs, a party or deponent can demand that the deposition be suspended for the time necessary to make a motion for a court order. Before so doing, though, counsel should be certain that the deposition transcript will reflect actions by opposing counsel sufficient to justify the termination of the deposition. The Rule 30(d)(4) standard is not mere annoyance, but unreasonable annoyance, embarrassment or oppression.

While statements made during the deposition are taken down by the reporter, special efforts may be required to make a record of certain types of abusive deposition conduct. A request that counsel not raise her voice to the witness will serve to make a record of this conduct. Examining counsel, too, should make a record of any abusive non-verbal conduct. An objection should be made on the record if counsel whispers to her client after a question has been asked, points to particular information in a deposition document, or signals in some other manner to the witness. If the attorney believes that other counsel may resort to abusive deposition tactics, the deposition can be videotaped to preserve, or, ideally, to prevent, such tactics. While it sometimes may be difficult to do so, counsel should attempt to retain a professional manner in the face of abusive deposition tactics and not sink to the level of opposing counsel.

The attorney defending the deposition may take steps short of terminating the deposition to ensure the accuracy of deposition testimony. Counsel should ensure that the witness has sufficient time to answer all questions and that his answers are not cut off by the examining attorney. If questions are asked about a document, the witness should be encouraged to take sufficient time to review the document before answering.

Attorneys are forbidden by Rule 30(d)(1) from making suggestive objections in an effort to guide the witness's answers. Nor should defending counsel respond to a question by stating to the witness, "If you know." While witnesses are to testify from their own personal knowledge, such a statement can become an abusive cue to the witness to respond to questions with the statement "I don't know."

Counsel usually should not confer with the witness once a question has been asked. If a misstatement is made by the witness, counsel can confer with the witness at a break and then question him later in the deposition to correct the misstatement. In some jurisdictions, though, it is considered improper to discuss the substance of the deposition with a witness once the deposition has begun. An objection can be made if opposing counsel confers with a witness during deposition questioning. If the activity continues, the examining attorney might ask the witness if counsel helped to refresh his recollection or if his answer is now different than it would have been without any consultation.

After the examining attorney has completed her questioning, other counsel will have an opportunity to ask their own questions. The attorney who has defended a discovery deposition should see this as a chance to obtain clarifications of previous witness testimony, rather than as a time to develop all of the testimony that eventually will be offered at trial. For this reason, defending counsel usually ask few, or no, questions of their own witnesses at their depositions. However, if a deposition transcript will be offered at trial and is not being taken merely for discovery purposes, counsel should fully question the witness just as she would at trial.

After giving the examining attorney a chance to ask any follow-up questions, counsel defending the deposition should be sure that the court reporter, pursuant to Rule 30(b)(4), states on the record that the deposition is complete. Statements by examining counsel that the deposition is "recessed" or "concluded for now" leave open the possibility that the deposition may be resumed at a later time. Defending counsel therefore should request that the deposition be concluded at the present time and express her willingness to remain until the deposition is complete.

CHAPTER NINE

REQUESTS FOR PRODUCTION, EXAMINATIONS, AND ADMISSIONS

I. RULE 34 REQUESTS TO PRODUCE

Interrogatory answers and deposition statements can be introduced against a party at trial or in connection with pretrial motions. However, time clouds our memories, and current statements may be inaccurate characterizations of past conduct. The most effective evidence in many cases may be a party's statements, beliefs, and actions as memorialized in contemporaneous written documents. Rule 34 of the Federal Rules of Civil Procedure permits a party to request documents falling within the general scope of Rule 26(b) that are within the "possession, custody, or control" of other parties to the litigation.

Rule 34(a)'s description of "documents" is quite broad, including "writings, drawings, graphs, charts, photographs, phono-records, and other data compilations from which information can be obtained, translated, if necessary, by the respondent through detection devices into reasonably usable form." A picture may be worth a thousand words in litigation as in other aspects of life, and Rule 34 permits requests for relevant photographs, video-tapes, and other recordings within a party's possession, custody, or control.

Of increasing importance in modern litigation is information that has not been reduced to print but is stored in computer data bases. This information, too, may be requested pursuant to Rule 34, although the court may require a requesting party to share the expense of creating a written printout of or otherwise translating the computerized information into "reasonably usable form."

Rule 34 also provides for requests to "inspect and copy, test, or sample any tangible things which constitute or contain matters within the scope of Rule 26(b) and which are in the possession, custody or control of the party upon whom the request is served." Thus, in a products liability action, the defendant could request the opportunity to inspect and test the allegedly defective brakes in the plaintiff's car. Additionally, Rule 34 authorizes requests to enter and inspect, measure, survey, photograph, test, or sample land or other property in a party's possession or control. If the plaintiff fell down the stairs of defendant's apartment house, a Rule 34 request could be filed to gain entry to that building for pretrial examination.

Rule 34 requests are similar to Rule 33 interrogatories, in that they only can be used by parties and directed to other parties. Rule 34(c), though, provides: "A person not a party to the action may be compelled to produce documents and things or to submit to an inspection as provided in Rule 45.'' Under Rule 45, a party's attorney can issue a subpoena for the inspection of documents, tangible things, or premises of a non-party. In many cases counsel may not even need to resort to formal discovery requests, but may be able to obtain non-party discovery informally.

As with interrogatories, Rule 34 document requests cannot be served before the time specified in Rule 26(d) unless the case is exempted from initial disclosures pursuant to Rule 26(a)(1)(E) or when otherwise authorized by the Rules, the court, or party agreement. Thus document requests typically cannot be served until after the parties have conferred concerning discovery and the other subjects set forth in Rule 26(f). Rule 34(b) provides that the production request shall ''set forth, either by individual item or by category, the items to be inspected, and describe each with reasonable particularity'' as well as ''specify a reasonable time, place, and manner of making the inspection and performing the related acts.'' Because Rule 34 responses generally are due within thirty days, the Rule 34(b) specification often merely provides that the requested documents shall be produced in the office of requesting counsel thirty days from the service of the production request.

The format for Rule 34 requests is quite simple, as is evidenced by Form 24 of the Appendix of Forms to the Federal Rules of Civil Procedure:

REQUEST FOR PRODUCTION
OF DOCUMENTS, ETC.,
UNDER RULE 34

Plaintiff A.B. requests defendant C.D. to respond within ___ days to the following requests:

(1) That defendant produce and permit plaintiff to inspect and to copy each of the following documents:

(Here list the documents either individually or by category and describe each of them.)

(Here state the time, place, and manner of making the inspection and performance of any related acts.)

(2) That defendant produce and permit plaintiff to inspect and to copy, test, or sample each of the following objects:

(Here list the objects either individually or by category and describe each of them.)

(Here state the time, place, and manner of making the inspection and performance of any related acts.)

(3) That defendant permit plaintiff to enter (here describe property to be entered) and to inspect and to photograph, test or sample (here describe the portion of the real property and the objects to be inspected).

(Here state the time, place, and manner of making the inspection and performance of any related acts.)

Signed: _____
                  Attorney for Plaintiff.

Address: _____

Rule 34(b) provides that a written response must be filed within thirty days after service of the request, although a different time may be directed by the court or agreed to by the parties so long as it does not interfere with any time set for completion of discovery, for hearing of a motion, or for trial. The Rule 34(b) written response is to address each item or category of materials requested and either state that inspection will be permitted as requested or object to the particular item or category of request.

Objections to Rule 34 requests can be based upon the discovery limitations contained in Rule 26(b)(2) or upon the grounds for protective orders set forth in Rule 26(c). If objections are made to specific requests, the requesting party can file a Rule 37(a) motion to compel production of the requested documents or tangible things. A typical objection might look something like this:

Response to Production Request 1. Objection. The defendant objects to this production request because the burden and expense of producing the documents requested outweigh any likely benefit within the meaning of Federal Rule of Civil Procedure 26(b)(2)(iii). This request seeks documents that concern a peripheral issue in this case. Because the defendant has no subject matter file containing the documents plaintiff seeks, any response would require a manual review of approximately four thousand separate documents written over a period of ten years.

The following sentence was added to Rule 34(b) in 1980: "A party who produces documents for inspection shall produce them as they are kept in the usual course of business or shall organize and label them to correspond with the categories in the request." This amendment stemmed from a concern by the Advisory Committee about the deliberate "mix[ing of] critical documents with others in the hope of obscuring significance." Even though such needle-in-the-haystack productions are not permissible, counsel should draft production requests as specifically as possible so that only those documents that they actually want are produced.

One of the most time-consuming aspects of discovery in major cases can be the review of documents produced by other parties. Rule 34 and Rule 45 do not require that documents be copied and given to a requesting party, but merely that relevant documents be produced for inspection and copying. Even if copies are given to the requesting party rather than merely produced for that party's inspection and copying, all of the documents produced must be read, organized, and indexed in some fashion so that they can be used effectively in the litigation.

A record of the documents produced in response to a Rule 34 request or a Rule 45 subpoena should be made by the responding party. This record can take the form of an index listing each document produced. If relatively few documents fall within the production request, counsel may merely copy those documents and send a set of copies to requesting counsel. In this case, a record of the documents produced can be made in a cover letter accompanying the documents or the documents can be bound and tabbed as a single set of papers. The documents produced also can be consecutively numbered with a page stamp to ensure that there will be no later question concerning the specific documents produced in response to the production request.

Responding counsel should try to prevent any later controversy in which opposing counsel credibly can argue that a particular document encompassed within her request was not produced. If the judge concludes that non-production has occurred, he could extend the discovery period, permit additional discovery, or invoke sanctions (including a prohibition against the use of specific documents at trial). A Rule 34 response therefore should include (1) the written response itself (stating whether or not production will be provided as requested), (2) the production of all or some of the documents and tangible things encompassed within the Rule 34 request, and (3) a written record listing each document produced.

II. RULE 35 EXAMINATIONS

While Rule 34 requests can be used to examine land or other tangible things within the possession, custody or control of another party, Rule 35 provides for the possible examination of that other party, himself. Rule 35(a) states in part: "When the mental or physical condition (including the blood group) of a party, or of a person in the custody or under the legal control of a party, is in controversy, the court in which the action is pending may order the party to submit to a physical or mental examination by a suitably licensed or certified examiner or to produce for examination the person in the party's custody or legal control." While Rule 35 examinations most often are undertaken by physicians, "suitably licensed or certified examiner[s]" under that Rule include other professionals such as psychologists, dentists, and occupational therapists.

Because of the potential sensitivity of physical and mental examinations, Rule 35(a) requires a court order for the examination of parties or those in the custody or under the legal control of a party. However, as with other disclosure and discovery, in many cases the parties will agree among themselves to permit Rule 35 examinations. In this event, counsel should be aware that Rule 35(b)(3) states that the reciprocal discovery provided under Rule 35(b) applies to voluntary examinations unless the parties' agreement expressly provides to the contrary.

Rule 35(a) contains several requirements for an order of examination. Initially, the party's mental or physical condition must be "in controversy." This requirement would be satisfied, for example, if the defendant sought an examination to determine the extent of physical injuries sustained by the plaintiff in a personal injury case. Although it did not uphold the order before it in that case, the Supreme Court in *Schlagenhauf v. Holder* (S.Ct. 1964) construed Rule 35 to encompass the examination of defendants, as well as plaintiffs. The defendant's mental or physical condition might be in controversy if there is a claim that defendant's condition led to an accident forming the basis of suit.

In addition to the requirement that a mental or physical condition be "in controversy," Rule 35(a) provides that an examination order "may be made only on motion for good cause shown and upon notice to the person to be examined and to all parties and shall specify the time, place, manner, conditions, and scope of the examination and the person or persons by whom it is to be made." In the motion seeking a mental or physical examination, the requesting party typically will propose the physician, psychologist, or other examiner and the details of the examination. The response of the person whose examination is sought or of the parties to the suit may challenge any of the proposed conditions or suggest other conditions for the examination. The court may accept or reject these proposals and conditions in whole or in part, and the final terms of any examination are to be set forth in the court's examination order.

If an examination is ordered, Rule 35(b) governs discovery concerning the examination results and any other relevant examinations of the same condition. Rule 35(b)(1) provides that a party examined pursuant to Rule 35 can request a copy of a detailed report setting forth the examiner's findings, "including results of all tests made, diagnoses and conclusions, together with like reports of all earlier examinations of the same condition." If the party examined requests such a report, though, the examining party then can request "a like report of any examination, previously or thereafter made, of the same condition, unless, in the case of a report of examination of a person not a party, the party shows that such party is unable to obtain it."

Requesting a copy of a Rule 35 examination therefore requires reciprocal disclosure by the examined party of other examinations. Rule 35(b)(2) specifically provides that by requesting a report of the examination or taking the deposition of the examiner, the examined party waives any privilege regarding the testimony of any person concerning the condition in question. However, without a report of the Rule 35 examination, it may be extremely difficult to challenge the examiner's testimony at trial or evaluate that person's conclusions prior to trial. Indeed, Rule 35(b)(3) explicitly leaves open the possibility of deposing the examiner pursuant to other provisions of the Federal Rules of Civil Procedure such as Rule 26(b)(4).

In most cases, Rule 35 will lead to a full exchange of reports concerning mental or physical conditions in controversy in a lawsuit. So that there will be no later questions concerning the reports that have or have not been requested pursuant to Rule 35, all requests should be made in writing. These requests can be memorialized in a letter to counsel that refers to the relevant provisions of Rule 35.

III. RULE 36 ADMISSION REQUESTS

The final discovery device provided by the Federal Rules of Civil Procedure is the Rule 36 request for admission. Rule 36(a) states, in part, "A party may serve upon any other party a written request for the admission, for purposes of the pending action only, of the truth of any matters within the scope of Rule 26(b)(1) set forth in the request that relate to statements or opinions of fact or of the application of law to fact, including the genuineness of any documents described in the request."

As with interrogatories and production requests, Rule 26(d) provides that requests for admission cannot be served before the parties have held their Rule 26(f) discovery conference. This Rule 26(d) limitation, though, does not apply if there is an order or party agreement permitting an earlier service of admission requests, the case is exempted from the initial disclosure provisions by Rule 26(a)(1)(E), or when a different time is otherwise authorized under the Federal Rules of Civil Procedure. As is also the case with interrogatories and production requests, a response to admission requests must be served within thirty days after service of the request (unless the court sets, or the parties agree in writing to, a different response time).

Responses to admission requests can take several forms. While Rule 35 requires a court order prior to obtaining a party examination, Rule 36 admissions can be effective even without a response. Rule 36(a) provides that requested matter is admitted unless, within the thirty day response period, "the party to whom the request is directed serves upon the party requesting the admission a written answer or objection addressed to the matter, signed by the party or by the party's attorney." Admission requests are thus a unique form of discovery in which "no news is good news."

Because of the self-executing nature of admission requests, they can be a powerful discovery tool. Admissions can narrow the scope of pretrial discovery and of the contested issues relevant to a pretrial motion or trial. Admissions obtained at the outset of a case can remove entire issues from the scope of discovery and thereby expedite pretrial proceedings. Admissions can provide the factual predicate for pretrial disposition by way of summary judgment or partial summary judgment. Service of admission requests prior to Rule 16 pretrial conferences may cause a judge to encourage, or counsel to accept, admissions narrowing the issues in a case.

Counsel may have limited knowledge concerning an opponent's case at the outset of an action, and it only may be possible to draft meaningful admission requests once other discovery has been completed. Admission requests filed at the completion of other discovery can help to tie up loose ends and frame the issues for trial in the most focused and favorable manner for the requesting party. If an opposing party is less than cooperative in agreeing to pretrial stipulations, proposed stipulations can be cast in the form of admission requests to encourage opposing counsel to give them serious consideration. Some counsel use more than one set of admission requests, serving a general set of requests at the outset of a case and following those initial requests with more detailed requests as additional facts are uncovered during discovery.

Rule 36(a) permits not only admission requests relating to "statements or opinions of fact" but also proposed admissions concerning "the application of law to fact." Despite the work-product protection of Federal Rule of Civil Procedure 26(b)(3), admission requests can be sought concerning even mental impressions, opinions, and conclusions that relate to "statements or opinions of fact or of the application of law to fact" within the scope of Rule 26(b).

Form 25 of the Appendix of Forms to the Federal Rules of Civil Procedure illustrates the general format of Rule 36 requests:

REQUEST FOR ADMISSION UNDER RULE 36

Plaintiff A.B. requests defendant C.D. within ___ days after service of this request to make the following admissions for the purpose of this action only and subject to all pertinent objections to admissibility which may be interposed at the trial:

1. That each of the following documents, exhibited with this request, is genuine.

(Here list the documents and describe each document.)

2. That each of the following statements is true.

(Here list the statements.)

Signed: _____

Attorney for Plaintiff.

Address: _____

In order to obtain useful admissions, admission requests must be carefully, and narrowly, drafted. Just as with a defendant's answer to the complaint, opposing counsel will construe any ambiguity in admission requests against the requesting party. If a party has made a statement about which counsel would like to obtain an admission, the admission request should contain the exact language of that prior statement to ensure that an admission is forthcoming.

Admission requests should be phrased in terms of specific facts, rather than characterizations. The defendant may refuse to admit that he "beat up plaintiff John Johnson." However, the defendant might have no choice but to admit a more strictly factual statement that "the defendant hit the plaintiff John Johnson at least three times in the head."

Another way to encourage admissions is to file, simultaneously with admission requests, an interrogatory asking for all facts upon which any denials of admission requests are based. Opposing counsel may find it easier to admit a particular request than to specify the reasons for a refusal to admit. Many attorneys also include a set of instructions and definitions at the beginning of admission requests, similar to those that preface some interrogatories and production requests. The instructions might include a reminder of the responding party's duties under Rule 36, such as the duty to conduct a reasonable inquiry concerning the admission requests and the duty to admit any portions of a request that are true.

While ambiguous admission requests usually result in disappointing admission responses, Rule 36(a) requires that admission answers must "specifically deny" matters that are not admitted "or set forth in detail the reasons why the answering party cannot truthfully admit or deny the matter." Thus there are four possible responses that can be made either singly or in combination to any admission request: (1) an admission, (2) a denial, (3) a statement that the answering party is without sufficient information or knowledge to either admit or deny the matter asserted, and (4) an objection. An objection to an admission request must include a statement of reasons for the objection. Objections to admission requests are similar to objections to interrogatories or production requests and generally are based upon the discovery limitations contained in Rule 26(b) and (c).

Rule 36(a) provides that denials "shall fairly meet the substance of the requested admission, and when good faith requires that a party qualify an answer or deny only a part of the matter of which an admission is requested, the party shall specify so much of it as is true and qualify or deny the remainder." A typical admission response therefore might look something like this:

> *Answer to Admission Request Number 1.* This admission request is denied, except that the defendant admits that he talked with the plaintiff on the telephone on April 9, 2001.

Rule 36(a) places a duty of "reasonable inquiry" upon the party served with admission requests. This rule prohibits a party from claiming that he is without sufficient information or knowledge to admit or deny the truth of an admission request "unless the party states that the party has made reasonable inquiry and that the information known or readily obtainable by the party is insufficient to enable the party to admit or deny." Nor may a party refuse to answer an admission request merely because the request may present a genuine issue for trial.

The discovery certification and sanction provisions of Rule 26(g) are applicable to admission requests and responses. There also are special provisions in Rule 36 and Rule 37 for challenging allegedly insufficient responses to admission requests. Rule 36(a) permits a requesting party to move to determine the sufficiency of the answers or objections to admission requests. The court either can rule on such a motion immediately or defer ruling until a later pretrial conference or other designated time prior to trial. Rule 36(a) incorporates the provisions of Rule 37(a)(4), which require the court to award the expenses of the motion to the prevailing party unless the opposition is "substantially justified," the moving party had not made a good faith effort to obtain the discovery without court action, or there are other circumstances that make an award of expenses unjust.

Rule 37(c)(2) is a special provision governing the expenses entailed by an unjustified failure to admit a Rule 36 request. This Rule provides that if a party fails to admit the genuineness of a document or the truth of a matter that later is proven to be genuine or truthful, the court shall award to the requesting party the reasonable expenses incurred in making that proof. However, Rule 37(c)(2) contains major exceptions precluding an award of expenses if "(A) the request was held objectionable pursuant to Rule 36(a), or (B) the admission sought was of no substantial importance, or (C) the party failing to admit had reasonable ground to believe that the party might prevail on the matter, or (D) there was other good reason for the failure to admit." These four exceptions mean that Rule 37(c)(2) sanctions are rarely assessed. Moreover, in cases that result in a general jury verdict, it may be impossible to know whether any specific fact was or was not proven at trial.

Rule 36(b) governs the effect of Rule 36 admissions. While a party may later challenge or explain his interrogatory answers or deposition statements, Rule 36(b) in part states: "Any matter admitted under this rule is conclusively established unless the court on motion permits withdrawal or amendment of the admission." In order to obtain leave to withdraw or amend an admission, Rule 36(b) requires (1) a showing that "the presentation of the merits of the action will be subserved" by the withdrawal or amendment and (2) failure by the party who obtained the admission to satisfy the court that "withdrawal or amendment will prejudice that party in maintaining the action or defense on the merits."

If counsel has merely neglected to respond to admission requests and seeks leave to file admission responses out of time, the court is likely to find the requirements of Rule 36(b) satisfied and permit the late filing of admission responses. However, if a substantial amount of time has passed since the admission responses were due, or if further discovery requests or decisions not to request discovery have been based upon the initial admissions, counsel will have more difficulty convincing a judge to permit the filing of untimely admission responses. If an admission has formed the basis for stipulations or otherwise has been incorporated in a Rule 16 pretrial order, an amendment of that order also may be necessary pursuant to Rule 16(e).

CHAPTER TEN

JUDICIAL INTERVENTION INTO THE DISCOVERY AND DIS-CLOSURE PROCESS

I. DISCOVERY AND DISCLOSURE DISPUTES

The discovery and disclosure provisions of the Federal Rules of Civil Procedure contemplate that relevant information will be exchanged between the parties without judicial intervention. The assumption is that disclosures will be provided, discovery requests will be made, discovery responses will be forthcoming, and any disagreements will be resolved by the parties. However, what if the parties cannot agree upon the propriety of a particular disclosure or discovery request or response? In these situations, the Federal Rules of Civil Procedure provide several routes for judicial intervention into the disclosure and discovery process.

Figure 10–1 illustrates possible responses to a discovery request, as well as the manner in which disputes concerning the propriety of the discovery request or response can be resolved. The far left column of Figure 10–1 illustrates the typical situation in which the party upon whom discovery is served answers the discovery request. This is how discovery usually works.

If counsel believes that another party's discovery request is improper, an objection can be made to that request pursuant to Rules 30(c), 33(b), 34(b), 36(a), or 45(c)(2)(B). The requesting party then may conclude that the grounds for the objection are well-taken or decide not to pursue the discovery for some other reason. Absent the rare situation in which the judge himself ascertains the discovery dispute and sua sponte enters a discovery order, this will be the end of the matter and the requesting party will not obtain the discovery initially sought. If, however, the requesting party still desires the discovery in question, a motion to compel a discovery response can be filed pursuant to Rule 37(a) of the Federal Rules of Civil Procedure. This is illustrated by the middle column of Figure 10–1.

FIGURE 10–1

DISCOVERY RESPONSES AND INTERVENTION BY THE COURT

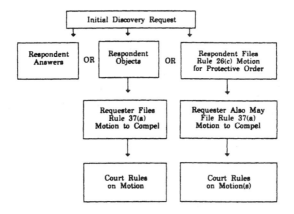

The party from whom discovery is sought need not merely object to an improper discovery request, but can take the initiative by filing a Rule 26(c) motion for a protective order providing that the discovery not be had. The party who requested the original discovery can oppose the motion for a protective order or file its own Rule 37(a) motion to compel the discovery in question. In either event, the parties' discovery dispute will be resolved by the court. This situation is represented by the column on the far right of Figure 10–1.

While Figure 10–1 specifically illustrates the manner in which the court may become involved in discovery disputes, Rules 26(c) and 37(a) also may be invoked with respect to Rule 26(a) required disclosures. Rule 37(a)(2)(A) permits a party to file a motion to compel Rule 26(a) required disclosures that are not voluntarily provided, while a Rule 26(c) motion for protective order can be filed to obtain an order that Rule 26(a) disclosures not be had or that they be provided only on specified terms and conditions.

Either a Rule 26(c) motion for a protective order or a Rule 37(a) motion to compel can be accompanied by a request for the award of expenses. Whether accompanied by such a request or not, Rule 26(c) and Rule 37(a) motions must be accompanied by a certification that the movant has in good faith conferred or attempted to confer with other affected parties in an effort to resolve the dispute without court action. Discovery and disclosure motions can be expensive and can delay pretrial proceedings, and busy judges are not appreciative of attorneys who insist upon judicial resolution of disputes that counsel could themselves resolve. Many attorneys memorialize their attempts to resolve discovery and disclosure disputes informally by sending a letter to opposing counsel. Such a letter not only can serve as a record of settlement efforts, but it may indicate to opposing counsel that the requesting party is serious about obtaining the information and convince opposing counsel to provide that discovery or disclosure voluntarily.

Before filing a motion to compel or for a protective order, counsel also should check the local rules of court. These local rules may govern the format of discovery motions and provide, for instance, that discovery disputes must be raised in short letters to the court rather than in formal motions.

II. RULE 26(c) MOTIONS FOR PROTECTIVE ORDERS

Rather than merely objecting, a party from whom discovery or disclosure is sought can file a motion for a protective order pursuant to Rule 26(c) of the Federal Rules of Civil Procedure. Rule 26(c) in part provides:

> Upon motion by a party or by the person from whom discovery is sought, accompanied by a certification that the movant has in good faith conferred or attempted to confer with other affected parties in an effort to resolve the dispute without court action, and for good cause shown, the court in which the action is pending or alternatively, on matters relating to a deposition, the court in the district where the deposition is to be taken may make any order which justice requires to protect a party or person from annoyance, embarrassment, oppression, or undue burden or expense * * * .

Following this general authorization, Rule 26(c) contains eight separate examples of the types of protective orders that district courts can enter. Among the specific types of protective orders listed in Rule 26(c) are orders "that the disclosure or discovery not be had" (Rule 26(c)(1)), "that the disclosure or discovery may be had only on specified terms and conditions, including a designation of the time or place" (Rule 26(c)(2)), "that the discovery may be had only by a method of discovery other than that selected by the party seeking discovery" (Rule 26(c)(3)), and "that certain matters not be inquired into, or that the scope of the disclosure or discovery be limited to certain matters" (Rule 26(c)(4)).

If the court denies a motion for a protective order, Rule 26(c) provides that it can order that specific discovery be provided, just as if a Rule 37(a) motion to compel disclosure or discovery had been filed. Rule 26(c) further states that the provisions of Rule 37(a)(4) concerning the award of expenses apply to a motion for a protective order as well as to a motion to compel. Under Rule 37(a)(4), the party who successfully brings or opposes a motion to compel is entitled to the expenses of that motion unless the court finds that the successful movant had not attempted to obtain the disclosure or discovery without court action or the losing person "was substantially justified, or that other circumstances make an award of expenses unjust."

One of the major reasons that protective orders are sought is to protect a party from "undue burden or expense" within the meaning of Rule 26(c). If the plaintiff in a simple automobile accident case were served with several hundred interrogatories, chances are that "good cause" could be shown for a Rule 26(c)(1) order that "discovery * * * not be had." There is, however, no bright-line test for discovery requests that violate Rule 26(c)'s "undue burden or expense" standard. Rule 26(b)(2)(iii) similarly instructs judges to limit discovery if "the burden or expense of the proposed discovery outweighs its likely benefit, taking into account the needs of the case, the amount in controversy, the parties' resources, the importance of the issues at stake in the litigation, and the importance of the proposed discovery in resolving the issues." Discovery motions typically are decided upon the specific facts presented, and the brief, affidavits, or declarations offered in support of a motion for a protective order should detail quite precisely why the provision of specific disclosures or discovery would create undue burden or expense.

In addition to orders totally prohibiting certain disclosure or discovery, Rule 26(c) protective orders can be tailored to restrict specific aspects of disclosure or discovery, as well as the time, place, and manner in which disclosure or discovery is provided. If a deposition is noticed for a time when the deponent or counsel cannot be present, a Rule 26(c)(2) protective order can be sought resetting the time or place of the deposition. However, if counsel confer concerning deposition scheduling, the need for protective orders of this nature should be obviated. In other situations, a person may be willing to produce certain information, but only if the requesting party shares in the expense of production. This situation may occur when relevant information is available in a computer data base, but a computer printout of that information will be costly to produce.

Rather than restricting the disclosure or discovery provided to the parties to a case, some protective orders restrict public access to that information. Rule 26(c)(6) provides for protective orders "that a deposition, after being sealed, be opened only by order of the court," while Rule 26(c)(7) authorizes an order "that a trade secret or other confidential research, development, or commercial information not be revealed or be revealed only in a designated way."

Many Rule 26(c) protective orders are not the result of contested motions, but are entered with the consent of all parties to a case. A party or third person may be willing to provide information to a litigant in a particular case, but not want the information to reach litigants in other cases, competitors, or the general public. The requesting party may be willing to agree that certain disclosure or discovery will not be used outside the confines of the present lawsuit or shared with others. Counsel therefore may submit to the judge an agreed protective order providing, for example, that any discovery responses that are used in the proceeding (and that therefore normally would be filed with the court pursuant to Rule 5(d)) will be sealed. Another common protective order provision is that the party receiving documentary discovery will not reveal the information to others and will return the documents to the party who produced them when the case is concluded.

In *Seattle Times Co. v. Rhinehart* (S.Ct.1984), the Supreme Court rejected a first amendment challenge to a state court's protective order prohibiting the defendant newspaper from publishing or disseminating information obtained in discovery. Noting that "pretrial depositions and interrogatories are not public components of a civil trial," the Court concluded: "Liberal discovery is provided for the sole purpose of assisting in the preparation and trial, or the settlement, of litigated disputes. Because of the liberality of pretrial discovery permitted by Rule 26(b)(1), it is necessary for the trial court to have the authority to issue protective orders conferred by Rule 26(c)."

Despite the Supreme Court's decision in *Rhinehart,* in recent years the use of blanket protective orders has become increasingly controversial. Defendants in some products liability cases have obtained protective orders restricting public access to information concerning allegedly defective products that are still being marketed. In other cases, discovery concerning issues of general public interest has been shielded from the public by protective orders.

For these reasons, many judges now scrutinize more closely proposed protective orders that would restrict public access to discovery. Some judges are less willing to sign blanket protective orders shielding all discovery from public dissemination, but instead require the parties to tailor proposed protective orders to specific material falling within Rule 26(c). Even if a judge agrees to seal discovery responses, those responses still may be unsealed by the court at a later time.

Nevertheless, there are many situations in which protective orders should be considered by parties or third persons from whom disclosure or discovery is sought. If a person has a strong argument against the discovery of important information, he or she may want to frame the issue before the court by filing a motion for a protective order rather than merely waiting for the requesting party to file a motion to compel.

If the party requesting discovery files a motion to compel, the person resisting discovery can file a motion for a protective order along with an opposition to the motion to compel. A motion for a protective order is not required in this later situation, though, for Rule 37(a)(4)(B) provides that if a court denies a Rule 37(a) motion to compel, it "may enter any protective order authorized under Rule 26(c)." However, Rule 37(d) provides that a party cannot totally ignore a discovery request by, for example, not attending a properly noticed deposition or failing to respond to interrogatories or production requests. Instead, a protective order should be filed to prevent possible waiver of objections to the requested discovery.

III. RULE 37 MOTIONS TO COMPEL

If a person refuses to provide disclosure or discovery, the requesting party can seek the court's assistance by filing a Rule 37(a) motion to compel. As with Rule 26(c) motions for protective orders, Rule 37(a)(2) requires those moving to compel to certify that they have conferred or attempted to confer with the party from whom the information is sought in an effort to secure the information without court action.

Rule 37(a)(2)(A) permits the filing of a motion to compel disclosure required by Rule 26(a). Rule 37(a)(2)(B) provides that a motion to compel can be filed if a party or third person fails to answer a deposition question, a corporation or other entity fails to make a Rule 30(b)(6) or Rule 31(a) deposition designation, or a party fails to answer interrogatories or properly respond to a Rule 34 production request. Under Rule 36(a), a party can move to determine the sufficiency of answers or objections to requests for admission. However, because admission requests are deemed admitted unless there is a timely answer or objection, there is no provision in Rule 37 for a motion to compel admission responses.

Rule 37(a)(3) makes clear that an evasive or incomplete answer is to be treated as a failure to answer for the purposes of Rule 37(a). In ruling upon a motion to compel, the judge can (1) grant the motion, ordering that the requested disclosure or discovery must be provided, (2) grant the motion in part, ordering that some portion of the requested disclosure or discovery must be provided, or (3) deny the motion.

Rule 37(a)(1) requires that motions to compel a party to provide disclosure or discovery are to be filed in the court in which the action is pending. However, this rule also provides that motions to compel a nonparty (such as a nonparty deponent) to provide discovery are to be filed in the district in which the discovery is being, or is to be, taken. If a deponent refuses to answer a particular deposition question, the examining attorney either can complete or adjourn the deposition before filing a motion to compel.

If the court denies a motion to compel, Rule 37(a)(4)(B) provides that the court may enter a protective order precluding or restricting the disclosure or discovery in question. More significantly, Rule 37(a)(4)(A) and (B) provide that the court "shall" award the reasonable expenses, including attorneys' fees, incurred in successfully obtaining or opposing the motion to compel unless the successful movant had not attempted to obtain the disclosure or discovery without court action or the court finds that the losing person "was substantially justified or that other circumstances make an award of expenses unjust." The judge has a great deal of discretion in deciding whether to award the expenses incurred in connection with a Rule 37(a) motion to compel or a Rule 26(c) motion for a protective order. In addition, the Rule 37(a)(4)(A) sanction provision not only applies if a motion to compel is granted but extends to situations in which "the disclosure or requested discovery is [only] provided after the motion [to compel] was filed."

If the decision is made to award the reasonable expenses incurred in connection with a motion, Rule 37(a)(4)(A) and (B) provide that those expenses can be awarded against the "party or deponent whose conduct necessitated the motion or the party or attorney advising such conduct or both of them" (if the motion is granted) or against the "moving party or the attorney filing the motion or both of them" (if the motion is denied). However, Rule 37(a)(4) further provides that expenses are not to be awarded without "an opportunity to be heard." The actual hearing on expenses typically is provided in the written briefs or letters filed in support of and in opposition to the motion to compel.

IV. RULE 37 SANCTION MOTIONS

What if the party seeking discovery obtains a Rule 37(a) order compelling discovery, but the information sought still is not provided? Rule 37 provides not only for a motion to compel, but for the imposition of sanctions if a person does not comply with a discovery order or a party totally refuses to provide requested discovery.

There are two different routes to Rule 37 discovery sanctions, both of which are illustrated in Figure 10–2. The more common route to Rule 37 sanctions occurs if a person who has been ordered to provide discovery fails to comply with that order. In this event, the court is authorized by Rule 37(b) to award a full range of sanctions. This route to sanctions is illustrated by the column on the left of Figure 10–2.

FIGURE 10–2

RULE 37 SANCTIONS

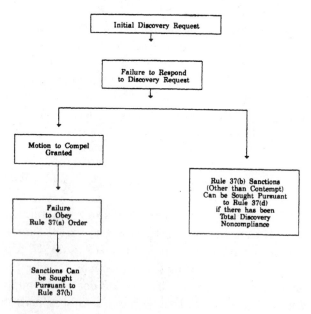

Rule 37(b)(2) provides that if a party, or an officer, director, or managing agent of a party, or a person designated to give deposition testimony under Rules 30(b)(6) or 31(a) refuses to obey a court order to provide or permit discovery or a Rule 26(f) discovery order, "the court in which the action is pending may make such orders in regard to the failure as are just." Rule 37(b)(2) lists the following orders that the district courts have authority to enter:

(A) An order that the matters regarding which the order was made or any other designated facts shall be taken to be established for the purposes of the action in accordance with the claim of the party obtaining the order;

(B) An order refusing to allow the disobedient party to support or oppose designated claims or defenses, or prohibiting that party from introducing designated matters in evidence;

(C) An order striking out pleadings or parts thereof, or staying further proceedings until the order is obeyed, or dismissing the action or proceeding or any part thereof, or rendering a judgment by default against the disobedient party;

(D) In lieu of any of the foregoing orders or in addition thereto, an order treating as a contempt of court the failure to obey any orders except an order to submit to a physical or mental examination;

(E) Where a party has failed to comply with an order under Rule 35(a) requiring that party to produce another for examination, such orders as are listed in paragraphs (A), (B), and (C) of this subdivision, unless the party failing to comply shows that that party is unable to produce such person for examination.

In addition to listing these potential discovery sanctions, Rule 37(b)(2) further provides that, unless the court finds that "the failure was substantially justified or * * * other circumstances make an award of expenses unjust," the court shall award the expenses, including attorneys' fees, caused by a failure to comply with a discovery order. These expenses can be awarded either in lieu of other sanctions or in addition thereto, and they can be assessed against the party who refused to obey the order, the attorney who advised that party, or both.

Rule 37(b)(2) sanctions can be imposed against parties by the court in which an action is pending. In addition, Rule 37(b)(1) provides that the failure of a deponent to be sworn or to answer a deposition question after being directed to do so by the court in the district in which the deposition is being taken may be considered a contempt of that court.

Failure to obey a discovery order is not the only basis for the imposition of sanctions against parties or their counsel. A less common route to discovery sanctions is provided by Federal Rule of Civil Procedure 37(d) and is illustrated by the column on the right of Figure 10–2. Rule 37(d) provides that the court in which an action is pending "may make such orders * * * as are just" if a party, an officer, director, or managing agent of a party, or a person designated to give deposition testimony pursuant to Rules 30(b)(6) or 31(a) fails:

(1) to appear before the officer who is to take the deposition, after being served with a proper notice, or

(2) to serve answers or objections to interrogatories submitted under Rule 33, after proper service of the interrogatories, or

(3) to serve a written response to a request for inspection submitted under Rule 34, after proper service of the request.

Not only does Rule 37(d) provide district courts with general authority to impose discovery sanctions, but that section specifically authorizes the imposition of all of the Rule 37(b)(2) sanctions except contempt. Rule 37(d) also requires the court to order the party failing to act or that party's attorney or both of them to pay the reasonable expenses, including attorneys' fees, caused by the failure, "unless the court finds that the failure was substantially justified or that other circumstances make an award of expenses unjust."

Rule 37(c)(1) deals with the failure to provide Rule 26(a) required disclosures in a manner comparable to Rule 37(d)'s handling of discovery noncompliance. Rule 37(c)(1) provides that if a party without substantial justification fails to disclose information required by Rule 26(a) or (e)(1), or fails to amend a prior discovery response as required by Rule 26(e)(2), the court may impose appropriate sanctions, including the Rule 37(b)(2) sanctions other than contempt. Thus neither Rule 37(d) nor Rule 37(c)(1) presuppose an initial Rule 37(a)(2) motion to compel as a prerequisite to sanctions. Rule 37(c)(1) additionally provides that, unless the failure to disclose or amend was harmless, the party that failed to disclose or amend cannot make use of that information at trial, at a hearing, or in connection with a motion. Finally, Rule 37(c)(1) permits the court to inform the jury of the failure to make a required disclosure.

Although the full arsenal of discovery sanctions other than contempt can be imposed for discovery noncompliance in violation of Rule 37(d), these sanctions are not routinely awarded in practice. A Rule 37(d) violation requires a virtual nonresponse to a discovery request. Rule 37(d) is triggered by gross discovery noncompliance, such as the refusal to even appear for a deposition or respond to interrogatories or a production request. Under Rule 37(b)(2), in contrast, sanctions can be awarded for failure to comply with a court order to answer even a single deposition question.

Counsel faced with discovery noncompliance falling within the literal terms of Rule 37(d) often file a motion seeking Rule 37(d) sanctions or, in the alternative, an order compelling discovery pursuant to Rule 37(a). Some judges are reluctant to sanction even gross discovery noncompliance if no court order has been violated. The typical progression toward discovery sanctions therefore proceeds from an initial Rule 37(a) order compelling discovery to a

Rule 37(b)(2) order assessing discovery sanctions. Failure to voluntarily comply with a discovery request is a serious matter, but it pales beside the violation of a court order.

Nevertheless, counsel faced with a discovery request should not presume that the request can be ignored with impunity. Rule 37(d) provides that the "failure to act described in this subdivision may not be excused on the ground that the discovery sought is objectionable unless the party failing to act has a pending motion for a protective order as provided by Rule 26(c)." Thus a valid discovery objection can be waived if it is not asserted in a proper and timely fashion.

Discovery and disclosure noncompliance need not be wilful to be sanctionable under Rule 37. In 1970, Rule 37 was amended by the substitution of the word "failure" for the word "refusal" throughout that rule. The Advisory Committee's Note to this 1970 amendment explains that, under amended Rule 37, "wilfullness [is] relevant only to the selection of sanctions, if any, to be imposed."

In its 1976 *per curiam* opinion in *National Hockey League v. Metropolitan Hockey Club, Inc.* (S.Ct. 1976), the Supreme Court upheld the dismissal of an action due to the plaintiffs' failure to comply with an order requiring them to answer interrogatories. The Court stated that "the most severe in the spectrum of sanctions provided by statute or rule must be available to the district court in appropriate cases, not merely to penalize those whose conduct may be deemed to warrant such a sanction, but to deter those who might be tempted to such conduct in the absence of such a deterrent."

There are several bases other than Rule 37 for the assessment of discovery sanctions against parties and their counsel. Rule 26(g) is an attorney certification provision specifically applicable to disclosures and discovery requests, responses, and objections. Rule 26(g)(1) provides that an attorney's signature on a Rule 26(a)(1) or (3) disclosure "constitutes a certification that to the best of the signer's knowledge, information, and belief, formed after a reasonable inquiry, the disclosure is complete and correct as of the time it is made." Pursuant to Rule 26(g)(2), an attorney's signature on a discovery document constitutes a certification that the document is "(A) consistent with [the Federal Rules of Civil Procedure] and warranted by existing law or a good faith argument for the extension, modification, or reversal of existing law; (B) not interposed for any improper purpose * * * ; and (C) not unreasonable or unduly burdensome or expensive, given the needs of the case, the discovery already had in the case, the amount in controversy, and the importance of the issues at stake in the litigation." If without substantial justification a certification is made in violation of Rule 26(g), the court "shall" impose upon the offending attorney, party, or both an appropriate sanction.

Rule 30(g) of the Federal Rules of Civil Procedure authorizes the assessment of sanctions in connection with depositions. Rule 30(g)(1) provides that a party may be required to pay other parties their reasonable expenses in attending a deposition that does not proceed because the party who noticed the deposition fails to attend. Rule 30(g)(2) provides for the award of similar expenses if a party gives notice of a deposition but the witness fails to attend because he or she was not subpoenaed.

Some federal statutes also provide a basis for discovery sanctions. Discovery abuse has been sanctioned under 28 U.S.C. § 1927, which permits federal courts to sanction attorneys who "multipl[y] the proceedings in any case unreasonably and vexatiously." Nor is a specific provision in federal rules or statutes necessary to the assessment of discovery sanctions. In *Roadway Express, Inc. v. Piper* (S.Ct. 1980), the Supreme Court held that federal district courts possess an inherent power to assess sanctions against attorneys for bad faith obstruction of the discovery process. More recently, in *Chambers v. NASCO, Inc.* (S.Ct.1991), the Supreme Court affirmed a sanction of almost one million dollars assessed for bad faith litigation conduct outside the discovery process. The majority in *Chambers* stated that "the inherent power of a court can be invoked even if procedural rules exist which sanction the same conduct."

Discovery operates most expeditiously and inexpensively when counsel make reasonable discovery requests and respond cooperatively to the discovery requests of other parties. Moreover, Rule 3.4(d) of the Model Rules of Professional Conduct specifically precludes counsel from making frivolous discovery requests or failing to make a reasonably diligent effort to comply with proper discovery requests. To the extent that Rule 3.4(d) guides discovery practice, discovery sanctions should become increasingly rare.

CHAPTER ELEVEN
PRETRIAL MOTION PRACTICE
I. PRETRIAL MOTIONS

Pretrial motions should not be filed in an ad hoc manner. Instead, counsel should consider the way in which pretrial motions can be used to further her client's litigation objectives. In devising a pretrial motion strategy, counsel should determine all of the motions that are potentially available in the lawsuit. Not only the motions that are available to her client, but motions that other parties are likely to file, should be considered.

Most of the common pretrial motions were considered in earlier chapters of this book. In Chapter 5, Rule 12 preanswer motions were discussed. These motions, particularly motions to dismiss, are often filed in response to the complaint. Rule 26(c) and Rule 37 motions often are filed to obtain a judicial resolution of discovery disputes, and these motions were considered in Chapter 10. Summary judgment motions are increasingly important in the federal courts, and Chapter 12 is devoted to such Rule 56 motions. This section explores the other major pretrial motions, which have not previously been discussed but with which counsel should be familiar.

A. Motions Based Upon a Party's Failure to Properly Contest a Lawsuit

The fact that a lawsuit has been filed does not mean that the action will be contested. Many cases are resolved by the filing of voluntary dismissals. In other cases, the lawsuit is dismissed involuntarily, because the plaintiff has failed to properly prosecute the case. Still other cases are resolved by default judgments, which are entered because the defendant has not properly defended the lawsuit. Litigation counsel therefore should be familiar with Rule 41 dismissal motions and Rule 55 motions for a default judgment.

Rule 41 of the Federal Rules of Civil Procedure provides for both voluntary and involuntary dismissals. Rule 41(a) permits a plaintiff to voluntarily dismiss an action after its filing. A plaintiff may decide to dismiss his own action if a settlement has been reached with the defendant, the plaintiff no longer has the resources to prosecute the action, personal jurisdiction or venue in the original forum is problematic, or the plaintiff desires to refile the action in another, more favorable, forum. Rule 41(a)(1)(i) generally provides that a plaintiff may voluntarily dismiss an action "at any time before service by the adverse party of an answer or of a motion for summary judgment, whichever first occurs." However, court approval of a dismissal may be specifically required by statute and is necessitated by the Federal Rules of Civil Procedure prior to the dismissal of class actions, shareholders' derivative actions, actions relating to unincorporated associations, and actions in which a receiver has been appointed.

Unless a statute or rule provides to the contrary, a Rule 41(a)(1)(i) dismissal is effective without any action by other counsel or the court. Typically the motion for voluntary dismissal merely consists of a single sentence such as the following: "The plaintiff, pursuant to Federal Rule of Civil Procedure 41(a)(1)(i), hereby voluntarily dismisses this action."

If the defendant has not filed an answer or a motion for summary judgment, the plaintiff unilaterally can obtain a voluntary dismissal even though there have been extensive pretrial proceedings. This should create an incentive for the defendant to answer the complaint as soon as possible and thereby lock the plaintiff into the lawsuit. If there is a reasonable likelihood that the plaintiff will seek a voluntary dismissal and there is a strong legal defense, the defendant might decide to answer and file a Rule 12(c) motion for judgment on the pleadings rather than file a Rule 12(b)(6) motion to dismiss. However, if the defendant has a compulsory counterclaim that could be more advantageously litigated in another forum, defense counsel might decide to file a motion to dismiss (even though the plaintiff can respond to such motion by filing a notice of voluntary dismissal that generally will permit the plaintiff to refile the lawsuit). If an answer is filed, it must contain any compulsory counterclaims or those counterclaims are waived.

If the defendant has answered or filed a motion for summary judgment, the plaintiff still can obtain a voluntary dismissal under Rule 41(a)(1)(ii) "by filing a stipulation of dismissal signed by all parties who have appeared in the action." Unless otherwise stated in the dismissal notice or stipulation, Rule 41(a)(1) dismissals are without prejudice to the later refiling of the same action. However, Rule 41(a)(1) provides that "a notice of dismissal operates as an adjudication upon the merits when filed by a plaintiff who has once dismissed in any court of the United States or of any state an action based on or including the same claim."

What if the defendant has filed an answer or motion for summary judgment (precluding a Rule 41(a)(1)(i) dismissal) and the defendant will not stipulate to a Rule 41(a)(1)(ii) voluntary dismissal? A dismissal is still possible by order of the court pursuant to Rule 41(a)(2). This rule gives the court authority to grant a motion for voluntary dismissal "upon such terms and conditions as the court deems proper." The rule also provides that the dismissal is without prejudice unless otherwise specified in the dismissal order. However, if the plaintiff later files an action based upon or including the same claim against the same defendant, Rule 41(d) gives the court authority to stay the second action until the plaintiff has paid the costs of the first suit.

The one restriction upon a court's power to grant voluntary dismissals is Rule 41(a)(2)'s provision that if a counterclaim has been pled prior to service of the motion to dismiss, the action cannot be dismissed over the defendant's objection "unless the counterclaim can remain pending for independent adjudication by the court." This restriction is triggered by compulsory counterclaims that are within the court's supplemental jurisdiction but over which the court has no independent jurisdictional power. Counterclaims themselves can be voluntarily dismissed, for Rule 41(c) extends Rule 41's voluntary and involuntary dismissal provisions to counterclaims, cross-claims, and third-party claims.

In many cases it will be the defendant, rather than the plaintiff, who seeks dismissal of an action. Rule 41(b) provides for involuntary dismissal if the plaintiff fails to prosecute his action or comply with the Federal Rules of Civil Procedure or any court order. Rule 41(b) further provides that involuntary dismissals are with prejudice (operate as an adjudication on the merits) unless (1) the dismissal order specifies to the contrary or (2) the dismissal is for lack of jurisdiction, improper venue, or failure to join a party pursuant to Rule 19.

The trial judge has a great amount of discretion in entering Rule 41(b) involuntary dismissals. Typically, actions are not dismissed because the plaintiff has failed to comply with a single rule or order, but because of a continuous course of bad faith or grossly negligent conduct on the part of the plaintiff or his counsel. In *Link v. Wabash R.R. Co.* (S.Ct. 1962), the Supreme Court upheld the dismissal of an action due to the failure of plaintiff's counsel to attend a pretrial conference after that attorney had caused other case delays.

In contrast to Rule 41 dismissals, which involve plaintiffs who have lost interest in their lawsuits or have failed to comply with governing rules or court orders, Rule 55 of the Federal Rules of Civil Procedure permits the entry of defaults and default judgments against a party from whom affirmative relief is sought (usually a defendant) who has failed to plead or otherwise defend. Contrary to the practice in some states, the Federal Rules of Civil Procedure prescribe a two-step process for obtaining a default judgment.

Initially, Rule 55(a) requires the clerk of court to enter a default against a party who fails to plead or otherwise defend against a claim for affirmative relief. The non-defaulting party then must use the default to obtain a default judgment. If the plaintiff's claim is for a "sum certain or for a sum which can by computation be made certain" and the defaulting party is not an infant or incompetent party, Rule 55(b)(1) requires the clerk to enter a default judgment upon request of the plaintiff and presentation of an affidavit establishing the amount due. Rule 55(b)(1) therefore might apply if the claim is for breach of contract and the contract contains a liquidated damages clause or damages can be precisely calculated. Rule 55(b)(1) would not apply if the plaintiff asserts a tort claim and seeks relief such as damages for pain and suffering that cannot be calculated with mathematical precision.

If the claim is not for a sum certain or a sum which can by computation be made certain, or if the defaulting party is an infant or incompetent person, the default judgment must be sought from the court pursuant to Rule 55(b)(2). Rule 55(b)(2) provides that default judgments cannot be entered against infants or incompetent persons unless a representative has appeared on their behalf. The court is given the authority to hold hearings pursuant to Rule 55(b)(2), which typically is done in order to determine the truth of the plaintiff's averments or the amount of damages to which the plaintiff is entitled. If the party against whom the default judgment is sought has appeared in the action, that party or his representative is entitled to written notice of the application for default judgment at least three days prior to the hearing on the application.

Rule 54(c) provides that a judgment by default "shall not be different in kind from or exceed in amount that prayed for in the demand for judgment." Rule 55(c) states that the court can set aside an entry of default for "good cause shown," while noting that a Rule 60(b) motion can be filed asking the court to set aside a default judgment. However, rather than put a client through the uncertainty of a motion to set aside a default or a default judgment, counsel should respond to all court papers in a timely fashion and thereby preclude the entry of defaults and default judgments in the first instance.

B. Motions for a Change of Forum

In some cases, counsel may have an argument that another court should hear and resolve the case. Because the action presumably was filed in the most favorable plaintiff's forum, defense counsel should consider alternative forums that might be more hospitable to the defendant. In comparing the possible forums, counsel should consider the probable judges and juries, any different law that might apply, the convenience of the forums for counsel, the parties, and witnesses, and the relative speed of the pretrial and trial processes.

There are several means by which counsel can attempt to obtain a change of forum. Section 1404(a) of Title 28 of the United States Code provides: "For the convenience of parties and witnesses, in the interest of justice, a district court may transfer any civil action to any other district or division where it might have been brought." Section 1404 transfers can be sought by any party or ordered by the court sua sponte. This section is a statutory exception to the rule that the plaintiff's original choice of forum is generally respected. For this reason, the party (either plaintiff or defendant) seeking to transfer a case must make a strong showing that another forum would be more convenient for the parties, witnesses, and courts.

Although it involved a *forum non conveniens* dismissal rather than a transfer under 28 U.S.C. § 1404, the Supreme Court's decision in *Gulf Oil Corp. v. Gilbert* (S.Ct.1947) listed many of the factors that courts consider when faced with Section 1404 transfer motions. The *Gulf Oil* factors include those going to the "private interest of the litigant," such as relative ease of access to sources of proof, availability of compulsory process, the possibility of a site view by the trier of fact, and "all other practical problems that make trial of a case easy, expeditious and inexpensive." In addition, the *Gulf Oil* Court listed "public interest" factors such as court congestion, the imposition of jury duty on persons from a community with no relation to the litigation, and the "local interest in having localized controversies decided at home."

Section 1404 provides for the possibility of transfer within the federal system, even though venue is statutorily proper in the original district. In contrast, 28 U.S.C. § 1406 provides for possible transfer from a federal district in which venue is improper to a federal district in which venue is proper. If a case is not transferred under Section 1406, the statute of limitations might run between the time that the initial action is filed and a second action is filed in the proper forum. Section 1406(a) requires district courts to dismiss a case in which venue is improper or, "if it be in the interest of justice, transfer such case to any district or division in which it could have been brought."

In addition to the transfer provisions of Sections 1404 and 1406, 28 U.S.C. § 1407 permits the transfer of cases that involve one or more common questions of fact to a single judicial district if the transfer is "for the convenience of parties and witnesses and will promote the just and efficient conduct of [the transferred] actions." In contrast to transfers under 28 U.S.C. §§ 1404 or 1406, the transfer permitted by 28 U.S.C. § 1407 is for coordinated or consolidated pretrial proceedings rather than for trial.

Not only can cases be transferred from one federal district court to another pursuant to Sections 1404 and 1406 of Title 28, but there are situations in which an action can be moved from one court system to another. Section 1441 of Title 28 is the general federal removal statute. This statute permits defendants to remove certain actions from state court to the federal district court embracing the place where the action is pending. Removal is only possible if the action falls within the original subject matter jurisdiction of the federal courts. If the action presents a federal question, 28 U.S.C. § 1441(b) permits removal to federal court without regard to the citizenship of the parties. If the basis of original federal subject matter jurisdiction is not federal question jurisdiction, 28 U.S.C. § 1441(b) only permits removal if none of the defendants is a citizen of the state in which the action was brought.

Both the federal and state courts have the power to dismiss lawsuits pursuant to the common law doctrine of *forum non conveniens.* This doctrine permits a court to dismiss an action, within its jurisdiction, if the forum would be very inconvenient because of factors such as those enunciated by the Supreme Court in *Gulf Oil Corp. v. Gilbert.* While this doctrine does not permit an actual transfer from one court system to another, after a *forum non conveniens* dismissal the same action often is filed in another court system. Indeed, one of the requirements for such a dismissal is the existence of another court that can entertain the action. For this reason, the original court may condition a *forum non conveniens* dismissal upon the defendant's agreement not to assert a statute of limitations defense in the alternative forum.

C. Motions Affecting the Timing of the Action

In addition to motions that may result in the pretrial disposition or change of venue of an action, important motions can affect the timing of the pretrial and trial process. If the plaintiff is about to suffer irreparable injury due to the defendant's alleged actions, a motion for a temporary restraining order or a preliminary injunction can be filed pursuant to Rule 65.

In many cases, counsel will desire to extend, rather than expedite, the pretrial process. Among the most important motions that attorneys file are motions for an extension of time. Rule 6(b) of the Federal Rules of Civil Procedure permits a court, "for cause shown," to enlarge the time for pretrial tasks. If a motion for extension of time is not made until after the act in question should have been done, Rule 6(b) requires that the failure to act must have been "the result of excusable neglect." Counsel should try to limit their requests for extensions of time. While judges understand that all attorneys occasionally need extensions of time, they become less sympathetic with each new extension request. Local rules of court may address the ability of counsel to stipulate to extensions of time to perform certain pretrial tasks without court approval.

D.   Motions Affecting the Trial of the Action

Some of the motions filed during the pretrial process will have a great impact upon the eventual trial of the action. It may be to a party's advantage to obtain a judicial ruling on a motion prior to trial. If counsel knows whether certain evidence will be admitted at trial or whether a specific witness will be permitted to testify, that attorney's trial strategy can be shaped accordingly. A pretrial ruling that certain evidence cannot be offered at trial may prevent the jury from inadvertently hearing the evidence if a witness answers a question before counsel's trial objection can be resolved. For this reason, counsel should consider making pretrial motions *in limine,* seeking evidentiary or other rulings prior to trial. The judge may defer ruling on some motions *in limine,* in order to consider the motions in the specific factual context of trial. Whether the judge grants, denies, or defers ruling on a motion *in limine,* local rules of court and judicial practice may require that the judge's ruling be reflected in the final pretrial order.

In addition to motions concerning the admissibility of trial evidence, the presentation of trial evidence can be structured by pretrial orders. Rule 42(a) of the Federal Rules of Civil Procedure permits the court to consolidate actions involving a common question of law or fact. Rule 42(b) provides that, "in furtherance of convenience or to avoid prejudice, or when separate trials will be conducive to expedition and economy," the court may order separate trials of claims or issues.

Apart from the efficiencies that may result from bifurcation or consolidation of actions or issues, Rule 42 orders may be strategically advantageous to a party. For example, if a plaintiff's evidence on liability is much weaker than his evidence concerning damages, it probably will not be to the plaintiff's advantage to bifurcate the issues of liability and damages at trial.

E. Other Miscellaneous Motions

In addition to the motions described above, various other motions may be appropriate in particular cases. A motion for class certification typically is filed in a class action, and a motion to proceed *in forma pauperis* may be filed to permit an impecunious plaintiff to prosecute an action without prepaying court fees and costs. Rule 7(b)(1) defines a motion as an "application to the court for an order," and most cases present many situations in which such an application seriously should be considered.

II. PRETRIAL MOTION STRATEGY

Once the potential motions that *can* be filed have been identified, a decision must be made as to the motions that actually *should* be filed. Counsel should develop a motion strategy in which individual motions complement one another. Motion strategy is one aspect of a comprehensive pretrial litigation plan.

In developing a motion strategy, counsel should consider the goals that pretrial motions can serve. Among the possible goals of pretrial motions are to (1) obtain a favorable pretrial resolution of an entire action (by, for instance, filing a successful motion to dismiss or for summary judgment); (2) narrow the issues between the parties (by, for instance, filing a successful motion for partial summary judgment); (3) lay the groundwork for an ultimately successful resolution of the action through settlement, during pretrial, or at trial; (4) obtain control of the pretrial proceedings (by using successful motions to put opposing counsel on the defensive); and (5) gain credibility with other counsel and the court (by using successful motions to demonstrate the strength of your case, resources of your client, and your own abilities as an attorney). Before filing any motion, counsel should be clear concerning the purpose or purposes that the motion is to serve.

The major factor in deciding whether to file a particular motion is the likelihood that the motion will be successful. Merely because there is a "colorable basis" for a motion does not mean that it should be filed. Even if the judge doesn't sanction an attorney for filing a particular motion, he still may resent the wasted time that the motion entailed. An attorney's credibility is one of her most important assets. Every time an attorney files an unsuccessful motion, she makes a withdrawal from her "credibility account" with the court.

In addition to the likelihood of success, counsel should consider the possible consequences that may result from filing a motion. What purpose will the motion serve, if it is granted by the court? Counsel should balance the negative consequences that may result from a motion against the potential gain if the motion is granted. There is more reason to risk a negative motion outcome if the motion is one that could resolve the action in favor of the moving party (such as a motion to dismiss or for summary judgment).

Filing a particular motion may cause other counsel, including counsel for co-parties, to respond in kind or otherwise delay a case. Even motions that are ultimately successful may have detrimental consequences. Motion practice can be expensive, can delay pretrial proceedings, and can divert the attention of the court and the parties from other aspects of the pretrial and trial process (including the merits of the case). The victory from a motion to dismiss may be short-lived if the court grants the motion but permits the plaintiff to file an amended complaint.

Nor should a party's motion strategy be inconsistent with that party's overall case theory. If the plaintiff desires an expedited case resolution, pretrial motions for extension of time should be avoided. Counsel should not lose sight of her ultimate litigation objectives by focusing merely upon the immediate gains that might result from particular motions.

Not only must counsel determine what motions she should bring on behalf of her client, but she should decide upon the best response to the motions filed by opposing counsel. The positions taken in response to the motions of other parties should be one aspect of, and consistent with, counsel's overall motion strategy. In preparing her litigation plan, counsel should have considered the pretrial motions that other parties are likely to file as well as her own responses to those motions.

By considering at an early stage of the case the motions that other parties are likely to file, counsel can prepare to meet those motions. Legal research, factual investigation, and formal discovery can be conducted to use in the eventual responses to the anticipated motions. The filing of one's own motions can be expedited in an effort to preempt likely opposition motions. An opposing counsel who must respond to your motions will have less time to prepare motions of her own.

Every motion filed by an opposing party should not necessarily be opposed. Indeed, Ethical Consideration 7–38 of the Model Code of Professional Responsibility provides that a lawyer should agree to reasonable requests for continuances, settings, the waiver of procedural formalities and similar matters that do not prejudice the rights of her client.

Before a motion is opposed, counsel should consider both the importance of the motion and the likelihood that the motion will be granted by the court. A dispositive motion that will end the lawsuit generally should be opposed, presuming there is a good faith basis for an opposition. On the other hand, there may be little reason to oppose motions seeking more limited relief. Why oppose a motion to amend the complaint if the court is likely to permit the amendment?

Federal Rules of Civil Procedure 26(c) and 37(a) require counsel to attempt to resolve their disputes before filing motions for a protective order or to compel discovery or disclosure. In most federal district courts, local rules similarly require opposing counsel to "meet and confer" before certain motions are filed. Even absent such a rule, it may make sense to discuss potential motions with opposing counsel in an effort to avoid the need for filing such motions. While attorneys shouldn't "give away the store" by agreeing to every motion filed by an opposing party, contesting even the most routine motions can greatly increase the length and expense of pretrial proceedings. Counsel who refuse to accede to reasonable requests for extensions of time will find opposing counsel similarly unwilling to agree to such motions. In lawsuits, as in life, what goes around, comes around.

Sometimes the best response to another party's motion is to file a motion of your own. Possible responses to an opponent's motion for summary judgment include a cross-motion for summary judgment and a motion to defer ruling upon the summary judgment motion until additional discovery can be obtained. The best response to a motion to dismiss may be a motion to amend the complaint to fix the defect alleged in the motion to dismiss.

While litigation plans often are modified as a case progresses, counsel should develop a litigation plan to ensure that her motions and motion responses are consistent with one another and with the long-term interests of her client.

III. THE WRITTEN MOTION PAPERS

Federal Rule of Civil Procedure 7(b) contains the basic requirements for civil motions. Rule 7(b)(1) provides that "unless made during a hearing or trial, [a motion] shall be made in writing, shall state with particularity the grounds therefor, and shall set forth the relief or order sought." Rule 7(b)(2) incorporates the provisions of Rule 10 concerning the form of motions (requiring a case caption and permitting adoption by reference), while Rule 7(b)(3) specifies that all motions must be signed in accordance with Rule 11. Whenever possible, counsel should file written motions, rather than make oral motions for the first time during hearings. If the trial court record does not indicate that a motion was made, the court of appeals may refuse to consider the issue raised by the motion.

More detailed motion requirements often are contained in local rules of court. Such rules may restrict the length of motion briefs, set schedules for filing opposition and reply briefs, specify the number and format of lines to be printed on a page, and prescribe a format for citing legal authority. Local rules also may require that a notice of hearing or proposed order be filed with the written motion.

The written motion itself is usually quite brief, as illustrated by the sample motion to dismiss set forth in Chapter 5, supra, p. 106. A sample notice of motion and certificate of service also are set forth in Chapter 5, supra, pp. 108, 109. The brief or memorandum filed in support of the motion will require the real work by counsel.

The most important thing to remember when drafting the motion brief is that trial judges are very busy people. The motion brief should be brief, and it should get to the point immediately. The brief's introductory paragraph should succinctly explain the case and describe the motion, the argument in support of the motion, and the relief sought. The introductory paragraph of a brief in support of a defendant's motion to dismiss might read something like this:

> Plaintiff Thomas Jones, a citizen of Missouri, seeks $150,000 from the defendant Midwest Chemicals, Inc. in this federal diversity action. However, as the affidavits offered in support of defendant's motion to dismiss show, the principal place of business of Midwest Chemicals is Missouri. Because the plaintiff and defendant are both Missouri citizens, the requirements of 28 U.S.C. § 1332 for diversity of citizenship are not met. Accordingly, the defendant asks the court to dismiss this action pursuant to Rule 12(b)(1) of the Federal Rules of Civil Procedure.

After such an introductory paragraph, the motion brief typically will contain a more detailed statement of the facts, including any procedural facts relevant to the present motion. The importance of the fact statement cannot be overemphasized. The brief should avoid argument, should never misstate the facts, and should not omit important facts that will be called to the court's attention by opposing counsel. Each factual assertion should be followed by a citation to the authority establishing that fact, such as an accompanying affidavit, declaration, discovery response, pleading, or other court paper.

While factual misstatements and overstatements do not belong in motion briefs, the facts should be set forth in as persuasive a manner as possible. The fact statement should be constructed so that the judge will be convinced of the correctness of your client's position before he even reads your legal argument.

The argument section of the brief follows the fact statement. The argument should be identified by a heading that summarizes the argument in support of the motion:

ARGUMENT

Because Both Plaintiff and Defendant
Are Citizens of Missouri,
The Court Should Grant
Defendant's Motion to Dismiss

.

In the argument portion of the brief, counsel should weave together the relevant facts and law into a persuasive argument. As when stating the facts, understatement, rather than overstatement, is the best course to follow in arguing one's case. Counsel's credibility with the court will suffer if it appears that the facts or law have been overstated or otherwise distorted.

The brief should focus on the major argument or arguments, rather than attempt a law review-like discussion of all the possible nuances of an issue. The main arguments of the opposing party should not be avoided. Instead, these arguments should be addressed head-on, after first developing your own arguments concerning the motion. If an opponent has an argument that you cannot overcome, the motion probably should not have been filed in the first place. Moreover, Rule 3.3(a)(3) of the Model Rules of Professional Conduct and Disciplinary Rule 7–106(B)(1) of the Model Code of Professional Responsibility require counsel to disclose to the court directly adverse legal authority within the controlling jurisdiction that is not disclosed by opposing counsel.

If there is controlling authority in the jurisdiction, there may be little reason to make an extended argument. This also may be the case if the judge, himself, or another judge on the same court has addressed the issue in question. The position taken by the Alaska Supreme Court may be of little relevance unless your case is in Alaska or there are no authorities within your own jurisdiction.

After the argument section of the brief, there should be a short concluding paragraph setting forth the relief sought in connection with the motion. For example:

CONCLUSION

For the reasons set forth above, the defendant Midwest Chemicals, Inc. requests that its motion to dismiss be granted.

The writing in any legal brief should be as clear and concise as possible. Argument headings can make the brief easier to follow. By planning motions well in advance and beginning work on them as soon as possible, counsel should have time to think through her arguments and prepare multiple drafts of major motion briefs.

String citations of authority should be avoided. Instead, limit yourself to the strongest authorities supporting particular arguments. Just as the judge will have limited time to read the parties' motion papers, he usually will not be able to conduct extensive legal research. A judge will be more likely to check a case or two if those cases are highlighted in the brief, rather than being buried among many authorities within string citations. In some jurisdictions counsel can rely upon unpublished authorities. However, copies of any unpublished authorities should be attached to the brief to assure that opposing counsel and the court have ready access to them.

Not only motion briefs, but other documents offered in connection with a motion, should be concise and well written. If material relevant to the motion is in the trial record, it may help the judge if that material is gathered into a motion appendix. A motion for summary judgment may be supported by statements from several depositions, particular interrogatory responses, and a few admissions. Even if this material has been filed with the court, the judge will be less likely to examine documents scattered throughout the case file than an evidentiary appendix that has been bound and tabbed for the judge's use in connection with the motion.

In the federal courts, 28 U.S.C. § 1746 provides that unsworn declarations signed under the penalty of perjury can be substituted for sworn affidavits whenever affidavits are required by rule or statute.

Therefore, although Rule 56 permits summary judgment motions to be supported or opposed by sworn affidavits, unsworn declarations can be used instead. As a practical matter, the only differences between affidavits and declarations are the final signature lines and the fact that notaries are not needed in connection with declarations.

Motion affidavits or declarations should get to the point, but contain sufficient details so that the conclusions offered by the witness are credible. The initial paragraphs of the affidavit or declaration should set forth the witness's background and explain why the witness is qualified to offer testimony. The affidavit or declaration should consist of relatively short, separately numbered paragraphs. This will make the document more understandable and also make it easier to cite to specific portions of the affidavit or declaration in the motion brief.

After the motion and supporting papers have been prepared, they must be filed with the court and served upon other parties. Federal Rule of Civil Procedure 5(e) authorizes local courts to permit motions and other papers to be filed by electronic means, as well as by hand or by mail. In some jurisdictions, the moving party must contact the judge's chambers prior to filing the motion to obtain a date for the motion hearing. Counsel then must file a notice of motion along with the motion itself, thereby notifying the other parties of the motion day.

Counsel should be sure that motions and motion papers are filed in a timely manner. Federal Rule of Civil Procedure 6(d) requires that written motions, other than those that may be heard ex parte, and notices of motion must be served at least five days before the hearing date. However, local rules of court often specify a greater period of advance notice, and Rule 6(d) permits the judge to order a different time period. Rule 56(c) contains a special time period for summary judgment papers, providing that summary judgment motions must be served at least ten days before the summary judgment hearing.

The typical response to a motion is an opposition brief, containing the party's motion argument, and, depending upon the motion, accompanying evidentiary material such as affidavits or discovery responses. The opposition brief should follow the same general format as the brief in support of the motion. Opposition briefs should start with a short introduction, followed by a fact statement, argument, and conclusion. Counsel need not merely rebut the moving party's argument point by point, but can make new arguments. Opposition counsel also should not feel that she must contest every argument made by the moving party. Instead, she should focus her brief on the strongest argument or arguments against the relief sought by the moving party.

In many jurisdictions, the moving party will be entitled to file a short reply brief. These briefs are not a platform to reiterate all of the points made in the original motion brief. Instead, reply briefs are to succinctly address major points made for the first time in the brief filed in opposition to the motion.

IV. MOTION ARGUMENT

Motion argument varies from court to court and from judge to judge. In some jurisdictions, growing judicial caseloads mean that there is a decreasing opportunity for oral motion argument. In other jurisdictions, docket pressures result in oral arguments that are shorter in length. In all jurisdictions, counsel should use the oral argument in a different manner than the written brief and get to the major points of the argument as quickly as possible.

In many courts, oral argument must be specifically requested or the judge will rule on the basis of the written motion papers. If a motion is important, counsel generally should request oral argument. The give-and-take of oral argument should permit counsel to address the judge's concerns with the motion and ensure that the judge really understands her client's arguments.

Oral argument is not merely an opportunity to repeat orally everything that has been said in the written motion papers. Instead, oral argument should hit on the most important aspects of a party's arguments. The oral argument should stress the strongest reasons why the motion should be granted or denied and, after establishing these, rebut the strongest counterarguments raised by opposing counsel. While secondary arguments can be raised during oral argument, counsel may merely mention them and, if the judge has no questions, refer him to the written brief on these less important points. Complex arguments are more difficult to make orally than in writing.

Even if docket pressures didn't cause judges to restrict oral argument, the human attention span is very limited. As the evangelist Billy Sunday reputedly said, "Very few souls are saved after the first ten minutes." Important points should not be buried in the midst of an extended, scatter-shot argument touching on every conceivable aspect of the motion.

To effectively plan oral argument, counsel should know what to expect from the judge. Will the argument be one of many on a crowded motion docket, will the judge take a quick break from an ongoing trial to hear the motion, or has the judge set aside an hour for just this motion? Is the judge someone who asks frequent questions during oral argument? Is the judge always, or rarely, prepared for oral argument?

After getting a general sense of what to expect from the judge, counsel should plan her actual argument. While counsel should avoid reading anything during oral argument, a written outline should be prepared to give structure to the argument. This outline can serve both as an organizational aid prior to oral argument and as a check list to ensure that all important points are made during the argument. Oral arguments can be practiced in advance. The realism of a moot court can be increased if it is held before colleagues. Even a non-lawyer spouse or friend can serve as the judge for such a session, particularly if he or she asks pertinent questions and otherwise attempts to simulate the give-and-take of an oral argument.

Counsel should arrive early for the actual argument. Why start the argument with one strike against you by appearing late? By arriving at the courtroom early, counsel can not only compose herself for the argument but may be able to watch other arguments and get a sense of how the judge handles oral argument.

Counsel should bring to the argument her case file and be thoroughly familiar with that file. When attorneys appear for oral argument, they may be asked about other aspects of the case such as the status of discovery or whether the case can be settled short of trial. Counsel should anticipate such potential questions and be ready to answer them. Counsel also should bring to the motion hearing extra copies of the motion papers and, perhaps, relevant authorities. These documents may be useful in making your own argument, and the judge may be more willing to consult a particular authority if you have it available for his study in the courtroom.

There should be a structure to oral motion argument, just as there should be a structure to the written motion briefs. However, arguments in the trial court generally are much less structured than appellate arguments, in which appellant's counsel speaks for a limited amount of time, followed by appellee's counsel, and, finally, by appellant's rebuttal. There may be much more back-and-forth between counsel during motion arguments, and the trial judge may let counsel argue for a much shorter, or longer, amount of time than would be permitted in the court of appeals.

Counsel should introduce herself at the beginning of the argument and then briefly describe the case and the pending motion: "Your honor, I'm Pam Jones, and I'm appearing here today on behalf of the defendant Midwest Chemicals, which has filed a motion to dismiss." Counsel's argument in support of, or in opposition to, the motion then should be summarized in a sentence or two: "We ask your honor to grant this motion because * * * ." This one or two sentence summarization of the argument is particularly important if there are multiple grounds offered in support of, or in opposition to, the motion. Organizing the argument in 1, 2, 3 fashion will help the judge, especially if he is given a preview of the organizational structure before counsel launches into the argument.

After setting the stage in this fashion, the facts pertinent to the motion should be recited. As with the written briefs, it is the fact statement that should predispose the judge to grant, or deny, the motion. The judge must understand both the nature of the case and how the present motion fits within that case. If the judge is well prepared, he may ask counsel to proceed to the legal argument. Absent such an indication from the judge, the factual statement should not be omitted or truncated.

The legal argument follows the factual statement and should build upon the facts previously set forth. The most important facts, and their legal significance, should be reiterated throughout the legal argument. Analogies may make an argument more understandable to the judge, and visual aids such as maps, charts, or photographs may be appropriate in connection with some motion arguments.

Counsel should conclude the argument with a sentence summarizing her argument and requesting a specific ruling from the court on the pending motion: "For the reasons that I've outlined in my argument, the defendant Midwest Chemicals is a citizen of Missouri, as is the plaintiff. Because both parties are citizens of the same state, this court doesn't have subject matter jurisdiction over this case. The defendant therefore asks the court to grant its motion to dismiss."

If counsel represents the party opposing the motion, a structured argument is still quite important. However, because the motion opponent will argue after the moving party, the opposition argument can, and should, more explicitly address arguments made in support of the motion. Counsel usually should put forth her client's strongest case, and only then address the arguments of opposing counsel. However, those arguments should be attacked head-on: "The defendant relies upon *Smith v. Jones* in support of its motion. However, there are three major reasons why *Smith* does not support defendant's motion in this case."

Sometimes the best response to particular arguments of opposing counsel will be to concede those arguments. There is no reason to challenge every assertion of opposing counsel. Such an across-the-board opposition may detract from your client's strongest points. In addition, a candid concession on collateral points should increase your credibility with the court concerning the truly important aspects of your argument. Sometimes an argument can be focused at the outset by delineating the points that are, and are not, in dispute:

> Your honor, we do not contest the fact that the national sales office of Midwest Chemicals is in Kansas. Where we disagree with the plaintiff is with respect to the characterization of Midwest's business activities within Missouri. As I'll show in my argument today, because the major manufacturing facilities and international headquarters of Midwest are located in Missouri, the defendant is a citizen of Missouri, rather than Kansas.

While a prepared structure is essential to oral argument, counsel needs to be flexible in actually giving the argument. Other counsel may raise new points for the first time during the oral argument, and, if significant, these matters should be addressed. If the new matter is both significant and something to which counsel cannot respond on the spot, she should request leave to file a short written response with the court within a few days after the hearing.

Even more important than the matters raised by opposing counsel are the questions and concerns of the court. While watching appellate argument my young son remarked to my wife, "If those judges don't stop asking Daddy questions, he'll never get a chance to give his argument." However, counsel should never consider the judge's questions to be mere hurdles to be run before the "real" argument can be given. The most important purpose of oral argument is to address the concerns of the judge who will decide the motion.

Rather than attempting to avoid questions or comments from the judge, counsel should try to elicit such reactions by maintaining eye contact with the judge and pausing at the conclusion of major portions of the argument. It can be unnerving when a judge expresses disagreement with your position during the oral argument. An even more frustrating situation, though, is when the judge doesn't express his concerns from the bench but only in his ultimate ruling, at which time there usually is nothing that can be done to change the judge's mind.

The judge should be the focus of the oral argument. His questions and concerns should be of paramount importance and be addressed immediately. Counsel should avoid responding to a judge's questions with "I'll get to that." This response suggests that the judge's question is not as important as counsel's current argument. In addition, if an immediate answer is deferred, counsel may never get back to the promised response.

The argument should be made to the judge, and not addressed to opposing counsel, the parties, or others in the courtroom. If there is occasion to refer to opposing counsel, that attorney should be respectfully referred to by her name and title rather than as "Mary" or "that lawyer for the other side."

At the conclusion of the argument, the judge may give an oral opinion from the bench, may announce a ruling and state that a written opinion will follow, or may take the motion under advisement. If the judge rules, he may ask the attorney who prevailed on the motion to submit to the court a proposed order reflecting that ruling. Generally the party who is asked to submit such a proposed order will be expected to provide a copy to other counsel so that they can confirm that it accurately reflects the judge's ruling. If there is uncertainty concerning any aspect of the judge's ruling, clarification should be sought while counsel are still before the judge in the courtroom. Such an immediate response from the court may save counsel the need to file a written motion for clarification at some future time.

CHAPTER TWELVE

SUMMARY JUDGMENT

I. RULE 56 SUMMARY JUDGMENT PROCEDURE

Among the most significant pretrial motions is the motion for summary judgment provided by Rule 56 of the Federal Rules of Civil Procedure. Rule 56 permits the entry of judgment short of trial, with attendant legal and judicial savings. Because of the increasing importance of summary judgment, counsel should be thoroughly familiar with summary judgment motions and summary judgment practice.

While the Federal Rules of Civil Procedure have always provided for summary judgment, there was a time when at least some federal courts were reluctant to grant Rule 56 motions, particularly in complex cases. The Supreme Court addressed this reluctance to grant summary judgment in a trilogy of 1986 cases: *Matsushita Elec. Indus. Co. v. Zenith Radio Corp.* (S.Ct.1986), *Anderson v. Liberty Lobby, Inc.* (S.Ct.1986), and *Celotex Corp. v. Catrett* (S.Ct. 1986). In each of these cases the Supreme Court reversed appellate courts that had overturned district court grants of summary judgment. As the majority stressed in *Celotex Corp. v. Catrett,* "Summary judgment procedure is properly regarded not as a disfavored procedural shortcut, but rather as an integral part of the Federal Rules as a whole, which are designed 'to secure the just, speedy and inexpensive determination of every action.' "

Rule 56 permits both claimants and defending parties to seek summary judgment as to all or part of a claim, counterclaim, or cross-claim. Rule 56(a) permits a claimant to file a motion for summary judgment "at any time after the expiration of 20 days from the commencement of the action or after service of a motion for summary judgment by the adverse party," while Rule 56(b) permits a party defending against a claim, counterclaim, or cross-claim to seek summary judgment on that claim at any time. In either case, Rule 56(c) requires that the summary judgment motion be served at least ten days before any summary judgment hearing. Local rules may contain additional requirements concerning the timing and length of summary judgment papers.

Summary judgment need not be sought on an entire claim, but partial summary judgment can be entered by the court. Rule 56(c) specifically provides: "A summary judgment, interlocutory in character, may be rendered on the issue of liability alone although there is a genuine issue as to the amount of damages." Even if a party requests summary judgment on an entire claim, the court may decide to render only partial summary judgment. Rule 56(d) provides that if summary judgment is not granted concerning an entire case, the court if practicable shall determine what material facts are, and are not, in good faith controverted. Pursuant to Rule 56(d), the judge then is to enter an order "specifying the facts that appear without substantial controversy," which facts shall be deemed established at trial.

The legal standard for the grant of summary judgment is contained in Rule 56(c). This rule provides that summary judgment shall be granted if the "pleadings, depositions, answers to interrogatories, and admissions on file, together with the affidavits, if any, show that there is no genuine issue as to any material fact and that the moving party is entitled to a judgment as a matter of law." Thus when presented with a motion for summary judgment, the court must consider both (1) the material facts and (2) the governing substantive law.

The Supreme Court in *Anderson v. Liberty Lobby, Inc.* (S.Ct.1986) equated a genuine issue of material fact with evidence that would preclude the grant of judgment as a matter of law at trial: "[S]ummary judgment will not lie if the dispute about a material fact is 'genuine,' that is, if the evidence is such that a reasonable jury could return a verdict for the nonmoving party." If there is no genuine issue between the parties, or if the only issues that exist involve nonmaterial facts, the factual portion of the Rule 56(c) standard is met. The Supreme Court noted in *Lujan v. National Wildlife Federation* (S.Ct.1990) that "the purpose of Rule 56 is to enable a party who believes there is no genuine dispute as to a specific fact essential to the other side's case to demand at least one sworn averment of that fact before the lengthy process of litigation continues."

In addition to establishing that there is no genuine issue of material fact, the party moving for summary judgment must show that he is entitled to a judgment under the governing substantive law. If there are no material factual disputes between the parties, legal questions concerning the claimant's right to relief may have been resolved by a Rule 12(b)(6) motion to dismiss or a Rule 12(c) motion for judgment on the pleadings. In fact, if the court considers matters outside the pleadings in connection with either of these two motions, the motion is to be treated as a motion for summary judgment. As a practical matter, the real questions posed by most summary judgment motions involve factual disputes rather than a difference as to the governing legal standard.

Summary judgment motions often are filed after discovery, although they need not be. Rule 56(c) permits the court to consider pleadings, discovery responses, and affidavits in ruling on a summary judgment motion. However, Rule 56(e) cautions: "When a motion for summary judgment is made and supported as provided in this rule, an adverse party may not rest upon the mere allegations or denials of the adverse party's pleading, but the adverse party's response, by affidavits or as otherwise provided in this rule, must set forth specific facts showing that there is a genuine issue for trial.''

Affidavits or declarations may or may not be offered in support of, or in opposition to, a motion for summary judgment. Rule 56(e) provides that summary judgment affidavits ''shall be made on personal knowledge, shall set forth such facts as would be admissible in evidence, and shall show affirmatively that the affiant is competent to testify to the matters stated therein.'' Rule 56(e) further provides that sworn or certified copies of papers referred to in a summary judgment affidavit should be attached to the affidavit.

What if the party opposing summary judgment does not have access to the facts necessary to oppose a motion for summary judgment? Rule 56(f) permits counsel opposing a summary judgment motion to file an affidavit explaining why certain facts cannot be presented. The court then may deny the summary judgment motion or order a continuance to permit counsel to obtain the affidavits or discovery necessary to oppose the motion.

Any attorney who is preparing or opposing a motion for summary judgment should be familiar with Rule 56(g) of the Federal Rules of Civil Procedure. Rule 56(g) requires the court to assess reasonable expenses, including attorneys' fees, if summary judgment affidavits are presented in bad faith or solely for the purpose of delay. If such affidavits are presented, the court also can adjudge the offending party or counsel in contempt of court. Even if there has been no bad faith, Rule 11 sanctions may be assessed if a summary judgment paper is signed in violation of the certification requirements of that rule.

II. EFFECTIVE USE OF SUMMARY JUDGMENT MOTIONS

Counsel should be able to determine whether a motion for summary judgment can be filed by a quick review of Rule 56 of the Federal Rules of Civil Procedure. A more difficult question is whether a Rule 56 motion actually *should* be filed. This is a question that counsel must answer for herself, without guidance from the Federal Rules.

Potential summary judgment motions should have been considered at the very outset of the case, when the litigation plan was developed. As with other pretrial motions, potential motions for summary judgment should be consistent with, and supportive of, a party's litigation theory and theme. By making an early decision to seek summary judgment, counsel can structure discovery and other pretrial proceedings to support a Rule 56 motion.

In deciding whether to file a motion for summary judgment, counsel should consider: (1) whether the motion is likely to be successful, (2) the significance of the relief that will be granted if the motion is successful, and (3) the problems that may be created if the motion is denied.

Some trial judges are especially receptive to motions for summary judgment. If the alternative to summary judgment is a long and costly trial, the judge may be even more predisposed to seriously consider the entry of summary judgment. Even if the motion is denied, its very filing may give the moving party some measure of control over the pretrial proceedings. Counsel who must respond to a summary judgment motion will have that much less time to file motions of their own. A defendant may be able to convince the court to stay discovery or other pretrial proceedings until a summary judgment motion raising threshold defenses is resolved. Even if the judge finds that there is a genuine issue of material fact, the decision denying summary judgment may include a favorable interpretation of the governing law.

There are, though, potential disadvantages to summary judgment motions. Ruling on a major motion for summary judgment may require a significant expenditure of judicial resources, and the judge may not be appreciative of the lawyer and party who required time to be spent on a motion that was not well-taken. Summary judgment motions can cause major pretrial delays. A summary judgment motion may encourage other parties to file cross-motions for summary judgment. Not only will summary judgment motions take time for the attorneys to brief, but the court may not be able to rule on the motions immediately. In some cases counsel may be better off proceeding to trial rather than precipitating the delay usually occasioned by summary judgment motions.

Counsel always should consider whether her client's argument will be stronger if presented by live witnesses at trial rather than in written summary judgment papers. Strong witnesses may be more convincing at trial than on paper. The judge will not be as favorably disposed to a trial argument that he already has rejected in connection with a summary judgment motion. On the other hand, some witnesses do not bear up well under the stress of trial, and their testimony can be presented more effectively in the much more controlled context of a summary judgment affidavit. Counsel also should consider how convincing the witnesses of other parties will be at trial. If opposing witnesses came across well at their depositions, counsel may want to move for summary judgment in an effort to resolve the case short of trial.

The timing of the summary judgment motion can be very important. Rule 56(a) precludes a claimant from filing a summary judgment motion before the expiration of twenty days from the commencement of the action or the service of a summary judgment motion by the adverse party. Rule 56(c) requires that a summary judgment motion be filed at least ten days before any summary judgment hearing. In addition to these requirements of Rule 56, the local rules of some courts limit the time for filing summary judgment motions. Some local rules require that summary judgment motions must be filed a certain number of days before trial, while others require that summary judgment motions be filed within a certain amount of time after the completion of discovery.

Counsel should consider seeking summary judgment early in the case, before wide-ranging discovery is undertaken by other parties. However, an early summary judgment motion may trigger a Rule 56(f) affidavit from opposing counsel, requesting discovery necessary to oppose the motion. Nevertheless, if the summary judgment motion is based upon a discrete issue, it may be possible to limit discovery to that single issue until the motion for summary judgment has been resolved.

Some attorneys file early summary judgment motions to "educate the court" about their legal theories and factual strengths. However, there's usually little to be gained from educating the judge about a theory that he probably will find to be without merit. Counsel should file summary judgment motions that the judge is likely to grant rather than merely attempt to educate the court about one's case.

If a case is likely to settle, a well-timed summary judgment motion may increase the moving party's settlement leverage. Opposing counsel may decide to settle a case rather than to expend a major amount of time and effort opposing a well constructed and supported motion for summary judgment. Counsel therefore should consider broaching the possibility of settlement with opposing counsel immediately after filing a strong motion for summary judgment.

Even if permitted to do so by local rules of court, the attorney who waits until right before trial to file a motion for summary judgment decreases the chances that the motion will be granted. If the motion is filed at the eleventh hour, opposing counsel can argue that there is no sense in delaying the trial for which the parties have prepared. The judge also may prefer to decide the issues presented by a summary judgment motion on the full record at trial, rather than on the basis of affidavits and other documentary proof.

The actual motion for summary judgment usually is quite straightforward. The motion is typically only a sentence or two, often something like this:

Chocolates Unlimited, the defendant in this action, hereby moves the court pursuant to Rule 56 of the Federal Rules of Civil Procedure to enter summary judgment on its behalf. In support of this motion, the court is respectfully referred to the accompanying Defendant's Brief in Support of Summary Judgment, the August 17, 2001, declaration of Thomas T. Tompkins, and Defendant's Summary Judgment Appendix of Discovery Responses.

In addition to the summary judgment motion, local rules of court may require the submission of a notice of hearing, a supporting brief, a proposed order, and a statement of material facts as to which there is no genuine issue. Counsel also must decide what evidentiary material will be offered in support of the motion.

Summary judgment evidence can include (1) affidavits or declarations prepared specifically for the summary judgment motion and (2) preexisting pleadings and discovery responses. Rules 56(a), (b), and (c) do not require that summary judgment motions be supported by affidavits, but give the moving party the option whether or not to offer affidavits in support of the motion.

Typically, affirmative evidence is not offered during the discovery process unless specifically called for by a discovery request. The moving party therefore usually prepares summary judgment affidavits to summarize that party's strongest evidence in support of summary judgment. Summary judgment affiants should be chosen with care to ensure that they have the concrete, first-hand knowledge required by Rule 56(e). Summary judgment affiants also are likely deposition targets for opposing counsel in the event of any further discovery.

Some judges are reluctant to grant summary judgment if a great amount of evidence is offered in connection with a summary judgment motion. A few judges even seem to follow the apocryphal "One Inch Rule," presuming that "there's a genuine issue of material fact in there somewhere" if the summary judgment papers are more than one inch thick.

Evidence offered in summary judgment affidavits is a form of voluntary discovery provided to other parties. While counsel should not withhold evidence that might convince the court to grant summary judgment, summary judgment affidavits may destroy the possibility of evidentiary surprises at trial and even may provide a basis for the trial impeachment of one's own witnesses. Counsel should consider not only the current usefulness of particular evidence in connection with the summary judgment motion, but the possible use that opposing counsel can make of that evidence if summary judgment is denied. Counsel also should consider whether a motion for summary judgment may trigger the filing of opposing affidavits that themselves contain valuable discovery.

Rule 56(e) contains specific requirements for summary judgment affidavits. This rule requires that summary judgment affidavits (or declarations filed pursuant to 28 U.S.C. § 1746) shall be made on the affiant's personal knowledge, set forth facts that would be admissible in evidence, and establish the competency of the affiant to offer testimony. Even absent Rule 56(e), it is hard to imagine a credible affidavit that would not satisfy the requirements of that rule.

The initial paragraph or paragraphs of the summary judgment affidavit should set forth the affiant's background, while the numbered paragraphs that follow should contain the affiant's relevant, first-hand testimony. If documents are referred to by the affiant, Rule 56(e) requires that sworn or certified copies of those documents be attached to the affidavit.

In addition to affidavits and declarations, discovery responses often are offered in connection with motions for summary judgment. An opposing party's discovery responses, given earlier in the pretrial proceedings, can be more convincing than his self-serving affidavits prepared specifically in connection with a summary judgment motion. For instance, if the plaintiff in a case involving an automobile accident stated at his deposition that he went through a red light, that deposition statement can be powerful evidence in support of a defense motion for summary judgment. Some courts have held that a genuine issue of material fact cannot be created by an affidavit that conflicts with the affiant's prior unambiguous deposition testimony.

Because the discovery responses of other parties can provide powerful summary judgment evidence, discovery requests should be framed to elicit responses that can be used most effectively in connection with summary judgment motions. Deponents should be encouraged to give complete answers, to preclude later summary judgment affidavits containing information the deponent "forgot" at his deposition.

After a particular topic has been exhausted at a deposition, the examining attorney can summarize the deponent's testimony to create a single question and answer that can be used conveniently in connection with a motion for summary judgment: "So the only times that you talked with the defendant were on December 2, 2000, and April 9, 2001?" An affirmative answer to this question could be used much more effectively in connection with a motion for summary judgment than could a series of questions and answers extending over several pages of the deposition transcript.

If an entire claim is not susceptible to a motion for summary judgment, counsel should consider the possibility of a motion for partial summary judgment. By such a motion, the disputed factual and legal issues can be narrowed and the case made more manageable for trial, resolution short of trial, or settlement. Motions for partial summary judgment can be addressed to individual issues, such as liability but not the amount of damages. Individual counts of the complaint or defenses in the answer also can be the subject of motions for partial summary judgment. A successful motion for partial summary judgment is worth many unsuccessful motions for summary judgment concerning an entire lawsuit.

There may be major advantages to be gained from a successful motion for partial summary judgment totally apart from the trial efficiencies that result from narrowing the issues in dispute. Even if all of the counts in a complaint do not lend themselves to summary judgment, a successful motion for partial summary judgment concerning a major count may cause the plaintiff to lose interest in the case. If certain issues are taken out of the case by partial summary judgment, an opposing party may be precluded from offering evidence at trial pertaining to those issues. Nor is the grant of a motion for partial summary judgment an immediately appealable final judgment. For this reason, a good time to raise settlement with opposing counsel may be immediately after prevailing on a motion for partial summary judgment.

Because of the possible effect of a motion for partial summary judgment on trial evidence, counsel may decide to withhold filing such a motion in certain situations. Presume that the plaintiff has a very strong case on liability but a much weaker case on damages. In this situation, a successful motion by plaintiff for partial summary judgment on the issue of liability would greatly limit the liability evidence that plaintiff could offer at trial. Plaintiff may be better advised to withhold the motion for partial summary judgment and offer all of his evidence at trial, because the jury's determination of damages may be influenced by the trial evidence concerning liability.

All counsel should be prepared to take advantage of Federal Rule of Civil Procedure 56(d). This rule requires the court, "if practicable," to specify the material facts that remain after it has ruled on a motion for summary judgment. Thus, even if summary judgment is not granted concerning an entire case, the summary judgment motion may provide a basis for significantly narrowing the issues that must be resolved at trial.

III. DEFENDING AGAINST MOTIONS FOR SUMMARY JUDGMENT

The key to defending against a motion for summary judgment is to convince the court that the case could be decided against the movant at trial if summary judgment is denied. Judges are rightly hesitant to grant summary judgment against a party they believe could prevail at trial.

Several strategies can be employed in defending against a motion for summary judgment. Counsel should consider whether (1) the moving party has complied with the procedural requirements of Rule 56 and any local rules of court, (2) the moving party is entitled to summary judgment under the Rule 56 standard, and (3) the summary judgment motion should be decided without permitting additional time for formal or informal discovery.

An opposing party's summary judgment papers should be checked for compliance with the specific requirements of Rule 56. Has the plaintiff filed his motion before the expiration of twenty days from the commencement of the action, contrary to Rule 56(a)? Has the motion been served less than ten days before the summary judgment hearing, contrary to Rule 56(c)? Do the supporting affidavits comply with the requirements of Rule 56(e)?

The motion papers also should be checked for compliance with local rules of court. Has the moving party failed to submit a statement of material facts as to which there is no genuine issue? Has opposing counsel properly noticed the motion for a hearing and complied with page limitations governing the supporting brief?

Summary judgment motions that are denied generally are unsuccessful not because of the above types of procedural failings, but because the Rule 56(c) summary judgment standard has not been met. Counsel faced with an opposing party's motion for summary judgment always should consider whether there is a genuine issue of material fact between the parties and whether the movant is entitled to judgment as a matter of law.

The courts are more likely to find a genuine issue of material fact precluding summary judgment if witness credibility is at issue. If intent, motive, or other state of mind must be determined, summary judgment is generally inappropriate. The demeanor of a witness cannot be evaluated upon the paper record presented in connection with a summary judgment motion.

Whether or not credibility is at issue, in *United States v. Diebold, Inc.* (S.Ct.1962) (*per curiam*) the Supreme Court recognized, "On summary judgment the inferences to be drawn from the underlying facts * * * must be viewed in the light most favorable to the party opposing the motion." Even if there are no facts in dispute, summary judgment is inappropriate if differing inferences reasonably can be made from the undisputed facts. The judge also may be reluctant to grant summary judgment in cases involving expert testimony or in which a jury trial has been sought.

Mere conclusory allegations unsupported by the summary judgment record are an insufficient basis for summary judgment. As Justice White, the swing vote in *Celotex Corp. v. Catrett* (S.Ct.1986), recognized in that case, "It is not enough to move for summary judgment without supporting the motion in any way or with a conclusory assertion that the plaintiff has no evidence to prove his case." However, the majority in *Lujan v. National Wildlife Federation* (S.Ct.1990) later noted that "*Celotex* made clear that Rule 56 does not require the moving party to *negate* the elements of the nonmoving party's case."

In arguing to the court that there could be different outcomes at trial if summary judgment is denied, the party opposing summary judgment can stress the self-serving nature of the movant's summary judgment affidavits and any lack of opportunity to cross-examine the summary judgment affiants. Inconsistencies between summary judgment affidavits and earlier discovery responses should be stressed. Spontaneous deposition testimony is given greater credence in connection with summary judgment motions than are affidavits prepared specifically in support of a summary judgment motion. However, the Supreme Court stressed in *Anderson v. Liberty Lobby, Inc.* (S.Ct.1986) that a plaintiff cannot defeat summary judgment "by merely asserting that the jury might, and legally could, disbelieve" the defendant.

Not only can the party defending against summary judgment focus on the failure of the movant to satisfy the summary judgment standard, but affirmative steps can be taken to defeat summary judgment. If the summary judgment motion challenges the legal sufficiency of the complaint, the plaintiff might voluntarily amend the complaint (if no answer has been filed) or seek leave to amend (if the defendant has answered). Unless a summary judgment motion is warranted by law, is not presented for an improper purpose, and any factual contentions have evidentiary support, Rule 11 sanctions can be sought. Rule 56(g) is a separate fee-shifting provision covering summary judgment affidavits presented in bad faith.

The affidavits offered in opposition to summary judgment should be carefully drafted. Especially when before judges with a propensity to grant summary judgment, attorneys defending against motions for summary judgment may be wise to present more of their evidence at the summary judgment stage, rather than withhold important evidence for trial. The attorney who withholds evidence may have summary judgment entered against her client and never have the chance to offer that evidence.

Even if the merits are not raised directly by a motion for summary judgment, summary judgment affidavits may allude to the merits of the lawsuit. If the defendant seeks summary judgment on technical legal grounds, the plaintiff's summary judgment papers might remind the court of the serious injuries he has sustained and other aspects of the merits that can be expected to arouse sympathy for the plaintiff. While totally irrelevant facts should not be interjected into summary judgment proceedings, a general description of the merits may be relevant if only to put the pending summary judgment motion in its proper context.

If the party opposing summary judgment has a particularly appealing case on the merits, counsel might request a hearing on the summary judgment motion to ensure that all the important facts are before the judge. If a hearing is held, either party can seek to offer oral testimony pursuant to Federal Rule of Civil Procedure 43(e). More typically, the judge will decide the summary judgment motion based upon affidavits and other written material offered in connection with the motion.

Some of the most effective techniques to defeat summary judgment are those that are employed before the summary judgment motion is even filed. Proper deposition preparation should prevent a client from making inadvertent deposition statements that can be used by opposing parties in seeking summary judgment. Counsel may decide to ask a question or two of her own client during a deposition, so that the deposition transcript accurately reflects facts that later may be important to a summary judgment motion.

The party opposing summary judgment can himself seek entry of summary judgment by filing a cross-motion for summary judgment. If a cross-motion for summary judgment is filed, the supporting papers usually should make clear that the cross-motion is not a concession that there are no genuine issues precluding summary judgment for the opposing party. However, if the parties' dispute concerns only legal, rather than factual, issues, there may be no need for a trial and the entry of summary judgment for one or the other of the parties may be appropriate.

Finally, a Rule 56(f) affidavit can be filed in response to a motion for summary judgment. Such an affidavit can be filed by counsel when she is unable to offer facts sufficient to justify opposition to the motion but she believes that those facts can be obtained through informal or formal discovery. A Rule 56(f) opposition stands a good chance of success if the party opposing summary judgment has not yet had a chance to obtain discovery from the moving party. For example, the plaintiff in an employment discrimination suit may not be able to offer certain specific facts showing discrimination without access to the defendant's personnel records. If the defendant moves for summary judgment prior to providing these records, the court may continue the summary judgment motion until plaintiff has had an opportunity to obtain the records and extract from them information relevant to the summary judgment motion.

A Rule 56(f) affidavit also may be successful if there is evidence that might be obtained from third parties that would support a summary judgment opposition. For example, if a person with information relevant to the summary judgment motion cannot be located or lives in a foreign country, the court may give the party opposing summary judgment a limited amount of time to attempt to obtain an affidavit from that person before ruling on the summary judgment motion.

In most cases, a successful Rule 56(f) summary judgment opposition will merely result in the court deferring its ruling on the summary judgment motion. However, in some cases the court ultimately may decide to proceed to trial without resolving the summary judgment motion, while in other cases a judicial ruling may be unnecessary because the case is voluntarily settled. Even if the court ultimately rules on the motion, the time gained by the Rule 56(f) opposition may permit the party opposing summary judgment to obtain facts that can be used to convince the court to deny the motion.

CHAPTER THIRTEEN

PRETRIAL CONFERENCES AND PRETRIAL ORDERS

I. PRETRIAL CONFERENCES

Over the course of a lawsuit, there may be numerous conferences with the court. These pretrial conferences may concern such matters as the scheduling and management of pretrial and trial proceedings, as well as the possible resolution of the case by settlement or other means short of trial. Rule 16 of the Federal Rules of Civil Procedure was greatly expanded in 1983 and expanded again in 1993, reflecting the increasing importance of pretrial conferences.

Rule 16(a) grants district courts the discretionary power to require attorneys and unrepresented parties to appear for pretrial conferences. In addition, Rule 16(c) recognizes the power of the court to require that a party or its representative be present or reasonably available by telephone in order to consider possible settlement at a pretrial conference. The local rules of some federal district courts and the standing orders of some judges therefore require the presence of both counsel and their clients at final pretrial conferences or other pretrial conferences at which settlement may be discussed.

Rule 16(a) specifies the following purposes and objectives for pretrial conferences:

(1) expediting the disposition of the action;

(2) establishing early and continuing control so that the case will not be protracted because of lack of management;

(3) discouraging wasteful pretrial activities;

(4) improving the quality of the trial through more thorough preparation, and;

(5) facilitating the settlement of the case.

Pretrial conferences typically involve a discussion between counsel and the court concerning ways to expedite the action (Rule 16(a)(1)–(3)), improve the quality of trial (Rule 16(a)(4)), and settle the case short of trial (Rule 16(a)(5)).

In addition to Rule 16(a)'s enumeration of general pretrial conference objectives, Rule 16(c) contains a long list of specific subjects that may be discussed at pretrial conferences. These include "the formulation and simplification of the issues," Rule 16(c)(1), "the possibility of obtaining admissions * * * , stipulations regarding the authenticity of documents, and advance rulings from the court on the admissibility of evidence," Rule 16(c)(3), "the control and scheduling of discovery, including orders affecting disclosures and discovery pursuant to Rule 26 and Rules 29 through 37," Rule 16(c)(6), "settlement and the use of special procedures to assist in resolving the dispute," Rule 16(c)(9), and "the form and substance of the pretrial order," Rule 16(c)(10).

Rule 16(c) further requires that at least one attorney for each party participating in a pretrial conference have authority to enter into stipulations and make admissions on behalf of her client.

The subjects discussed at a pretrial conference will depend upon how early in the case the conference is held, the purpose for which the conference is held, any governing local rules or standing orders, and the practices of the district judge or magistrate judge who presides at the conference. If the conference is held at the very outset of the case, the major subjects discussed may concern scheduling of pretrial and trial proceedings. Later conferences may be held to address specific problems that have arisen in the pretrial process, such as disputes concerning discovery or pretrial motions.

At any pretrial conference, the presiding judge may ask counsel and the parties about the chances of settlement and whether settlement can be facilitated by the judge. The desire to use a pretrial conference to discuss settlement is one of the reasons a judge may require parties to attend that conference. Merely seeing the plaintiff in a personal injury case may cause the defendant or the defendant's insurer to reassess the defense exposure if the case is tried. A plaintiff who witnesses the preparation and professionalism of defense counsel at a pretrial conference may reassess his chances of prevailing at trial. While judges attempt to avoid unfairly pressuring parties to settle, their discussions with parties, counsel, and insurance representatives at the pretrial conference may cause parties to more realistically assess their cases and resolve their disputes short of trial.

Most judges ultimately schedule a final pretrial conference to, in the words of Rule 16(d), "formulate a plan for trial, including a program for facilitating the admission of evidence." Rule 16(d) provides that final pretrial conferences "shall be held as close to the time of trial as reasonable under the circumstances," although different judges interpret this provision somewhat differently. If the final pretrial conference is held well before trial, it may be impossible to resolve all trial issues at that conference. On the other hand, counsel may need a few days or weeks to conform their trial presentations to judicial rulings made at the final pretrial conference.

If a party or attorney does not participate in good faith in a pretrial conference, sanctions can be assessed pursuant to Rule 16(f). The potential sanctions can include any of the sanctions specified in Rule 37(b)(2)(B), (C), and (D), such as an order prohibiting the introduction of specific evidence at trial, striking pleadings, dismissing the action, entering a default judgment, or, if a court order has been violated, treating the offending conduct as contempt of court. In addition to or in lieu of any other sanction, the judge is to require the payment of reasonable expenses incurred due to noncompliance with Rule 16, unless the noncompliance was substantially justified or other circumstances make an award of expenses unjust.

II. PREPARATION FOR, AND HANDLING OF, PRETRIAL CONFERENCES

Preparation for a pretrial conference presumes that there is a pretrial conference for which to prepare. In appropriate cases, counsel may want to request a pretrial conference if one has not been scheduled by the court. The intervention of the judge may be helpful in moving opposing counsel off an unreasonable position or in facilitating agreement among counsel concerning case settlement or individual pretrial disputes. However, if settlement is not achieved at the pretrial conference, it may be difficult to try the case before the judge who conducted pretrial settlement discussions. For this reason, in some courts a district judge or magistrate judge other than the trial judge presides over pretrial settlement conferences. Even if this is not local practice, counsel might request that the case be assigned to someone other than the trial judge for a pretrial settlement conference.

The appropriate preparation for a pretrial conference depends upon the particular type of conference for which one is preparing. The final pretrial conference at which a final pretrial order will be adopted requires more extensive preparation than intermediate pretrial conferences addressed to discrete issues. In preparing for the conference, counsel should familiarize herself with relevant local rules of court, standing orders of the judge who will preside at the conference, and the specific order scheduling the conference.

Counsel should never presume that a pretrial conference will be limited to those matters listed in the order scheduling the conference. Rule 16(c) lists a great number of topics that may be discussed at any pretrial conference. Counsel should be thoroughly familiar with the case file and should bring it to the pretrial conference. Not only can Rule 16(f) sanctions be assessed if a party or attorney is substantially unprepared to participate in a pretrial conference, but judges are quite naturally displeased by such behavior. Moreover, even though the Rule 16(e) "manifest injustice" standard only must be met in order to modify final pretrial orders, obtaining modification of other pretrial orders sometimes can be a difficult task.

Many judges use pretrial conferences to check, generally, on the status of cases. Attorneys therefore should be ready to address questions about the progress of discovery, whether pretrial motions will be filed, and when the case will be ready for trial. Because questions about the trial may arise, the attorney who will try the case should handle the pretrial conference. In fact, Rule 16(d) requires that at the final pretrial conference at least one of the attorneys who will conduct the trial for each party shall appear.

Among the common topics of discussion at the final pretrial conference are the dates for trial and for remaining pretrial tasks, such as the completion of discovery and submission of the final pretrial order (if a proposed order has not been submitted prior to the final pretrial conference). Counsel therefore should be sure to bring their appointment calendars to all pretrial conferences.

While attorneys should participate in good faith in the pretrial process, there is a natural reluctance to agree to pretrial orders that will restrict counsel's later litigation options. If counsel stipulates to facts in the pretrial order, it will be difficult, if not impossible, to challenge those facts at trial. Counsel may have to walk a fine line at some pretrial conferences and be able to differentiate, on the spot, between matters that they cannot in good faith dispute and those proposed stipulations or procedures that will disadvantage their clients and that they can in good faith oppose.

If an attorney is not sure about the wisdom of a particular proposal made for the first time at a pretrial conference, she might request some time to think about the proposal or to consult with her client. The 1983 Advisory Committee note to Rule 16 recognizes that that rule should not "be read to encourage the judge conducting the [pretrial] conference to compel attorneys to enter into stipulations or to make admissions that they consider to be unreasonable, that touch on matters that could not normally have been anticipated to arise at the conference, or on subjects of a dimension that normally require prior consultation with and approval from the client." Counsel, though, should be careful about suggesting that they are without authority to enter into stipulations at the pretrial conference. Rule 16(c) requires that at least one of the attorneys for each party participating in any pretrial conference "shall have authority to enter into stipulations and to make admissions regarding all matters that the participants may reasonably anticipate may be discussed."

Because settlement is frequently considered at pretrial conferences, counsel should discuss this subject with their clients before the conference so that they can respond to settlement proposals or inquiries that may be made at the conference. If a client is not required to attend the conference, he should be available by telephone to respond to settlement proposals that may arise at the conference.

Counsel should leave the pretrial conference with a mental "to do" list of remaining business. Discovery may have to be completed within dates set at the conference, and counsel may be required to file particular pretrial motions by a date certain. Witnesses may have to be notified of the trial date, and the client should be informed about the outcome of the conference. Counsel also may be required to draft a proposed pretrial order, reflecting the subjects discussed and rulings made at the pretrial conference.

III. PRETRIAL ORDERS

During the pretrial process, the judge may issue many orders. The judge may extend the time for answering the complaint, compel discovery responses, or deny a motion to dismiss or for summary judgment. These all are pretrial orders—orders that the court issues prior to trial. The focus of this section, though, is on Rule 16 orders issued by the court to control later pretrial and trial proceedings.

The initial order entered in many civil cases is the Rule 16(b) scheduling order. While most of the other provisions of Rule 16 are not mandatory, Rule 16(b) requires that, except in "categories of actions exempted by district court rule as inappropriate," the district judge or magistrate judge is to enter a scheduling order. Rule 16(b) scheduling orders are to limit the time for joining additional parties, amending the pleadings, filing motions, and completing discovery. In addition, these orders may modify the times for disclosures and the extent of discovery to be permitted, set dates for pretrial conferences and trial, and include other appropriate matters.

Rule 16(b) provides that the scheduling order is to issue "as soon as practicable but in any event within 90 days after the appearance of a defendant and within 120 days after the complaint has been served on a defendant." The scheduling order is to issue after the court has received the parties' Rule 26(f) discovery plan or consulted with counsel and any unrepresented parties, although this consultation may occur over the telephone or through the mail. Rule 16(b) provides that the dates set in a scheduling order are not to be modified except by leave of the court "upon a showing of good cause."

Local rules of court and the standing orders of individual judges often address Rule 16(b) scheduling orders. Most district courts exclude certain categories of cases from scheduling order requirements. As the Advisory Committee recognized when the 1983 amendments to Rule 16 were promulgated, "Logical candidates for [exclusion from mandatory scheduling requirements] include social security disability matters, habeas corpus petitions, forfeitures, and reviews of certain administrative actions."

Rule 16(b) scheduling orders are not the only pretrial orders contemplated by Rule 16. Rule 16(e) provides:

> After any conference held pursuant to this rule, an order shall be entered reciting the action taken. This order shall control the subsequent course of the action unless modified by a subsequent order. The order following a final pretrial conference shall be modified only to prevent manifest injustice.

After every pretrial conference, the court thus enters an order setting forth the rulings made at the conference, which rulings will govern future pretrial proceedings.

After the final pretrial conference, the court enters a final pretrial order. While earlier pretrial orders have governed the ongoing pretrial proceedings, the focus of the final pretrial order is upon the trial of the action. Local rules of court, standing orders of individual judges, and judicial directions in individual cases govern the contents of the final pretrial order. Local rules and standing orders may provide a specific format for the final pretrial order. An example of such a final pretrial order is set forth in Rule 16.1 of the United States District Court for the Western District of Washington.

Hon. [name of judge]

UNITED STATES DISTRICT COURT
WESTERN DISTRICT OF WASHINGTON
AT _____

_____,) Plaintiff,)	No. _____
)	
vs.)	PRETRIAL ORDER
)	
_____,) Defendant.)	

JURISDICTION

Jurisdiction is vested in this court by virtue of: (State the facts and cite the statutes whereby jurisdiction of the case is vested in this court).

CLAIMS AND DEFENSES

The plaintiff will pursue at trial the following claims: (E.g., breach of contract, violation of 42 U.S.C. § 1983). The defendant will pursue the following affirmative defenses and/or claims: (E.g., accord and satisfaction, estoppel, waiver).

ADMITTED FACTS

The following facts are admitted by the parties: (Enumerate every agreed fact, irrespective of admissibility, but with notation of objections as to admissibility. List 1, 2, 3, etc.)

The plaintiff contends as follows: (List 1, 2, 3, etc.)

The defendant contends as follows: (List 1, 2, 3, etc.)

(State contentions in summary fashion, omitting evidentiary detail. Unless otherwise ordered by the court, the factual contentions of a party shall not exceed two pages in length. * * *)

ISSUES OF LAW

The following are the issues of law to be determined by the court: (List 1, 2, 3, etc., and state each issue of law involved. A simple statement of the ultimate issue to be decided by the court, such as "Is the plaintiff entitled to recover?" will not be accepted.) If the parties cannot agree on the issues of law, separate statements may be given in the pretrial order.

EXPERT WITNESSES

(a) Each party shall be limited to _____ expert witness(es) on the issues of _____.

(b) The name(s) and addresses of the expert witness(es) to be used by each party at the trial and the issue upon which each will testify is:

(1) On behalf of plaintiff;

(2) On behalf of defendant.

OTHER WITNESSES

The names and addresses of witnesses, other than experts, to be used by each party at the time of trial and the general nature of the testimony of each are:

(a) On behalf of plaintiff: (E.g., Jane Doe, 10 Elm Street, Seattle, WA; will testify concerning formation of the parties' contract, performance, breach and damage to plaintiff.)

(b) On behalf of defendant: (follow same format).

(As to each witness, expert or others, indicate "will testify," or "possible witness only." Also indicate which witnesses, if any, will testify by deposition. Rebuttal witnesses, the necessity of whose testimony cannot reasonably be anticipated before trial, need not be named.)

EXHIBITS

(a) Admissibility stipulated:

Plaintiff's Exhibits

1. Photo of port side of ship. (Examples)

2. Photo of crane motor.

3.   Photo of crane.

Defendant's Exhibits

A–1. Weather report. (Examples)

A–2. Log book.

A–3. X-ray of plaintiff's foot.

A–4. X-ray of wrist.

(b) Authenticity stipulated, admissibility disputed:

Plaintiff's Exhibits

4.   Inventory Report. (Examples)

Defendant's Exhibits

A–5. Photograph. (Examples)

(c) Authenticity and admissibility disputed:

Plaintiff's Exhibits

5.   Accountant's report. (Examples)

Defendant's Exhibits

A–6. Ship's log.

(No party is required to list any exhibit which is listed by another party, or any exhibit to be used for impeachment only. * * *)

ACTION BY THE COURT

(a) This case is scheduled for trial (before a jury) (without a jury) on _____, 19__, at _____.

(b) Trial briefs shall be submitted to the Court on or before _____.

(c) (Omit this sub-paragraph in non-jury case.) Jury instructions requested by either party shall be submitted to the court on or before _____. Suggested questions of either party to be asked of the jury by the court on voir dire shall be submitted to the court on or before _____.

(d) (Insert any other ruling made by the court at or before pretrial conference.)

This order has been approved by the parties as evidenced by the signatures of their counsel. This order shall control the subsequent course of the action unless modified by a subsequent order. This order shall not be amended except by order of the court pursuant to agreement of the parties or to prevent manifest injustice.

DATED this ___ day of _____ [insert month], 19__ [insert year].

_____

United States District Judge/Magistrate Judge

FORM APPROVED

_____

Attorney for Plaintiff

_____

Attorney for Defendant

Local practice varies as to the drafting of pretrial orders. Typically, counsel are required to draft the final pretrial order. Often plaintiff's counsel will be required to prepare the initial draft of the order and submit that draft to defense counsel for her approval. Even if there is not such a local practice, by volunteering to prepare the initial proposal counsel may be able to include language in the order favorable to her client. Regardless of who initially drafts the proposed order, a meeting between counsel may be required to reach agreement on the order.

In some jurisdictions, the district judge or magistrate judge prepares the final pretrial order in the first instance. Some judges dictate the order from the bench at the conclusion of the pretrial conference. The above form order contemplates that counsel will sign a proposed final pretrial order and submit it to the judge for his or her approval.

In addition to the final pretrial order itself, some local rules and judges require the preparation of additional pretrial documents. The above form order contemplates the submission of separate trial briefs, proposed jury instructions, and voir dire questions. In non-jury cases, the judge may require counsel to submit proposed Rule 52(a) findings of fact and conclusions of law either before or after trial.

The failure to list particular contentions, witnesses, or exhibits in a final pretrial order may result in the court's refusal to consider such matters at trial. Rule 16(e) only permits the modification of final pretrial orders "to prevent manifest injustice." Efforts to amend final pretrial orders thus may prove unavailing. This is especially true if the party opposing the proposed modification would be prejudiced by that amendment and such prejudice cannot be lessened by, for instance, an extension of time or a limited reopening of discovery.

Preparation of a final pretrial order can entail a great amount of work. However, because the final pretrial order will control the trial of the case, the time invested in that order is time well spent. In developing a litigation plan at the outset of the case, counsel should consider the matters that ideally should be included in the final pretrial order. Counsel's goal should be to structure pretrial proceedings so that she successfully can seek inclusion in the final pretrial order of as many items identified in her litigation plan as possible.

The very act of preparing a final pretrial order requires attorneys to come to grips with the strengths and weaknesses of their cases. This may lead to a better trial or a settlement or other resolution short of trial. This, after all, is the purpose of Rule 16 pretrial conferences and orders.

IV. JUDICIAL INVOLVEMENT IN THE PRETRIAL PROCESS

The original version of the Federal Rules of Civil Procedure that became effective in 1938 gave parties and their counsel great control in the handling of their cases. Rule 16 merely gave district courts the authority to require attorneys to appear for pretrial conferences, enter pretrial orders, and establish pretrial calendars.

In explaining the rationale for the extensive expansion of Rule 16 in 1983, the Advisory Committee noted that "there has been a widespread feeling that amendment is necessary to encourage pretrial management that meets the needs of modern litigation." The Advisory Committee relied upon empirical studies suggesting that "when a trial judge intervenes personally at an early stage to assume judicial control over a case and to schedule dates for completion by the parties of the principal pretrial steps, the case is disposed of by settlement or trial more efficiently and with less cost and delay than when the parties are left to their own devices."

Because Rule 16 is generally discretionary in nature, judges can tailor pretrial conferences and orders to individual cases. In a complex case, the judge may hold several pretrial conferences and require an extensive pretrial order. In simpler cases, there may be only a Rule 16(b) scheduling order and a final pretrial conference and order.

Rules and statutes other than Rule 16 encourage judicial management of the pretrial process. Rule 42 of the Federal Rules of Civil Procedure permits the court to consolidate or bifurcate cases to further trial convenience and economy. Section 1407 of Title 28 of the United States Code permits consolidated pretrial proceedings in a single federal judicial district of multidistrict litigation involving one or more common questions of fact. Local rules of many courts provide that a single judge is to hear all related civil cases filed in a given district. The *Manual for Complex Litigation, Third* encourages federal district judges to adopt proven case management techniques to resolve complex civil litigation.

Congress also has recognized a need for increased judicial management. The Civil Justice Reform Act of 1990 originally was codified at 28 U.S.C. §§ 471–482; all but 28 U.S.C. § 476 expired December 1, 1997. In this act Congress required each of the ninety-four United States District Courts to implement a civil justice expense and delay reduction plan to "facilitate deliberate adjudication of civil cases on the merits, monitor discovery, improve litigation management, and ensure just, speedy, and inexpensive resolution of civil disputes."

Despite the enthusiasm with which increased judicial management has been embraced in many quarters, it may come at a cost. Judicial management advocates assert that early judicial involvement in cases leads to a larger number of settlements and more efficiently and better tried cases. However, time spent on pretrial management is time that otherwise could have been spent trying cases. The appropriate degree of judicial management therefore depends upon the predilections of individual trial judges and the potential benefits that judicial management can produce in specific cases. In recognition of this fact, only pretrial scheduling orders are required by Rule 16, and other

Rule 16 orders and conferences are discretionary with the judge.

Recent efforts by, and directions to, the federal judiciary to assert control over civil dockets are in large measure a result of caseload pressures within the federal courts. Not only the numbers, but the types, of cases pending in the federal district courts have led to increased emphasis upon judicial management. If caseload pressures on the federal courts continue, so, too, will the attempts to judicially manage the pretrial and trial processes.

The great emphasis upon judicial management already has changed the nature of much civil litigation. Counsel are no longer given unfettered discretion to structure and control their cases, and many judges have become active participants in decisions about the issues and evidence that will be explored during pretrial and presented at trial. Judges and lawyers alike should be careful that a single-minded focus on case disposition statistics and judicial efficiencies does not result in the denial of a full hearing for some litigants. To avoid such a result, civil litigation must be conducted pursuant to Rule 1 of the Federal Rules of Civil Procedure "to secure the just, speedy, and inexpensive determination of every action."

CHAPTER FOURTEEN

NEGOTIATION AND SETTLEMENT

I. PRETRIAL SETTLEMENT NEGOTIATIONS

All good things must come to an end, even civil litigation. More often than not, the way in which civil litigation comes to an end is through a negotiated settlement. More often than not, such a negotiated settlement comes while the case is still in its pretrial stages. Regardless of whether any particular case settles, civil litigators spend a major part of their time in settlement negotiations.

Because so many lawsuits settle, counsel should consider the possibility of settlement from the very outset of a case. If counsel believes that a case is likely to settle, her litigation positions and actions may be different than if she believes that there is little chance of settlement short of trial. By settling a lawsuit in its early stages, all parties may be able to achieve a more favorable outcome than if the case proceeds to trial. The further a case proceeds toward trial, the more expensive the litigation becomes. Not only is litigation expensive in terms of monetary costs, but lawsuits often engender both mental and physical turmoil. In addition, a settlement may be tailored to the parties' individual circumstances, in contrast to an all-or-nothing judicial resolution of the dispute. Pretrial settlement therefore should be considered in all cases.

A. Evaluating a Case for Settlement

How does an attorney know whether she can obtain a more favorable result for her client in settlement than at trial? Each case must be evaluated, with counsel estimating (1) whether plaintiff or defendant is likely to prevail if the litigation continues, (2) the probable amount of the monetary judgment or other judicial resolution absent a settlement, and (3) the probable litigation expenses if no settlement is reached.

Estimating the likely outcome of a case requires an evaluation of such factors as the governing law, applicable facts, and the likely ruling of the judge or jury. Counsel's focus should not be exclusively upon the trial judge and jury, especially if the opposing party stands a good chance of upsetting the trial judgment on appeal. Counsel also should consider the probability of particular trial outcomes. An attorney who believes her client has a 90 percent chance of prevailing at trial should demand more in settlement than if she believes her client has only a 60 percent chance of receiving the same trial outcome.

The likely outcome of formal adjudication will be greatly affected by the manner in which counsel conduct the pretrial proceedings. Aggressive pursuit of formal or informal discovery may reveal information that greatly enhances one party's chances of success at trial. Effective use of pretrial motions may result in judicial rulings that greatly reduce a party's trial exposure on the claims that remain pending. Counsel should use the pretrial process to strengthen the positions of their clients in both settlement negotiations and formal adjudication.

In evaluating a case for settlement, the attorney should step back from the role of advocate and consider how the case will look to the judge or jury if no settlement is reached. In conducting such an evaluation, counsel may wish to consult reporting services that contain the actual jury verdicts and judgments rendered in particular types of cases in a given jurisdiction.

Counsel should consider a likely range of trial outcomes, rather than a single dollar amount. While such estimates are always only that, a party's settlement position will be clarified if counsel can estimate, for instance, that a plaintiff has a seventy-five percent chance of recovering $100,000 to $120,000. Multiplying the likely recovery of $100,000 to $120,000 by the seventy-five percent chance of obtaining such a recovery yields figures of $75,000 to $90,000. These figures should not be plaintiff's ultimate settlement demand, though, because if settlement is achieved short of trial plaintiff will be spared the additional costs and fees necessary to bring the case to trial. The estimated costs therefore should be subtracted from the figure arrived at by discounting the probable trial outcome by its likely probability. In the above example, if

$15,000 in costs and fees will be necessary to take a case to trial, $15,000 should be subtracted from $75,000 to $90,000. Thus a settlement for more than $60,000 to $75,000 should be very seriously considered by the plaintiff.

Defense counsel can evaluate a case for settlement in a similar manner. A rough settlement figure can be calculated for the defendant based upon (1) the amount plaintiff is likely to recover at trial, multiplied by (2) the likelihood (expressed as a percentage) that such recovery will be obtained, to which figure should be added (3) the costs and fees that the defendant will have to commit to the case if there is no settlement. If defense counsel evaluates the case in the above example in the same manner as plaintiff's counsel, she reasonably can recommend settlement offers to her client between $90,000 and $105,000 ((75% of $100,000 to $120,000) + $15,000). Because plaintiff's and defendant's settlement ranges overlap, serious efforts to settle this case should be successful.

Different counsel have different formulae for evaluating cases for settlement. For instance, an insurance company may base its settlement offers in routine tort cases upon a standard formula of four times the amount of plaintiff's provable special damages and lost wages.

The evaluation of cases for settlement, though, typically requires more than a series of simple calculations. Although it is likely that a party will achieve a particular outcome at trial, there may be serious questions about the ability of that party to actually take the case to trial. Counsel should consider not only the legal and factual strengths of the case that is likely to be presented at trial, but the practical difficulties that trial may present for both her client and the opposing party.

Time is a factor in many settlements. If settlement is discussed well before trial, the time value of money should play a role in the settlement negotiations. Assuming an interest rate of five percent, a current $100,000 settlement offer is comparable to a $105,000 judgment received one year from now. The parties should adjust their settlement offers accordingly.

Time may work to the disadvantage of a plaintiff who needs money now and cannot wait for trial or of a defendant who, perhaps for public relations reasons, desires an immediate resolution of plaintiff's claims. A party may wish to settle a case not only to avoid the resulting publicity but to avoid the very real stresses of public testimony and cross-examination or the impact of a trial on other pending or potential litigation.

Litigation can have a debilitating psychological effect on all parties, and, if a fair settlement can be achieved, it may be in everyone's interest to put the dispute behind them. On the other hand, some parties may want the public vindication that only a successful trial outcome can bring. No one can guarantee that any trial will be successful, however, and the degree to which the parties are risk averse will have a major impact upon how they evaluate settlement. Even if plaintiff prevails at trial, the victory may be short-lived if the defendant has no insurance coverage and cannot personally satisfy the judgment.

A party's position can be greatly affected not only by that party's staying power but by the commitment and capabilities of that party's counsel. In order to be the most effective advocate for a client, the attorney must be committed to that client's cause. The "best" attorney in a given situation may not necessarily be the attorney with the most experience or the most refined lawyering skills, but the attorney who demonstrates to opposing counsel that both she and her client are ready, willing, and able to take a case to trial. This commitment and capability are not only conveyed across the negotiating table, but throughout the entire pretrial process. If a defendant believes that plaintiff and his counsel will go to trial unless a particular settlement is offered, the defendant presumably will offer such a settlement or step up its preparations for trial.

Increasingly, parties have found it in their best interest to negotiate structured settlements. In such a settlement, the plaintiff does not receive the full settlement amount in a single lump sum. Instead, the defendant typically buys an annuity contract, which will pay the plaintiff a set amount on a periodic basis such as once a month or once a year. Structured settlements permit a defendant to purchase an annuity contract that will provide the plaintiff with periodic payments that total significantly more than the annuity purchase price.

Many plaintiffs are attracted to structured settlements because the resulting annuity can provide a guaranteed income stream for many years. A structured settlement can ensure that there will be income to meet future medical expenses and will preclude the possibility that a single lump sum settlement will be dissipated unwisely. Even more significantly for plaintiffs, the future income stream provided in the structured settlement of a personal injury claim is not subject to federal income tax. If, on the other hand, the plaintiff receives a present lump sum payment, the future interest earned on that lump sum is taxable.

To evaluate a structured settlement offer, the present cost of the future income stream must be calculated. This is not only necessary for determining the fairness of the structured offer, but also provides a basis upon which reasonable attorneys' fees for plaintiff's counsel can be calculated.

B. Negotiating the Settlement

Once a case has been evaluated for settlement, negotiation can begin. As with all other aspects of litigation, negotiation strategy should be planned carefully. Counsel should consider whether to raise the issue of settlement, and, if so, when and how this should be done.

During any successful negotiation, the attorneys reveal information about their respective cases. Providing an opponent with such "free discovery" can come back to hurt a client if the case goes to trial rather than settles. For this reason, counsel should realistically evaluate the chances of settlement before entering into serious settlement negotiations with opposing counsel.

The timing of settlement negotiations can be crucial. If negotiations are conducted at the very outset of the dispute, the parties may not have sufficient information to evaluate a claim. If settlement is not discussed until the eve of trial, the parties may have committed so much to the case and their positions may have so hardened that settlement is not a realistic possibility. The best time to discuss settlement will vary from case to case, but often negotiation "windows of opportunity" exist immediately before the complaint is filed, after the answer has been filed but before discovery has been undertaken, after the parties have been deposed, or before the court has ruled on a dispositive motion. Local rules requiring the parties to notify the court of any settlement a certain amount of time before the trial date also can affect the timing of settlement negotiations.

How does one actually initiate settlement negotiations? Some attorneys are hesitant to raise settlement with opposing counsel for fear that a settlement overture will be seen as a sign of weakness. However, there are very few cases in which it is not in the interest of all parties to consider settlement. In many cases, settlement offers will be expected.

Opposing counsel are more likely to conclude that one's litigation position is weak based upon the conduct of pretrial proceedings than because of the initiation of settlement discussions. Most judges strongly suggest, while other judges and some local rules require, that counsel discuss settlement. This gives counsel an independent reason to broach the subject of settlement.

Some attorneys do not like to initiate settlement negotiations because they prefer not to make the opening settlement offer. These attorneys prefer to respond to an opponent's initial offer, often out of concern that their own initial offer might be based upon a faulty estimation of the value of their own case. Other attorneys, though, prefer to make the initial offer so that opposing counsel will begin thinking in terms of that offer rather than of an unrealistic opening offer that opposing counsel otherwise might make.

Whoever makes the first offer, there should be a principled basis for all offers. Offers that are pulled out of thin air are treated accordingly. By making totally unrealistic offers, counsel wastes time and undermines her general credibility both in the negotiation and in the lawsuit of which the negotiation is just one part. A major aspect of counsel's job in any negotiation is to convince opposing counsel that there is a principled basis for her offers and that those offers should be treated seriously.

Because negotiations typically involve bargaining and a series of concessions, the initial offer should be beyond, but not unreasonably beyond, the bargainer's bottom-line settlement position. If the plaintiff has determined that he must receive $100,000 in settlement, his opening offer should not be $100,100. Not surprisingly, research indicates that the most successful plaintiffs' attorneys start with high, yet reasoned, initial demands and make smaller concessions during the negotiation.

Not only must the initial offer leave some room for movement during the negotiation, but that offer should not be so unreasonable that the other party breaks off settlement negotiations. What offers are unreasonable will vary from case to case, attorney to attorney, and time to time. Asking $1,000,000 for a claim that objectively might be valued at $100,000 is a much more risky negotiation strategy to employ the day before trial than at the time the complaint is filed.

A principled basis should exist for not only settlement offers, but for all settlement concessions: "I've thought some more about the timing of the settlement. I'd be willing to recommend to the plaintiff that he accept $10,000 less in settlement if your client can provide him with the settlement check by next Friday." In the absence of such a principled basis for concessions, the negotiation may degenerate into a game of split the difference: "You've offered $10,000 and our last demand is for $50,000. Let's settle for $30,000."

Negotiation offers should be specific. Assuming there is a principled basis for the offer, a precise offer to settle a case for $51,250 will be received more seriously than an offer to "see if I can sell my client on an offer somewhere around $50,000." Round, general numbers suggest that the attorney making the offer has room left to bargain, while precise offers indicate that one's settlement limit has been reached. Offers should not be made in the alternative. When plaintiff's counsel says, "My client will accept $10,000 or $12,000," the case is not going to settle for $12,000.

In cases that present multiple issues, counsel may want to begin the negotiation with a discussion of the issues that can be most easily resolved. For instance, if the plaintiff has suffered an easily quantifiable amount of property damage or has incurred specific medical expenses, these matters might be considered at the outset of the negotiation. By reaching agreement on these issues, a cooperative working relationship may be established that will smooth the path to resolution of other outstanding issues. The investment in the negotiation process necessary to resolve initial issues may encourage the parties to keep negotiating in an attempt to reach agreement on the remaining issues.

Counteroffers can differ from a prior offer in various ways. In addition to varying the monetary amount of a prior offer, a counteroffer can restructure that prior offer. For instance, rather than offering the plaintiff a lump sum settlement, a defendant might counteroffer with a proposal to pay a certain amount now and additional amounts at some time in the future.

Cooperative or problem-solving negotiation has received increasing attention in recent years. All too often, legal disputes are perceived by the parties as a zero sum game in which every dollar that the plaintiff receives in settlement is another dollar that the defendant must pay. This is an accurate characterization of only some lawsuits. In every case, counsel, both individually and in discussions with opposing counsel, should attempt to generate creative dispute resolutions in which one party's gain does not require a comparable loss from other parties.

A consumer dispute can be used to illustrate a problem-solving approach to legal negotiation. Presume that the plaintiff alleges that his car has been improperly serviced by the defendant auto dealer, resulting in a minor accident. Rather than focus on a strictly monetary settlement, a settlement package might be devised that includes the plaintiff's purchase of a new car at dealer cost. In this type of settlement the plaintiff has obtained a benefit (a reduced price on a new car) that cost the defendant little or nothing. The defendant also might offer to service the new car for a certain length of time without charge, although the plaintiff might be wise to insist on an extended manufacturer's warranty permitting him to obtain service from another dealer.

To successfully employ problem-solving in legal negotiation requires counsel to focus on the parties' real needs, as opposed to their expressed demands. A pending dispute between two businesses may be of less significance than the preservation of their ongoing business relationship. Parents who have lost a child due to the defendant's alleged negligence may make large monetary demands in the resulting lawsuit. Their actual needs, however, may be strictly non-monetary. The defense attorney who recognizes this fact might suggest a creative settlement such as a memorial or a scholarship fund that addresses the real needs of the bereaved parents. No person, even a party to a lawsuit, is driven solely by economic forces.

C. Negotiation Tactics and Techniques

During legal negotiation, counsel should try to learn the opposing party's real bargaining range and simultaneously convey to opposing counsel the strength of her own client's negotiation position. By so doing, counsel's aim should be to move the bargaining range of opposing counsel closer to her own client's bargaining range. Numerous negotiation tactics and techniques for achieving this goal have been advocated by and for legal negotiators.

Any discussion of negotiation tactics must be prefaced with the admonition to separate negotiation style and tactics from negotiation substance. Attorneys can take a very aggressive or competitive substantive position in a negotiation and yet be extremely pleasant and cooperative. Conversely, quite obnoxious attorneys may not obtain particularly good substantive negotiation results.

As with pretrial and trial advocacy generally, most attorneys have difficulty assuming a negotiation style at odds with their basic character. Attorneys should be aware of their lawyering style, though, because this knowledge may help counsel deal more effectively with others. Negotiation style may change over the course of a negotiation or vary from issue to issue within the negotiation. In addition, an attorney's negotiation style may vary depending upon the style adopted by opposing counsel. An attorney who is cooperative at the beginning of a negotiation may become quite competitive if she believes her concessions have not been reciprocated by opposing counsel.

As in other aspects of life, negotiation success sometimes depends more on perception than reality. Even though your client is desperate to settle a case, this fact will not hurt that client in legal negotiations unless opposing counsel perceives this negotiation weakness. Successful negotiators therefore carefully consider the information that they provide to opposing counsel and attempt to garner as much information as possible from opposing counsel during the negotiation.

The active listening techniques discussed in Chapter 2, supra, p. 25, can be usefully employed during negotiation. Counsel should listen and watch carefully not only what opposing counsel says, but what she doesn't say and what she does and doesn't do during the negotiation. Does opposing counsel's behavior indicate that she would rather be somewhere else and thus rid of this lawsuit? Has opposing counsel really prepared for trial or would she prefer to settle this case because she is not prepared for, or is afraid of, trial? Simply asking questions can be a most effective negotiation tactic. Knowing the reasons for an opposing party's negotiation position may permit counsel to craft a counteroffer tailored to that party's real needs rather than to his unrealistic negotiation demands.

Counsel must be ready to advance the position of her own client during the negotiation, as well as deal with the arguments and positions advanced by opposing counsel. Because legal negotiation requires effective persuasion, counsel should consider bringing to the negotiation all potentially persuasive arguments and evidence. Charts, exhibits, and calculations that will be offered at trial frequently are the basis of negotiation discussions.

In some cases, counsel prepare evidence specifically for the negotiation. In many cases, the settlement demand or offer is made in a carefully drafted letter to opposing counsel. Because these settlement letters may be read by both one's own client and the opposing party, they should be persuasive without being demeaning or needlessly offensive.

In major personal injury cases, plaintiff's counsel may package her best arguments and evidence into a settlement brochure or videotape that is provided to opposing counsel. Under Rule 408 of the Federal Rules of Evidence, evidence of a settlement offer or of conduct or statements made during settlement negotiations is not admissible to prove liability for, or the invalidity of, the underlying claim. Rule 408 does not, though, preclude later use of evidence otherwise discoverable merely because it was presented during settlement negotiations. Moreover, if the case does not settle, the opposing party will have been provided an advance preview of counsel's strongest trial evidence.

Negotiation authority becomes an issue in some negotiations. Such a tactic occasionally is used by car salesmen: "I'm sorry, but the manager wouldn't approve the deal that you and I worked out. He told me, though, that he could approve it if you offered an additional $800." Similar tactics are sometimes used in legal negotiations: "My client rejected the offer. I know he's being a bit unreasonable, but I'm sure he'd settle if your client could offer another $2000." This tactic can be prevented if counsel confirms at the outset of the negotiation that opposing counsel has full settlement authority. If the problem nevertheless occurs, counsel can expose the negotiation ploy as just that and refuse to negotiate against herself and the prior settlement figure.

Some attorneys attempt to threaten opposing counsel during legal negotiations. Many threats are best ignored, particularly if they are isolated incidents. A short break may permit everyone to calm down. If counsel believes that a threat cannot go unanswered, she might implicitly challenge the threatening statement by repeating it back in question form: "You are saying that if we don't reach a settlement by 5:00 you'll file a motion for a temporary restraining order tomorrow morning?" A more drastic approach is to simply end the negotiation: "If that's really what you think about my client, there's no point in talking further." Before a negotiation is ended, though, counsel should consider whether she may want to preserve the possibility of resuming the negotiation at a later date.

Because threats can rupture the cooperative spirit necessary to reach a negotiated settlement, they should be used sparingly. It is usually unproductive to shout at an opposing counsel, "If your client doesn't accept this offer, we'll see you at trial!" Instead of threatening, consider merely predicting likely future events for opposing counsel: "We've come a long way in these negotiations, but your latest offer is simply nothing that my client will accept." Often subtle threats are the most effective: "Let's talk a little about the briefing schedule for the summary judgment motion that I need to file if we can't settle this thing."

If counsel makes a threat of any kind, she should be prepared to carry through on that threat. To be an effective negotiator, opposing counsel must credit your negotiation statements and positions. Nothing destroys an attorney's credibility more quickly than promising, predicting, or threatening something that doesn't come to pass.

Special problems can arise in multiple party cases. A favorite tactic of plaintiffs' counsel is to "divide and conquer" by pitting co-defendants against one another. A plaintiff may offer a favorable settlement to one defendant to obtain that defendant's cooperation in the prosecution of plaintiff's claim against the other defendants. Under a "Mary Carter" or "Gallagher" agreement, the plaintiff agrees to settle with one defendant for a set amount, but any recovery the plaintiff receives from the other defendants is set off against this initial settlement. See generally *Booth v. Mary Carter Paint Co.* (Fla.App.1967) (*per curiam*); *City of Tucson v. Gallagher* (Ariz.1972). If the case goes to trial and the settling defendant remains in the lawsuit, that defendant has an incentive to help plaintiff maximize his recovery at trial from the other defendants. Because of the potential abuse from such agreements, some states have declared them void while others require their disclosure to the court and other parties.

Even if there is only a single plaintiff and defendant, there still may be multiple interests involved in the negotiation. The attorneys may have needs that differ from those of their clients. If opposing counsel does not want to try a case because of conflicting personal or professional commitments, she may agree to a less favorable settlement than she otherwise would find acceptable. Attorneys should be aware of potential conflicts and ensure that other commitments do not interfere with the zealous representation of their clients during legal negotiations.

Whatever negotiation tactics are employed, the negotiation should be carefully planned. Counsel must plan not only her opening offer and bottom-line position, but the intermediate concessions she is willing to make to achieve a negotiated settlement equal to or better than her bottom-line position. Real negotiations rarely go exactly as planned, and attorneys must be flexible in the actual negotiation process. However, advance planning will help counsel maximize negotiation success.

Not only should potential concessions be planned, but the timing of any concessions should be considered in advance of the negotiation. A major concession early in a negotiation may not produce a reciprocal concession from opposing counsel. However, a concession offered the day before trial may break a negotiation stalemate and lead to settlement.

Counsel should think about the time and location of the negotiation. Most attorneys are more comfortable, and feel more in control, when negotiating in their own offices. If the negotiation is conducted in one's own office, counsel should have ready access to documents relevant to the negotiation and to a secretary who can prepare a memorandum of agreement or other settlement papers. However, if a negotiation is held in your own office, it may be difficult to refuse to produce a relevant document that is in a file cabinet in an adjoining room. By negotiating at an opponent's office, counsel also may gain insights concerning the resources available to opposing counsel for a given case.

The timing of the negotiation session can create settlement pressures on one or both counsel. Negotiating on a Friday afternoon may increase settlement pressures, especially if the trial is scheduled for the next Monday. There might be even greater settlement pressure on opposing counsel if her college reunion were the intervening weekend.

Time plays an important part in virtually all negotiations. Firm trial dates lead to settlements because counsel know that they will incur the risk and cost of trial if they do not settle. The impact of the trial date will vary from case to case. Many personal injury cases settle in the days immediately before trial. The greatest impetus to settle major commercial cases, however, may come several weeks or months before trial, because such cases may require not only more extensive trial preparation but more extended internal discussions before the parties can approve a proposed settlement.

Defense counsel can create time pressures for a plaintiff by making a settlement offer in the form of an offer of judgment pursuant to Rule 68 of the Federal Rules of Civil Procedure. A plaintiff has ten days in which to accept a Rule 68 offer of judgment. If the plaintiff rejects the offer of judgment but does not receive a more favorable judgment from the court, he cannot recover his costs (including attorneys' fees) incurred after the offer was made. Indeed, the plaintiff must pay the costs incurred by the defendant after the making of the offer, although these costs typically do not include attorneys' fees but are restricted to such court costs as filing and reporter fees.

Someone has suggested that the rules of the National Basketball Association could be revised to give each team 100 points at the outset of the game, which then would be played for only two minutes. So it is with legal negotiation, in which the parties may negotiate for extended periods, but the negotiation only gets serious in its very final stages. One of the keys to effective legal negotiation is being able to sense when an opponent believes there are only two minutes left in the game.

II. THIRD–PARTY SETTLEMENT FACILITATION

Despite the fact that most cases are settled short of trial, some cases are not voluntarily settled that could, and perhaps should, be resolved by other means than formal adjudication. This may be because the parties have incomplete or incorrect information about their own case, the opposing party's case, or the court's probable handling of the lawsuit. The parties also may be locked into an adversarial relationship that precludes serious settlement talks. When these or other barriers to settlement exist, a neutral third party may be able to effectively facilitate a negotiated settlement.

The judge is the individual most likely to facilitate settlement. Because many counsel are hesitant to initiate settlement discussions, judges often raise the possibility of settlement. In fact, Rule 16(a)(5) provides that one of the objectives of pretrial conferences is "facilitating the settlement of the case." In some standard final pretrial orders counsel must certify that they have discussed settlement. If the court has not scheduled a pretrial or settlement conference, counsel might consider requesting such a conference so that settlement can be explored.

The degree to which a judge intervenes in settlement discussions can change settlement dynamics quite dramatically. Different judges adopt different settlement approaches. Some judges discuss settlement with the parties and attempt to move them toward settlement. This direct approach can be quite effective, because the parties and their counsel may obtain an evaluation of the case from the judge who actually will try that case if it is not settled. However, once the judge intervenes in settlement negotiations, counsel may find themselves negotiating with not only opposing counsel but with the judge as well. If a judge is likely to intervene in settlement negotiations, counsel may not want to make her best settlement offer prior to the anticipated judicial intervention. This will permit counsel to "give up" something in later negotiations if requested to do so by the judge.

Many judges will not themselves discuss settlement with the parties, because of their concern that they may not be able to approach the case with an open mind if they have been privy to pretrial settlement offers. Some judges also are concerned that there not be a perception that the judge has coerced a settlement or that the parties will be penalized at trial for refusing to settle a particular case.

The fact that the trial judge does not participate in settlement negotiations does not mean there will be no judicial involvement in this process. In many jurisdictions cases are referred to magistrate judges or others for settlement discussions. These settlement conferences may be held at the request of the parties or at the suggestion of the court. In jurisdictions in which a magistrate judge, rather than the trial judge, conducts pretrial conferences, settlement discussions often are a part of these conferences. The judge's pressure on the parties to settle can be quite subtle and even unspoken. The setting of a firm trial date is the judicial action that is most effective in pushing parties to settlement.

Persons other than a judge can be used to facilitate settlement. Either before or after the filing of suit, the parties may agree to submit their dispute to a neutral third party for arbitration or mediation. Increasingly, courts require the parties to engage in alternative dispute resolution processes. These processes include court-annexed arbitration (in which a third party hears the case and renders an opinion) and mediation (in which a third party talks with the parties and attempts to help them reach their own settlement).

In addition to these more traditional dispute resolution techniques, courts recently have experimented with dispute resolution techniques such as summary jury trials and judicial mini-trials. A summary jury trial is a proceeding in which persons chosen from the jury pool hear a very abbreviated version of the parties' evidence, which may be presented by live witnesses or by attorney summaries. The summary jury trial verdict gives counsel a rough indicator of how a "real" jury might decide the case and provides a starting point for serious settlement negotiations between the parties. A mini-trial is a similarly truncated proceeding, but a judge, other judicial officer, or another neutral third party hears the evidence and renders an advisory verdict.

The aim of all these dispute resolution techniques is to facilitate settlement of a dispute short of formal judicial adjudication, thereby saving the parties and the court the time and expense of formal adjudication.

III. NEGOTIATION ETHICS

Most legal negotiation takes place outside the confines, and thus beyond at least some of the constraints, of the formal legal process. For this reason, ethical questions often arise during the negotiation process.

Counsel cannot forget that her primary duty is to her client. The very first rule of the ABA's Model Rules of Professional Conduct, Rule 1.1, requires an attorney to provide competent client representation. Attorneys must thoroughly prepare for legal negotiation, so that they can bring to bear the legal knowledge and skill necessary for the effective representation of each of their clients.

Rule 1.4 of the Model Rules of Professional Conduct imposes upon counsel the duty to keep her client reasonably informed about the status of his case and explain the case so that the client can make informed case decisions. See also Model Code of Professional Responsibility EC 7–8. Settlement offers must be relayed to the client, and Model Rule 1.2(a) squarely places the decision whether to accept a settlement offer with the client. See also Model Code of Professional Responsibility EC 7–7.

In order to avoid later confusion, counsel should relay settlement offers to the client in writing. Such a letter to the plaintiff should not only contain the defendant's offer but itemize the expenses and fees due plaintiff's counsel and the net amount the plaintiff actually would receive under the offer. While an attorney has a duty to explain a proposed settlement to her client and advise the client concerning the proposal, she should never forget that it is the client, rather than the attorney, who must make the final settlement decision.

If the attorney represents more than one client, she should be familiar with Rule 1.8(g) of the Model Rules of Professional Conduct, which prohibits lawyers from participating in the making of any aggregate settlement for multiple clients unless each client consents after consultation and relevant disclosure. See also Model Code of Professional Responsibility DR5–106(A).

Not only does the attorney owe her clients such duties, but ethical proscriptions govern her dealings with opposing counsel and parties. Rule 4.1(a) of the Model Rules of Professional Conduct and Disciplinary Rule 1–102(A)(4) of the Model Code of Professional Responsibility prohibit attorneys from knowingly making false statements of material fact and engaging in misrepresentation. See also Model Code of Professional Responsibility DR 7–102(A)(5). However, a comment to Rule 4.1 of the Model Rules of Professional Conduct recognizes that certain statements made in negotiations, such as estimates of value or statements concerning a party's settlement intentions, are not considered material facts subject to the general prohibition of Model Rule 4.1.

Model Rule 4.1 thus differentiates between estimates or intentions and statements of material fact, the line between which may not always be clear. As a rough rule of thumb, though, counsel might consider whether the statement she is about to make concerns positioning within the negotiation itself (an estimate or intention) or a fact existing outside the negotiation about which false statements cannot be made. Model Rule 4.1 would preclude an attorney from making the following statement if she knew that it was untrue: "The plaintiff paid $22,750 for the car that was destroyed in the wreck." However, counsel would not be constrained by the Model Rules from making (even untrue) statements such as these: "The plaintiff's claim is worth $150,000" or "Plaintiff is not going to settle this lawsuit for less than $125,000."

Rather than risk making a misstatement of material fact, counsel can simply refuse to answer a question calling for sensitive information. This can be done by ignoring the opposing attorney's question, changing the topic, or answering the question with a question of your own such as "Why do you ask?" Counsel also can confront the question head-on: "Oh, counsel, you know that I can't share that sort of privileged information with you in these negotiations." Another technique used by some attorneys in this situation is to offer to "trade" confidential information for information that an opposing attorney will not be willing to surrender: "I'll be glad to tell you about Global's future marketing plans if you'll give me Allied's customer list."

Regardless of its characterization under the Model Rules or Model Code, certain negotiation conduct, such as the misrepresentation of insurance policy limitations, has been held actionable in later civil litigation. Counsel also runs the risk that a settlement will be vacated if her failure to make a negotiation disclosure is found to be equivalent to an affirmative misrepresentation. The likelihood that the settlement will be vacated is increased if the judge actually approves the settlement based upon explicit or implied statements that counsel knows to be false. Finally, counsel should never insist upon a settlement that is so one-sided as to be unconscionable and thus unenforceable as a matter of contract law. If the settlement seems too good to be true, it probably is.

IV. MEMORIALIZING THE SETTLEMENT

Once settlement is reached, the parties' agreement still must be memorialized. A settlement agreement is a contract between the parties, and general contract principles apply to the written settlement documents. Although there may be no requirement that a particular settlement be reduced to writing, settlement agreements typically are drafted to protect all parties from later misunderstandings about the settlement terms.

Upon settlement, the plaintiff typically will be required to execute a release relinquishing his claims against the defendant. If the plaintiff has potential tort claims against more than one person, his settlements with individual defendants may be reflected in covenants not to sue rather than releases. As their name implies, covenants not to sue provide that, in return for a valuable consideration, the claimant will not sue or continue suit against a particular person. These covenants were developed to avoid the inadvertent release of all potential defendants by the execution of a release with a single defendant. While such an inadvertent release of joint tortfeasors is no longer a major concern in most states, some attorneys still prefer to use covenants not to sue rather than releases to effectuate a settlement with fewer than all potential defendants.

The law concerning contribution among joint tortfeasors should be checked before drafting the settlement documents. In some states, a plaintiff still may have to agree to indemnify a settling defendant if contribution is later sought from that defendant to satisfy a judgment rendered against non-settling defendants. Such an indemnification clause should not be necessary in states that have adopted the Uniform Contribution Among Tortfeasors Act or similar statutes. So there is no question as to the law governing the settlement, a choice of law clause can be included in the release, covenant not to sue, or settlement agreement.

If the settlement involves mutual promises by the parties, a settlement agreement containing those promises and signed by all parties may be in order. This agreement may include not only the parties' mutual promises, but a statement that, by entering into the settlement agreement, no party admits or concedes the validity of the claims, defenses, or allegations of any other party.

In addition to the release, covenant not to sue, or settlement agreement, a court document must be executed to formally resolve any litigation filed as a result of the parties' dispute. In most federal cases this second document will be a notice or stipulation of dismissal filed pursuant to Rule 41 of the Federal Rules of Civil Procedure.

Rule 41 generally only requires a notice of dismissal (if the opposing party has not filed an answer or a motion for summary judgment) or a stipulation signed by all parties (if an answer or summary judgment motion has been filed). A Rule 41(a)(1)(i) notice of dismissal typically provides nothing more than the following: "Plaintiff, pursuant to Rule 41(a)(1)(i) of the Federal Rules of Civil Procedure, hereby dismisses this action, with prejudice." While Rule 41(a)(1)(i) dismissals usually are considered without prejudice unless the dismissal notice provides to the contrary, settlements generally are premised on a dismissal with prejudice that will preclude the plaintiff from refiling the action at a later date.

In some situations, the parties may prefer that the judge enter an order dismissing the lawsuit. Such an agreed order can include the terms of the parties' settlement and provide that the judge before whom the action is pending will hear any later action for enforcement of the settlement agreement. In some cases, rules or statutes specifically require court approval of any settlement. For instance, Rule 23(e) requires that the court approve the dismissal of class actions, while Rule 23.1 requires judicial approval of the settlement of shareholder derivative actions.

The major disadvantage of filing the parties' settlement agreement with the court is that the settlement terms then may not remain confidential. Confidentiality is often insisted upon as a condition of settlement, particularly if there are claimants situated similarly to the plaintiff who may wish to use the settlement as a basis for negotiating their own settlements. While the judge may agree to seal the settlement agreement, that same judge may later be convinced by a party to the settlement or others to unseal the agreement.

The same care should be devoted to drafting the settlement documents as to the documents embodying any other legal contract. Settlement agreements, releases, and covenants not to sue should specify the claim or claims that are being settled and contain an integration clause providing that the document represents the entire agreement between the parties. Settlement documents should be explicit about whether litigation is being dismissed with or without prejudice and about who will bear the court costs of the dismissed action.

To avoid any later confusion, precise language is necessary concerning all settlement terms. Any portion of the settlement attributable to personal injury damages should be unambiguously identified to ensure that these damages are not considered taxable income to the plaintiff. A defendant's insurance coverage generally extends only to compensatory damages, and punitive damages are taxable income to the plaintiff. Settlement agreements therefore typically designate as much as possible of the settlement money as compensatory, rather than punitive, damages.

While counsel are the parties' agents for the purposes of settlement, later questions concerning the parties' agreement to the settlement can be resolved by having parties, as well as counsel, sign the settlement agreement. Some counsel include language in the settlement documents that the parties have read and understand the legal document they are signing. The copy of the settlement agreement signed by the parties should be self-contained, with additional documents such as a dismissal notice or stipulation referenced in, and attached to, the agreement.

Whatever settlement documents are contemplated, counsel generally should offer to draft those documents. There are minor terms in all settlements that may not have been addressed in the settlement negotiations. By drafting the settlement documents, an attorney may be able to obtain the most advantageous terms on such matters for her client. Even on matters about which the parties have negotiated, the attorney drafting the settlement documents may obtain language in the settlement agreement that is favorable to her client.

Continuing the counseling begun at the initial client interview, counsel should ensure that the client thoroughly understands all settlement terms and that, by settling, he is relinquishing his right to a judicial resolution of his claims. If counsel has done a good job during the negotiations and other pretrial proceedings, the client should be quite pleased with the settlement negotiated on his behalf.

*

INDEX

References are to Pages

PROCESS
See Filing and Service of Process

RELEASE, 17

RELIEF
Generally, 75–81
Attorneys' fees, 75, 78–79, 248–249, 253, 296, 310
Costs, 75, 78
Damages,
    Generally, 75–76, 364
  Compensatory, 75, 364
  Liquidated, 76
  Nominal, 76
  Punitive, 76, 80, 87, 364
  Special, 75
  Statutory, 76
Declaratory judgments, 78
Equitable, 76–78
Execution on judgment, 79
Injunctions,
    Generally, 76–78
  Permanent, 76–77
  Preliminary, 54, 77–78, 79–80, 269
  Temporary restraining orders, 54, 77–78, 269
Prayer for relief, 89

REMOVAL, 74, 268

REPRESENTATION AGREEMENT
See Attorney–Client Relationship

RULE 11
Generally, 89–94, 157, 277, 310
Certification requirement,
  Evidentiary support, 8–9, 53, 90
  Motions, 42, 92
  No improper purpose, 90
  Warranted by law, 3, 43, 90
Defenses, application to, 114, 115, 119
Sanctions, 91–94, 297, 310

SANCTIONS
See also Rule 11
Discovery, 91–94, 179, 192, 225, 234–236, 249–258
Pretrial conferences, 264, 317–318, 319

†